P9-CCI-204

ICFA Continuing Education
Good Ethics: The Essential Element of a Firm's Success

November 30–December 1, 1993
Washington, D.C.

Robert E. Angelica, CFA, *Moderator*
Robert A. Anselmi
William E. Avera, CFA
J. Carter Beese, Jr.
David H. Beevers
Karin B. Bonding, CFA, *Conference Moderator*
Michael S. Caccese
Judith D. Freyer, CFA
Paul G. Haaga, Jr.
Richard P. Halverson, CFA, *Moderator*
Lea B. Hansen, CFA, *Moderator*
Thomas J. Healey, CFA
Brian E. Hersey, CFA
Chiles T.A. Larson, *Moderator*

Scott L. Lummer, CFA
Gary G. Lynch
Susan D. Martin, CFA, *Moderator*
Iain W. McAra
Ian R. O'Reilly, CFA, *Moderator*
Ermanno Pascutto
William F. Quinn
Elliot L. Richardson
Martin F. Ryan
Stanley Sporkin
Lori A. Tansey
R. Charles Tschampion, CFA
O. Ray Vass

Edited by H. Kent Baker, CFA

To obtain an AIMR Publications Catalog or to order additional copies of this publication, turn to page 128 or contact:

AIMR Publications Sales Department
P.O. Box 7947
Charlottesville, VA 22906
U.S.A.
Telephone: 804/980-3647
Fax: 804/977-0350

The Association for Investment Management and Research comprises the Institute of Chartered Financial Analysts and the Financial Analysts Federation.

This publication is designed to provide accurate and authoritative information in regard to the subject matter covered. It is sold with the understanding that the publisher is not engaged in rendering legal, accounting, or other professional service. If legal advice or other expert assistance is required, the services of a competent professional should be sought.

ISBN 1-879087-38-3

Printed in the United States of America

April 1994

Table of Contents

(continued on next page)

Foreword

AIMR is very pleased to offer readers this collection of wide-ranging presentations from the seminar on *Good Ethics: The Essential Element of a Firm's Success*. The scope of material reaches from the philosophical underpinnings of our individual and collective ethical behavior to specific issues of ethical concern to today's investment professionals. Readers will be interested to note the various definitions of ethics. Most authors make distinctions among the "ethics" mandated by government regulation, the ethics developed and enforced by self-regulating organizations such as AIMR, and the ethics that determine a person's behavior even when no one is watching.

An important aspect of this volume is the insights it offers about relating ethical ideals and standards to day-to-day practice. The authors not only take pains to explain what SEC regulations and AIMR standards mandate, but they also discuss the parameters within which judgments must still be made.

These presentations make clear that a primary ingredient in moving ethical ideals into practice and maintaining ethical behavior in a firm is a clear statement of ethical positions combined with a compliance or ethics program to educate employees and enforce the policies. Such statements and programs demonstrate vigilant commitment to ethical standards in case questions arise about employees' ethical behavior—and they are good business.

For the convenience of readers, we have included the AIMR Code of Ethics and Standards of Professional Conduct so frequently mentioned or discussed in the proceedings in Appendix A, and the Performance Presentation Standards in Appendix B. These materials come from two AIMR publications, also frequently referenced in this proceedings, that set forth the cornerstones of AIMR's Professional Conduct Program.

- *Standards of Practice Handbook*, 6th ed. (Charlottesville, Va.: Association for Investment Management and Research, 1992).

- *Performance Presentation Standards* (Charlottesville, Va.: Association for Investment Management and Research, 1993).

In addition to the material in the appendixes, these books contain extensive explanations and discussions of the two sets of standards.

A third volume that is frequently referred to is a Research Foundation monograph reporting the results of a survey concerning ethical education and behavior:

- E. Theodore Veit and Michael R. Murphy, *Ethics in the Investment Profession: A Survey* (Charlottesville, Va.: The Research Foundation of The Institute of Chartered Financial Analysts, 1992).

Ordering information for all of these publications appears at the end of this proceedings.

We wish to thank all the seminar speakers for the time and effort they devoted to a subject that to some might seem to be of little concern but that to AIMR governors and members is the vital mark of professionalism. The care taken by speakers to relate concepts to reality and to explain concepts, perceptions, and standards was educational and useful. We are grateful also for these authors' patient help in preparing this volume for production.

Thanks are also due to the conference moderator, AIMR's Karin B. Bonding, CFA, and to the moderators of the seminar sessions: Robert E. Angelica, CFA, AT&T Investment Management Corporation; Richard P. Halverson, CFA, C.H. Brown Company; Lea B. Hansen, CFA; Chiles T.A. Larson, Chiles T.A. Larson and Associates; Susan D. Martin, CFA, AIMR; and Ian R. O'Reilly, CFA, Wood Gundy Inc.

Finally, AIMR wishes to thank H. Kent Baker, CFA, of The American University for his help in editing this proceedings, for his comprehensive overview, and for preparing the self-examination section.

Katrina F. Sherrerd, CFA
Senior Vice President
Publications and Research

Biographies of Speakers

Robert E. Angelica, CFA, is president of AT&T Investment Management Corporation and vice president and treasurer of the AT&T Foundation. Previously, Mr. Angelica has served as district and division manager in the Investment Management Division at AT&T and as an investment analyst in the Securities Investment Department of Mutual Benefit Life Insurance Company. He is a member of the Board of Governors of the Association for Investment Management and Research, director of the Financial Analysts Federation, director of the Institute for Quantitative Research in Finance, and a member of the advisory board of the Rodney White Center for Financial Research at the Wharton School of the University of Pennsylvania. Mr. Angelica holds a B.A. in economics from Rutgers University and an M.B.A. in finance from New York University.

Robert A. Anselmi is a managing director and general counsel for J.P. Morgan Investment Management. Prior to joining J.P. Morgan, he served as a vice president of Morgan Stanley & Company. Mr. Anselmi received his B.S., M.B.A., and J.D. degrees from Fordham University.

William E. Avera, CFA, is president and founder of Fincap, an economic, financial, and policy consulting firm. Previously, Dr. Avera served as director of the Economic Research Division at the Public Utility Commission of Texas. He has also served as manager of Financial Education for International Paper Company in New York City and has held faculty positions at the University of Texas at Austin and the University of North Carolina at Chapel Hill. Dr. Avera holds a Ph.D. in economics and finance from the University of North Carolina.

J. Carter Beese, Jr., is commissioner of the U.S. Securities and Exchange Commission and is active in investment management, derivative markets, cross-border financing, and corporate governance. Prior to his appointment, Mr. Beese was a partner of Alex. Brown & Sons, where his responsibilities included business development in corporate finance, investment management, and institutional brokerage. He has served as director of the Overseas Private Investment Corporation and also on the SEC's Emerging Markets Advisory Committee. Mr. Beese holds a B.S. in political science and finance from Rollins College and also attended Trinity College in Dublin.

David H. Beevers is president and director of Capital International Limited and chairman of the board of the Capital International Emerging Markets Fund and New Europe East Investment Fund. Previously, Mr. Beevers was a partner and director of Joseph Sobag & Company in the United Kingdom. He received a law degree from Cambridge University.

Karin B. Bonding, CFA, is vice president of the CFA Continuing Education Program in the Education and Programs Department of the Association for Investment Management and Research. Ms. Bonding's previous employers include Lombard, Odier & Cie in London and Frank Russell International. Ms. Bonding was a Fulbright exchange student at Ohio State University.

Michael S. Caccese is a senior vice president and general counsel of the Association for Investment Management and Research. Previously, he served as senior vice president and associate general counsel of Frank Russell Company and was regulatory compliance officer for a NYSE and several National Association of Securities Dealers broker/dealers and SEC-registered investment advisors. Prior to joining Frank Russell, Mr. Caccese served as corporate counsel at Federated Investors, and he also worked at the SEC's Division of Enforcement. He is a member of the American Bar and International Bar associations. He holds a J.D.D. from Temple University Law School and a B.A. from Pennsylvania State University.

Judith D. Freyer, CFA, is vice president for investments and treasurer of the Board of Pensions of the Presbyterian Church (USA). Previously, Ms. Freyer was director of investor relations and institutional investments for UGI Corporation. She serves on the executive board and Investment Committee of the Philadelphia Council, Boy Scouts of America, and the Pension Committee of the National Council of the Churches of Christ in the USA. She holds a B.A. from Manhattanville College, an M.A. in economic history from the University of Pennsylvania, and an M.B.A. from Boston University.

Paul G. Haaga, Jr., is senior vice president and director of Capital Research and Management Company. He is also chairman of fixed-income funds in The American Funds Group and president and director of Capital Income Builder and Capital World Growth and Income Fund. Formerly, he was a partner with Dechert Price & Rhoads and a senior attorney for the SEC. Mr. Haaga received an A.B. in economics from Princeton University, a J.D. from the University of Pennsylvania, and an M.B.A. in finance and commerce from the Wharton School of the University of Pennsylvania.

Richard P. Halverson, CFA, is president of the investment advisory firm of C.H. Brown Company. Previously, he served as executive vice president of the First Trust Company of St. Paul and as vice president and portfolio manager at Waddell & Reed. Mr. Halverson is chairman of the Association for Investment Management and Research's Professional Conduct Committee and a member of the Professional Ethics Committee. He received a B.S. in banking and finance from the University of Utah and an M.B.A. from Harvard University.

Lea B. Hansen, CFA, is an independent financial analyst. She has previously been a commissioner with the Ontario Securities Commission, served as director, executive vice president, and financial analyst at Brown, Baldwin, Nisker Limited, and served as a financial analyst for Dominion Securities Limited. Ms. Hansen is on the board of governors of the Association for Investment Management and Research.

Thomas J. Healey, CFA, is a partner at Goldman, Sachs & Company and head of the Pension Services Group. He previously headed the real estate capital markets operations at Goldman, Sachs. Mr. Healey also served as assistant secretary for domestic finance at the U.S. Treasury Department. He is a director of the Securities Investor Protection Corporation and serves on several charitable boards. Mr. Healey received an A.B. from Georgetown University and an M.B.A. from Harvard University.

Brian E. Hersey, CFA, is director of Investment Manager Research for Towers Perrin's Asset Consulting Practice, serving as the primary liaison with the investment management community. Before joining Towers Perrin, Mr. Hersey served in various business development and corporate finance positions at Aetna Life Insurance Company. He holds a B.A. in English from Wesleyan University and an M.S. in business policy from Columbia University.

Chiles T.A. Larson is president of Chiles T.A. Larson and Associates, which provides consulting services to several organizations, including the Association

for Investment Management and Research, in media and government relations. Prior to establishing his own firm, he served as deputy director of the SEC's Office of Public Affairs. Mr. Larson has also served as director of public relations and advertising for Legg Mason. He is a graduate of the College of William and Mary.

Scott L. Lummer, CFA, is managing director of the Consulting Services Group of Ibbotson Associates. Previously, he served on the faculty of Texas A&M University and as senior consultant for Manufacturers Trust Company. Dr. Lummer has authored articles for numerous publications, including the *Journal of Financial Economics, Financial Management,* the *Journal of Investing,* and the *Journal of Applied Corporate Finance.* Dr. Lummer holds a B.S. in mathematics and a Ph.D. in finance from Purdue University.

Gary G. Lynch is a partner with Davis Polk & Wardwell, where he counsels clients about the requirements of U.S. securities regulations and represents clients in SEC investigations and SEC and private securities litigation. Mr. Lynch has held several positions at the SEC, the most recent of which was director of the Division of Enforcement. He is a member of the American Bar and the International Bar associations and holds an A.B. from Syracuse University and a J.D. from Duke University.

Susan D. Martin, CFA, is a consultant to the Association for Investment Management and Research on the Performance Presentation Standards. Ms. Martin has previously served as a vice president in the Education and Programs Department of AIMR and was a member of the Management Committee. Prior to joining AIMR, Ms. Martin was at the investment advisory firm of Manning & Napier Advisors. She holds a B.A. from the State University of New York at Albany and an M.B.A. from Rochester Institute of Technology.

Iain W. McAra is a senior performance analyst for Baring International Investment, Limited. Previously, he worked in the performance analysis group at Citibank Investment Bank Limited. Mr. McAra has also worked in the areas of technical analysis and derivatives for Union Bank of Switzerland. He is a graduate of London University.

Ian R. O'Reilly, CFA, is vice president and director at Wood Gundy Inc.. Previously, he served as vice president and senior investment analyst at Dominion Securities. He is on the board of governors of the Association for Investment Management and Research, and is also a member of the Professional Conduct Committee. Mr. O'Reilly holds an M.A. in mathematics and economics from the University of Dublin.

Ermanno Pascutto is executive director of the Hong Kong Securities & Futures Commission Corporate Finance Division. He has also served as deputy chairman and chairman of the SFC Takeovers Committee. Mr. Pascutto previously served as executive director of the Ontario Securities Commission and directed the Canadian securities regulatory body. He is a graduate of the University of Toronto Faculty of Law.

William F. Quinn is the founding president of AMR Investment Services, which manages pension assets and short-term cash assets for American Airlines and outside clients. Mr. Quinn created the American AAdvantage Funds and serves as president and trustee. Previously, he was employed with Arthur Young and Company. Mr. Quinn is the founder of the Dallas/Fort Worth Metroplex Plan Sponsors Group and a member of the Financial Executives Institute's Committee on Investment of Employee Benefit Assets. He holds a B.S. in accounting from Fordham University.

Elliot L. Richardson is senior resident partner at Milbank, Tweed, Hadley & McCloy. He has served as a personal representative for the United Nations monitoring the electoral process in Nicaragua, as ambassador-at-large and special representative to the Law of the Sea Conference, as Secretary of Commerce; ambassador to the Court of St. James, U.S. Attorney General, Secretary of Defense, Secretary of Health, Education and Welfare, and attorney general of Massachusetts. He is the author of numerous articles on government, law, and foreign policy and of *The Creative Balance* (New York: Holt, Rinehart, and Winston, 1976). Mr. Richardson holds an A.B. from Harvard College and an LL.B. from Harvard Law School.

Martin F. Ryan is managing director of Russell Data Services responsible for analysis and verification services to plan sponsors and money managers. Previously, he served as president of Investment Data Systems and president of Pro Computing Corporation, a microcomputer software-development firm. Mr. Ryan holds a B.S. in general science from the U.S. Military Academy.

Stanley Sporkin is U.S. District Judge of the U.S. District Court for the District of Columbia. Prior to his appointment, he served as general counsel for the Central Intelligence Agency and as director of enforcement with the SEC. In addition to being a Certified Public Accountant, Mr. Sporkin holds a B.A. from Pennsylvania State University and is a graduate of Yale Law School.

Lori A. Tansey is a senior consultant at the Ethics Resource Center responsible for marketing, ethics training, and monitoring internal operations. She previously served as director of the center's Advisory Services Group. Prior to joining the Ethics Resource Center, she served in Procter & Gamble's brand management operations. Ms. Tansey holds an A.B. in political science from Duke University.

R. Charles Tschampion, CFA, is a vice president of General Motors Investment Management Corporation responsible for pension portfolio strategy and manager relations. He has held several positions in GM's treasury operations, including manager of the corporation's cash portfolio. Mr. Tschampion is co-chair of the Association for Investment Management and Research's Performance Presentation Standards Implementation Committee, a director of the Brazilian Investment Fund, a member of the investment subcommittee for the Lehigh University Endowment Fund, and a member of the editorial board for *The CFA Digest*. He holds a B.S. in industrial engineering and an M.B.A. from Lehigh University.

O. Ray Vass is first vice president and director of compliance and regulatory policy at Merrill Lynch, Pierce, Fenner & Smith. Previously, he was vice president and director of compliance at Paine Webber. Mr. Vass is also a member of the Securities Industry Task Force on Continuing Education. He holds a B.S. in mechanical engineering and an M.B.A. from the University of Maryland.

Good Ethics: An Overview

H. Kent Baker, CFA
University Professor and Chair, Department of Finance and Real Estate
Kogod College of Business Administration
The American University

"Ethics" means a set of guiding moral principles or values. "Ethical behavior" refers to behavior that conforms to those values, and both terms are often used to imply *good* ethics or *good* ethical behavior. The presentations in this seminar explain why good ethics, or shortened to *ethics*, in the investment industry in particular, is good business. As several authors emphasize, investment professionals must live up to the highest possible standards of ethical behavior and practices in order to maintain public trust. Only by following high ethical standards will the U.S. financial services industry remain the best in the world. The investment business, however, is an industry in which opportunities to be unethical arise every day. The challenges this dilemma creates for individuals, firms, professional organizations, and regulators pervade the presentations that follow.

This proceedings opens with four expositions on ethics and public trust in general and on ethical and regulatory issues in the securities industry. The following two authors then discuss public perceptions of the investment industry. The role of AIMR's standards in upholding ethics and the perception of ethical behavior of the industry is then discussed. The first of these presentations reviews the AIMR Code of Ethics and Standards of Professional Conduct (which are contained in Appendix A to this book) and is followed by a discussion of how buy-side and sell-side participants practice the code and standards.

The presentations then focus on compliance guidelines and programs, and on regulation and ethical standards around the world. Next, attention shifts to the ethical implications of using soft dollars. The final section deals with implementating AIMR's Performance Presentation Standards (which are presented in Appendix B).

Together, these presentations provide a captivating look into the ethical practices within the industry and suggest areas for future reform.

Definition and Background

The first presentation provides a lively introduction to the relationship of ethics to public trust and confidence in the U.S. financial services industry. The Honorable Elliot Richardson examines the issue of the ethical behavior of all those placed in a position of public trust. He contends that nothing is wrong ethically with simply having a conflict of interest. Only behavior is ethical or unethical. In conflict-of-interest situations today, however, people are presumed to act in their own self-interests rather than in the interests of their clients. Rules of conduct, including conflict-of-interest rules, serve the purpose of helping to disarm public suspicion. They should not, however, be mistaken for ethical precepts. According to Richardson, the two fundamental elements of ethical principles are trust and accountability.

William Avera also stresses the tremendous importance ethics has for the investment industry because of the industry's complete dependence on handling other people's money. Ethical behavior among investment professionals is critical to maintaining public trust. Without that trust, people will take their money away from intangible assets and investment managers and put it in physical assets. The investment business inhabits a hostile environment, however, for maintaining public trust. Threats to ethical behavior in the industry include dealing with large amounts of money, extreme competitiveness, and attracting people who are success oriented.

The critical nature of maintaining public trust led AIMR's forerunners to institute the Professional Conduct Program. The primary purpose of the program is to provide a framework in which to make ethical decisions in a hostile environment. With the AIMR code and standards, the association is trying to reinforce public expectations about investment management being an ethical business. Key elements of the desired ethical conduct are as follows:

- Conduct yourself with integrity and dignity and act ethically in all dealings.
- Perform financial analysis, and encourage others to do similarly, in a professional and ethical manner that reflects credit on the profession.
- Act with competence and strive to maintain and improve competence in yourself and others.

- Use proper care and exercise independent professional judgment.

The Honorable Stanley Sporkin continues the discussion of approaches to ethical dilemmas in the investment industry. He examines ethical dilemmas in two specific aspects. The first is the commission compensation system for broker/dealers. The current system is geared to producing commissions by generating purchases and sales of securities. This system creates the potential for churning and improper allocations. The most ethical conduct usually occurs when the compensation and incentives are the least tied to generating income for the money management organization. Unfortunately, no easy answer to the compensation dilemma exists. Some potential solutions include using fixed salaries and having strict licensing requirements and oversight.

A second area requiring reform is the way in which portfolio managers and investment advisors conduct their personal investment activities. Sporkin makes four suggestions about how money managers should handle their own accounts:

- Place their own portfolios in blind trusts or engage others to manage their accounts.
- Report their investment holdings to their employers.
- Disclose personal investment decisions to clients and to the SEC.
- Set up a fair and appropriate system for making allocations among accounts.

Carter Beese contends that individual failures to maintain high ethical standards erode public confidence in the marketplace; therefore, self-policing and government regulation have major roles to play in the long-term continued success of the U.S. capital markets. When individual and firm ethics do not adequately promote investor protection and public confidence, self-policing needs to provide that protection. When self-policing fails, the SEC has an obligation to advance cost-effective regulation to achieve those goals.

Beese discusses several areas that currently require self-policing by the investments industry: market transparency for municipal securities, sales practices, supervisory standards, suitability, and investor education. He illustrates the role of the SEC by discussing three areas of action or proposed action by the commission to ensure the integrity of the securities markets: insider-trading prohibitions, restrictions on payment for order flow, and the treatment of derivative products.

Public Perceptions of the Investment Industry

The next two discussions deal with perceptions of ethical problems in the industry that may undermine public confidence in the markets and providers of financial services. Scott Lummer examines three aspects of public perceptions of the investment industry. First, he evaluates whether any trends are noticeable in the public's perception of ethics violations in the industry. He concludes that the public's perceptions of ethics differ depending on whether "the public" is a plan sponsor, an individual investor, or the press. Second, Lummer discusses the actions being taken to create ethical values in the industry. He finds more attention to ethics training today than in the past but also sees room for improvement in college curriculums and the programs of securities firms. Third, he analyzes the roots of the public's negative perceptions about investment professionals. He attributes the causes to poor public relations and a lack of ethics training.

Finally, Lummer notes AIMR's activities to encourage industrywide ethical behavior through its Professional Conduct Program and educational materials, but he urges companies within the industry to do more than at present to counteract the current unfavorable perceptions. At the company level, the focus should be on continuing education, continual management, and leadership.

Gary Lynch views the public's perception of the investment industry as having undergone dramatic change in the past decade. Notorious cases of securities law violations of the 1980s and the attendant publicity severely damaged the industry in the eyes of the public and of Congress. As a result, the penalty structure in U.S. regulation of the securities markets changed completely. Not only did the penalties become tougher, but the SEC also now has the power to levy a penalty in any matter brought before it. Partly because of the press, the public's attention is much more focused on ethics in the investment industry than in the past. The biggest challenge for the future will be to educate the public and Congress about how the securities industry operates and about modern investment products.

Interpretation and Implementation of Standards

Investment professionals who set out to apply ethics in their daily business face the challenge of translating ideas about ideal behavior into actual behavior. In this connection, Avera's second presentation summarizes the guidelines for applying ethics that AIMR's Professional Conduct Program affords and discusses some commonly asked questions about applying the Standards of Professional Conduct.

Avera also discusses the program's enforcement as an important element in reassuring the public that the profession is committed to upholding the standards. As a self-regulatory organization, AIMR requires all members to participate in its program for professional responsibility and to sign an annual statement about their professional conduct. To add credibility to its Professional Conduct Program, AIMR has a self-enforcement system consisting of five major elements. Enforcement is

- based on self-reporting and peer reporting,
- regional in nature,
- supported by a professional staff,
- confidential, and
- carried out by peer review.

Avera reviews several commonly raised issues about ethical behavior and illustrates how, in many situations, the standards can *guide* behavior but individual judgment is nevertheless required. One such issue is the proper allocation of initial public offerings. According to the standards, investment professionals should have a reasonable basis for their actions, give priority to customers, and treat all customers fairly. Another issue is the length of time investment professionals should wait before taking action in a personal account. The standards do not mandate a specific time because the timing will depend on the circumstances. A third issue involves when a gift is too valuable to accept. The gift should be nominal.

Judith Freyer examines the responsibilities of plan sponsors and other fiduciaries to further the application of high ethical standards in day-to-day business. Pension plan sponsors, as the final buy-side entities, often have a different perspective about the investment industry and its ethics. Plan sponsors must follow the adage "let the buyer beware" and closely watch and understand what they are buying.

Freyer analyzes the tension between morality imposed by external controls and morality imposed from within. She notes that laws, regulations, and external controls are ineffective when societal or professional norms are inadequate. If investment professionals do not have the moral discipline within (i.e., the small voice within that delineates right from wrong), they will equivocate on tough issues or end up being paralyzed by their own indecision. The AIMR Code of Ethics and Standards of Professional Conduct provide a framework for ethical conduct that combines external and internal controls.

To illustrate how external and internal disciplines really work in the financial marketplace, Freyer cites results of a survey of the profession on ethical influences and behavior.[1] According to this survey, senior management is the single most important source of ethical training for investment analysts; the home environment is the most effective source. The most important deterrent to unethical behavior is fear of the law; a published code of ethics ranked last. The survey also shows that the failure to use diligence and thoroughness in making recommendations is the most often cited ethical violation.

Ray Vass focuses on the compliance and ethics function in a broker/dealer firm. He stresses that investment professionals should be held to a higher standard than legality. Considering the increasing negative publicity about the industry's perceived lack of ethics, acting ethically is more than ever in the best interests of those in the securities industry.

The compliance function in a broker/dealer organization deals primarily with conduct and sales practices. The concepts and rules of conducts cannot be exact, however, and compliance is not easily measured. At Vass's firm, the policies about ethical behavior rest on three major concepts designed for the long-term benefit of the firm:

- The customer's interest must come first.
- Good compliance is good business.
- No one's bottom line is more important than the reputation of the firm.

Compliance Guidelines

AIMR's General Counsel Michael Caccese discusses the securities firm's need for a compliance program, the elements of an effective compliance program, and the special role of a compliance officer. He also gives an overview of Chinese Wall procedures for separating the various departments in today's diversified financial services firms.

A formal compliance program has both advantages and disadvantages. Perhaps the greatest benefit of such programs is that they provide an effective way for firms to meet their legal requirements to supervise their employees and to guide employees' behavior. Compliance programs can also foster an ethical culture within the firm and deter crime, negative publicity, and misconduct. In addition, a compliance program may serve as an affirmative defense to lessen penalties for violations involving supervisory failure. A major disadvantage is that a firm *must* follow its compliance program once the program is in place.

Developing an effective compliance program in-

---

[1] E. Theodore Veit and Michael R. Murphy, *Ethics in the Investment Profession: A Survey* (Charlottesville, Va.: The Research Foundation of The Institute of Chartered Financial Analysts, 1992).

volves six steps:

- Obtain board and CEO support.
- Review business activities and the regulatory environment.
- Review competitors' programs.
- Draft the program.
- Carry out the program.
- Keep the program current.

Compliance officers are important in carrying out an effective program and have a legal responsibility to enforce compliance. A compliance officer is a supervisor who can affect behavior and respond to misconduct. There are two types of compliance officers—direct and indirect supervisors. Caccese discusses three cases that provide guidance about who is a compliance officer.

Caccese notes that Chinese Walls, departmental layouts and policies that limit the flow of confidential information to those who "need to know," are often part of effective compliance programs. A Chinese Wall has two parts: a physical separation of the part of the organization that receives inside information from the rest of the organization, and a written policy stating the trading procedures relating to the prevention of insider trading.

Paul Haaga and Lori Tansey discuss compliance guidelines from the points of view, respectively, of a broker/dealer and a designer of such programs. Haaga focuses on insider-trading policy and transactions reporting to illustrate the policies and compliance processes of a diversified securities firm. He points out that a violation of the insider-trading law involves material nonpublic information and a breach of duty. The procedures he outlines involve a reporting obligation and preclearance for personal securities transactions.

Haaga concludes by providing the following tips for creating and maintaining an effective compliance department:

- Select the right people for the compliance program.
- Create the right environment to educate and motivate the right people.
- Keep the compliance people involved in the business of the company.
- Keep the manuals manageable.
- "Demythify" the rules through communication.
- Involve the compliance department head directly in company management.
- Provide skills training for those involved in compliance.

Tansey begins her presentation by discussing U.S. Sentencing Guidelines for ethics violations. She then focuses on how to develop and maintain the effectiveness of an ethics or compliance program to deter and detect violations. U.S. Sentencing Guidelines for ethics violations became law in November 1991 and accomplished two things. First, they dramatically increased the fines and penalties for corporations convicted of misconduct. Second, they outlined the actions corporations can take to lessen any penalties and fines levied against them for violations.

Tansey posits that a firm that decides to tackle the challenge of establishing an ethics/compliance program and then measure its effectiveness must first understand the three primary reasons for ethical misconduct: ignorance, greed, and the individual's desire for the corporation to succeed. Tansey discusses the following mandates established by the U.S. Sentencing Guidelines for developing an effective ethics/compliance program:

- Establish standards and procedures for employees and agents.
- Designate a high-level employee to ensure compliance.
- Do not delegate discretionary authority to known or likely offenders.
- Practice effective communication of standards.
- Monitor and audit systems.
- Apply consistent and appropriate disciplinary mechanisms.
- Provide continual program improvement.

To determine whether an ethics or compliance program is effective requires identifying the objectives of the program, establishing what needs to be evaluated or measured, and deciding the tools and methods needed for measuring.

Regulation and Ethical Standards around the World

The first presentation devoted to worldwide standards focuses on the rapid growth of non-U.S. private pension plans. Brian Hersey notes that many markets are in the beginning stages of globalizing their pension-asset management practices. The major catalysts for the growth in non-U.S. private pension assets are the overall maturing of plans abroad and legislative actions to shift retirement burdens to the private sector.

Although countries are at different stages of development in establishing standards of practice, Hersey notes that the general trend is toward adopting practices similar to those in the United States. A totally uniform set of standards is unlikely to unfold soon because many impediments to universal standards remain among countries. Key issues in relating

AIMR's standards to global investment practices are the use of material nonpublic information, the presentation of performance, priority of transactions, and disclosure of conflicts. Hersey contends that, despite the absence of broad-based compliance with AIMR's standards in many markets, AIMR member organizations should not be disadvantaged in competing for global investment business.

Europe

David Beevers offers an overview of the regulatory status in the United Kingdom and the European Union (EU). The governing U.K. statute is the relatively recent Financial Services Act, which created a two-tier system. The Securities and Investment Board, as the senior regulator, supervises the frontline of regulation by various self-regulating organizations. The second tier contains several other institutions involved in regulation, such as the Bank of England and the London Stock Exchange. The current regulatory system in the United Kingdom results in overlapping regulators and a complexity of rules. Beevers contends that the United Kingdom needs a simpler system set on a statutory base and containing more emphasis on promoting high ethical standards.

In continental Europe, the approaches to regulation and ethical standards diverge widely. To help overcome this divergence, the Investment Services Directive will in 1996 begin the process of introducing a framework of rules for operating the general securities business in Europe. A potential problem in EU regulation, however, is that each member state will draft and enforce the rules, which could cause further divergence. Beevers recommends that the basic framework of laws for the EU embody a consensus on ethical standards.

Hong Kong

Ermanno Pascutto examines the Hong Kong securities markets and discusses the role of the Securities & Futures Commission (SFC) in promoting an efficient market for investors. This large and rapidly growing market was virtually unregulated until the SFC was established in 1989. The mission of the SFC is to promote efficiency and fairness in the markets. Much of the SFC's work has involved overhauling the regulatory framework, implementing international standards, and improving standards of corporate and professional behavior. Both the Stock Exchange of Hong Kong and the SFC recently introduced codes of conduct. Although the Hong Kong market is generally in line with international standards of market regulation and practice, the process of reform must continue.

Pascutto also reviews changes in the regulatory structure in Hong Kong, with emphasis on the corporate governance of listed companies and regulation of intermediaries. A high level of corporate control exists in the Hong Kong market because most companies are under the effective or legal control of a single shareholder or group of shareholders acting together. The central corporate-governance concerns in Hong Kong are the accountability of directors or controlling shareholders to public minority shareholders and equity between controlling and minority shareholders. The SFC uses a "fit and proper" test in regulating intermediaries to ensure that they have appropriate qualifications.

The Ethical Implications of Using Soft Dollars

Three presentations deal with the current issue of soft dollars. The first, by Robert Anselmi, presents the ethical implications of using soft dollars from the perspective of a fiduciary, namely, J.P. Morgan Investment Management. Anselmi views soft dollars as generally encompassing the payments a fiduciary causes clients to make to a broker that exceed the lowest available commission for executing a securities trade. The three most common uses of soft dollars are to pay for proprietary research searches, for third-party research services, and for directed brokerage. J.P. Morgan bases its soft-dollar practices on two basic principles:

- Commissions are the property of the client and should be used for the benefit of the client, not the money manager.
- Managers have a responsibility to clients to minimize transaction costs.

Thomas Healey discusses the history of soft-dollar arrangements and their ethical implications for brokers. He defines a soft-dollar arrangement as one in which a broker receives commissions above the charge for execution services and, in return, provides other products and services to investment managers and plan sponsors. He links the genesis of soft-dollar arrangements to the abolition of fixed commissions.

Although soft-dollar arrangements have legitimate uses, Healey posits, increased use creates potential problems, including:

- conflict of interests between the client and the investment manager,
- decreased quality of trade execution,
- decreased market liquidity,
- increased market volatility,
- an incentive to consultants to make recommendations on the basis of soft-dollar use, and

- an incentive to increase portfolio turnover.

A proposed solution for combating these problems is to disclose information about soft-dollar practices to clients.

William Quinn discusses the ethical problems for clients that result from using soft-dollar arrangements. He sees two troublesome aspects. First, the arrangement is virtually hidden. Thus, clients cannot determine whether they are getting good value for the dollars spent. Second is a lack of disclosure about soft-dollar arrangements.

Quinn identifies five potential areas of abuse relating to soft dollars, many of which coincide with those discussed by Healey. Quinn states that the biggest potential problem area comes from the divergent interests of the money manager and the client. To avoid the conflicts inherent with soft-dollar arrangements, Quinn's firm follows a three-point policy:

- Managers are to direct no commissions to pay for research.
- Managers are periodically to report unsolicited research services received.
- Managers are to direct no commissions on behalf of the firm; the firm will pay cash for services it needs.

Quinn believes that eliminating soft dollars whenever possible is a better solution than requiring full disclosure because too many parties are involved to allow proper policing of disclosure. Finally, as a result of the investment management industry's failure to self-police the use of soft dollars, the industry now awaits regulations requiring disclosure of such arrangements.

AIMR Performance Presentation Standards

AIMR's Performance Presentation Standards (PPS) became part of the Standards of Professional Conduct for domestic portfolios on January 1, 1993. Two authors discuss the implementation of the PPS in the United States almost a year later.

Martin Ryan provides an update on the implementation of the PPS in the United States from a consultant's viewpoint. He focuses on the role the plan sponsor plays in further implementation of the PPS. Ryan notes that implementation of the PPS has encountered some problems. For example, some confusion exists about what the standards are and how they are being implemented. The two areas causing the most confusion are how many composites a manager should have and whether those composites should be verified. Nevertheless, Ryan concludes, implementation is progressing.

Ryan suggests that the key to increasing adoption of the PPS rests with plan sponsors. They must understand the data and must realize that composites have different risk and return characteristics from individual portfolios. They must also understand that risk is a function of the period being measured and the portfolios used in the calculation. Finally, plan sponsors must understand the composition of a composite. Ryan concludes by discussing a graphical approach for displaying dispersion within composites.

Charles Tschampion begins by discussing the ethical framework for the PPS: full disclosure, fair representation, comparability, and minimum requirements. He then turns to a current major implementation issue—verification. The standards recommend, but do not require, verification of claims that performance complies with the PPS. Verification consists of two levels. Level I verification applies to the firm; Level II pertains to the firm and to specific composites; thus, Level II involves the investment management process as well as the measurement of performance.

Tschampion also explains the PPS enforcement program. Enforcement consists of three elements: peer pressure, the SEC, and AIMR. The ultimate enforcers, however, are the clients.

Tschampion concludes by examining the ongoing activities of the PPS Implementation Committee. To respond to industry change, the committee has appointed several subcommittees to examine implementation issues involving the following: bank trusts, real estate, venture capital and private placements, wrap fees, taxable portfolios, and international application.

Compliance with the international aspects of the PPS was mandated for AIMR members as of January 1, 1994. The final presentation in the proceedings is an update by Iain McAra of PPS implementation outside the United States and Canada. McAra begins by reviewing the basic purposes of the PPS: to promote full and fair representation in the reporting of investment results, and to ensure uniformity in reporting to enable comparisons among investment managers. He notes that, to comply with the PPS for international portfolios, firms face added complexity because they must deal with exchange rates and base currencies, country weights, hedging, and various local laws. This added complexity means that the PPS contain additional requirements for international performance reporting and that compliance requires additional disclosures. Thus, applying the standards to international portfolios requires flexibility and sophisticated data gathering.

In conclusion, McAra outlines three conditions needed for the PPS to become the industrywide standard for performance presentation in the future:

- vigilance to assure the proper and consistent use of the standards within the industry,
- insistence that verification be performed on a total-entity basis, and
- efforts to establish the PPS as the global standard.

The Nature of Ethical Principles

Elliot L. Richardson
Partner
Milbank, Tweed, Hadley & McCloy

Laws and regulations can enforce minimal standards of behavior that may be based on ethical standards, and many aphorisms suggest how to act as if one has an ethical backbone, but neither approach can supply a good sense of ethics. Ethics in investment management shares with ethics in government the concepts of public trust and accountability. The profession of investment management, however, has articulated its own specific ethical precepts related to the particular obligations imposed on the profession by the need for trust and accountability.

A close examination of the relationship between good ethics and good performance is a valuable exercise. This presentation focuses on this relationship as it applies to those who have been placed in a position of public trust. Much of what I have to say draws upon my recent experience in chairing a working group on ethics in government for the Council for Excellence in Government, which is composed of several hundred individuals who have held senior positions in a great variety of federal departments and agencies.

Rules, Words of Wisdom, or Ethics?

Inside the Beltway, the word "ethics" is used in a context having nothing to do with ethics as most of us understand the term. The Washington version of the word applies to rules, not principles; appearance, not behavior. Its most frequent application is to conflicts of interest. In fact, however, nothing is ethically wrong with merely having a conflict of interest, but in Washington, the general assumption is that not only is having a conflict of interest wrong but merely having the *appearance* of a conflict of interest is wrong.

Although they do not involve ethical questions, appearances can, of course, be important. When he asked me to leave the U.S. Department of Defense and take on the job of Attorney General of the United States, President Richard Nixon left to me the question of whether to appoint a special prosecutor for Watergate or to assume authority for the investigation myself. I decided that because I had been a

Nixon appointee throughout the first term of his presidency, public confidence required giving the responsibility for the Watergate investigation to somebody else.

After an exhaustive search, I came up with Harvard Law School professor Archibald Cox as the special prosecutor. Cox had been Solicitor General of the United States under the John Kennedy and the Lyndon Johnson administrations. A Massachusetts Yankee, he had himself sworn in as special prosecutor in his old U.S. Justice Department office and held a reception afterward in which all the guests were either members of the Kennedy family or members of the Kennedy administration. He was surprised, if not insulted, however, when Nixon developed the idea that Cox was a Kennedy operative who was out to get him. Nixon never changed that belief, and it certainly had something to do with Cox's firing and my resignation.

I could never persuade Nixon or anybody in the White House that Cox would actually rather have cut off his right arm than take any action out of personal bias or vindictiveness toward Nixon—any action that was not fully justified, indeed compelled, by the evidence. That attitude is the substance of ethical commitment.

Only a generation ago, fiduciaries would have been insulted by the suggestion that conflicts of interest present ethical dilemmas, because that suggestion implies that they would favor their personal interests over their fiduciary responsibilities in a situation of conflict, which of course, they would never have dreamed of doing. In conflict-of-interest situations today, most people are presumed to act in their own self-interest rather than in the interest of their clients, which is why conflicts of interest are presented as ethically wrong. Conflicts of interest are not, however, inherently unethical; only behavior is ethical or unethical.

During a discussion about this issue with members of the Council on Excellence working group on ethics, I suggested a review of a government ethics manual to determine exactly what it said about ethics. We chose to review the SEC manual, which was about 45 pages long. Only one and a half pages dealt with ethics. Much of the manual addressed conflicts of interest, and the rest dealt with "rules of conduct," such as who, if anybody, should be allowed to pay for one's lunch, airplane ticket, or hotel room and whether one is allowed to accept an honorarium or royalties on a book.

The notion that rules of conduct involve ethical principles makes sense only if you assume that the recipient of, say, a lunch will then pervert or subvert his or her public responsibility for the benefit of the person who buys the lunch. In other words, the premise of this notion is that public servants have no ethics at all.

The alternative is, of course, to drop the idea that these rules have anything to do with ethics and accept, instead, that they have a different function. The rules help maintain confidence in government on the part of a rather suspicious general public by saying to holders of public office, "We do not want you to occupy a situation or put yourself in a position in which somebody on the outside who does not know that you really are an honorable person might think that you are not and that you might thus be tempted to subvert your public position to favor that other person who has done something for you." That purpose, and that alone, is the function of these rules of conduct; therefore, when addressing the questions of ethics and ethical principles, we obviously need to look in a different direction from these rules.

The point is not that rules of conduct, including conflict-of-interest rules, should be wiped off the books; they do help disarm public suspicion. But because they have come to be viewed as addressing ethical actions, ethics as such has barely been discussed.

Another approach to ethical questions agrees with what I have said about rules but then adopts an equally serious mischaracterization of ethical principles. This point of view is epitomized by the commonly accepted piece of advice in Washington that all you need to know about ethics is to ask yourself, when you are thinking about doing something, "How would I like to see this on the front page of tomorrow's *New York Times*?" This approach may lead you to refrain from taking the action, but you are not doing so because you are an ethical person. You are doing so because you are a careful person who does not want to be embarrassed by what other people may consider inappropriate or improper behavior.

Exactly the same proposition is summed up by Cervantes' axiom: Honesty is the best policy. If "policy" is the reason you are honest, then again, you are not behaving on the basis of any ethical principle; you decided that to act as if you are honest is smart, a matter of intelligent self-interest.

The classic of all these prudential aphorisms is one by H.L. Mencken in which he defines conscience as "the inner voice which warns us that somebody may be looking."

James Madison, referring to the role of the system of checks and balances, pointed out that, under it, ambition is made to counteract ambition and thus "to supply the defect of better qualities." That is what the admonitions do, and in that role, they are useful. Just as the utility of rules of conduct should not be denied, so neither should shrewd maxims be banished. They no doubt do good; they encourage you to approximate ethical behavior without ethics, sometimes so successfully that nobody on the outside will even know the difference. Rules of conduct and prudential admonitions should not be mistaken, however, for ethical precepts.

True Ethical Principles

The two fundamental elements of ethical principles are trust and accountability. The importance of trust is captured in the program description for this seminar: "Ethics means a set of moral principles or values that guides behavior. . . . Ethical behavior is critical to maintaining the public trust." These statements capture more than the trust between an advisor or service provider and an individual client; they also relate to the trust the general public places in the investment management profession as a whole, trust in the very function of investment management.

I tried to make the same point in the *Statement of Principles of Ethics in Government for the Council on Excellence in Government*.[1] My version is: "Public service is a public trust." It is a cliché, but it is also a fundamental truth. The highest obligation of every individual in government is to fulfill that trust. Each person who undertakes the public trust assumes two paramount obligations—to serve the public interest, and to perform with integrity.

The second element, accountability, is a corner-

[1]Available from the author.

stone of our democracy. The unique aspect of our political system is that government derives its powers from us, the people. We delegate to our public servants responsibility for things that concern us in common, that need to be done for society as a whole. Those to whom we have delegated power remain accountable to us. Accountability in this broad context (between us—the people of the United States—and the people to whom we delegate responsibility) is analogous to the kind of accountability in the investment management profession that is being discussed at this seminar.

As to the kinds of tough ethical problems this seminar is addressing, the *Statement on Principles of Ethics in Government* has the following practical advice for those in a position of public trust: "The true public servant will not act out of spite, bias, or favoritism, will not tell the boss only what she/he wants to hear, respects the confidence and views of others, does not succumb to peer or political pressure, contributes to a climate of mutual trust and respect, refuses to let official actions be influenced by personal relationships, including those arising from past or prospective employment, has the courage of his/her convictions, is not seduced by flattery, unflinchingly accepts responsibility, does not try to shift blame to others, can distinguish between the need to support an unwelcome decision and the duty to blow the whistle, and never forgets that she/he is working for the people, all the people."

I would add, however, Oliver Wendell Holmes, Jr.'s wise observation that "general propositions do not decide concrete cases." These propositions about ethics in practice are all valid, but they are obviously not self-executing, and the public servant or investment manager can have tough calls—for example, distinguishing between the need to support an unwelcome decision and the duty to blow the whistle. No general rules can automatically resolve a difficult issue.

Professional Ethics

There is an element in the realm of professional ethical principles that distinguishes those principles from the ethical standards appropriate in day-to-day life in our homes and communities. This difference is clear in the *Ethics in the Investment Profession* survey.[2] Having been based on AIMR's Code of Ethics and Standards of Professional Conduct,[3] the ques-

tions asked in the survey related directly to the kinds of ethical problems presented to investment managers and advisors. These questions specifically address the duty of the investment manager or advisor to the client.

This type of duty exists in other professions. Doctors and lawyers, for example, have specific kinds of responsibilities toward their patients or clients. Therefore, it is entirely appropriate to think in terms of the ethical problems that are special or peculiar to a profession.

Each profession has responsibilities that call for articulating its own ethical precepts. In investment management, one such precept addresses the "failure to use diligence and thoroughness in making recommendations." An outsider might think that failing to do a diligent, thorough job because of laziness or lack of time is not a breach of ethics, although it may be the basis for discipline. In a situation in which investment advice is being given, however, and investment recommendations that entail various risks are being made, the profession has decided that an advisor/manager is not fulfilling a prime duty to the client unless the advisor/manager acts with diligence and thoroughness. Thus, diligence in this context *is* an ethical obligation.

Another concept in the investment management profession relates to *disclosure*. One of the survey questions asked how frequently the respondent believes a "failure to disclose conflicts of interest to clients and/or employer" occurs. This approach is the right one to take regarding conflicts of interest. It recognizes that the conflict is not unethical but that a failure to disclose that conflict is a lapse in appropriate ethical behavior.

Conclusion

This brief discussion of good ethics in investment management and good ethics in government sought to highlight their common denominator. In both situations, ethical obligations attach to a position of trust. Investors have to be able to trust their investment advisors. We the people have to be able to trust our public servants. Rules, regulations, and laws can enforce minimal standards of behavior that correspond to the fulfillment of ethical obligations. They cannot supply a sense of moral obligation. That sense is the subject and the substance of good ethics.

---

[2]E. Theodore Veit and Michael R. Murphy, *Ethics in the Investment Profession: A Survey* (Charlottesville, Va.: The Research Foundation of The Institute of Chartered Financial Analysts, 1992).

[3]See Appendix A.

Question and Answer Session

Elliot L. Richardson

Question: Has the federal government been too concerned about the appearance rather than the reality of ethical behavior? If so, how can that problem be addressed at the leadership level so that the focus is on the real core of ethical behavior rather than a "prudential approach"?

Richardson: First, the present rules have gotten ridiculously cumbersome. Most of the rules are needed, but they have been pushed to a point where I sometimes believe that the Ethics in Government Act had better be called the "No Ethics and Government Act" because its premise is that no one in government has any ethics. The assumption, for example, that anyone who owns a handful of shares in a nationally traded company will use the influence of his or her government position to benefit that company is ridiculous. This assumption has led, however, to the government's policy requiring divestiture of such ownership. These types of rules have been pushed too far and should be cut back.

To address the situation, the leaders in the government, starting with the President and going on to heads of departments and agencies, need to convey to their appointees the sense that they are in public service to serve, that their commitment is to the merits of the issues they address. The leaders must also level with the American people, give us the facts about the problems we face, and make clear the costs and benefits of competing choices.

The leaders have a special responsibility within their organizations to advocate core values, ex-

emplify guiding principles, evaluate their subordinates' performance in light of those standards, and seek others with strong ethical values to work in the organization. My working group's statement, for example, suggests various ways that ongoing training, sources of advice, regular meetings, and off-the-record discussions with peers can help create a context in which the tough calls can be addressed.

Question: What are the most common ethical situations or problems you have faced, and how did you deal with them?

Richardson: I have not faced many. The hardest problems for me were those in which I thought the public interest called for a given course of action and I suspected that the President or some other superior would not agree with me for various reasons, so I might get overruled. Then, the question was: What should I do? I faced this problem a number of times. First, I would try to head the disagreement off, to assure that I won at the end of the day. Ironically, Nixon saved me from resigning during the Dwight Eisenhower Administration over a decision taken at a cabinet meeting. Prior to the meeting, I had my resignation all written because I thought we were going to lose, but thanks to Nixon's timely interventions, we didn't, so I did not have to resign.

Most other types of ethical problems were not really problems for me. Telling people what they do not want to hear can be difficult, but it is a question of facing up to what you have to do.

Sometimes people surprise you; they may, in fact, be grateful for honesty. Two of my most loyal friends to this day are subordinates whom I demoted because they could not handle their jobs. They were decent, intelligent people, and as it turned out, they knew they were not handling their responsibilities. They were grateful to be given jobs they *could* handle.

Question: What advice would you give the youth of the country?

Richardson: That phrase, "the youth of the country," embraces an enormous number of unique individuals, each of whom has a number of reasonable, appropriate, legitimate options. Thus, I would try to get them to realize that nobody else can make choices for them. They have to catch themselves out of the corner of their own eyes. They have to gauge how they react to the spin that is being given to them by other people who start sounding as if this or that is what they should do. If they note that they are resisting that advice, they should heed their reactions. At the same time, young people need to discover their own interests, capabilities, and inclinations.

One point I emphasize to young people is that jobs differ greatly in their ambience; by that, I mean the jobs' tempos, characters, and ratios of intellect and articulateness to physical components. Take, for example, piano playing versus surgery; surgeons must accumulate 12 postbaccalaureate years, but they end up like pianists, using their hands.

Or take the special characteristics of politics. I've turned down judgeships, professorships, and consideration for college presidencies because I like to be in situations that give me short feedback loops. I like to be able to do something and quickly see what happens, react to it, and take further action.

These are the kinds of job characteristics that young people today must consider. Because they have so many options, the choice is harder, in many respects, than in the past.

Another point I would emphasize to today's youth is that they should not be in a hurry. They should consider the *other* end of their lives. Look at the people who retire at 54 and the people who are still working at 84. Young people should realize that it does not matter if they make several different starts and decide those are not what they want to do, as long as they give their best at the time to whatever they do do.

Definition of Industry Ethics and Development of a Code

William E. Avera, CFA
President
Fincap, Inc.

The investment management business depends in a fundamental way on public trust, but the environment in which analysts operate is hostile to ethical behavior: It is highly competitive and involves huge amounts of money and overachieving practitioners. The AIMR Code of Ethics and Standards of Professional Conduct were designed to deal with this dilemma. Financial analysts must be perceived to reflect each characteristic mentioned in the Code of Ethics if the profession is to maintain public trust.

Ethics is a particularly important topic for the investment industry and securities analysts because the whole industry is predicated on dealing with other people's money. This presentation discusses the importance of that public trust and how realization of its importance led to what is now the AIMR program of a code and standards for financial analysts.

Public Trust

One of the most important developments of modern society is the willingness of people to invest their wealth in intangible instruments like stocks and bonds rather than in tangible assets like gold, silver, and livestock. This transition contributed significantly to the economically advanced, global society in which we live. It also generated the growth of the modern investment industry.

Survival of the investment industry depends on public trust. If investors cease to trust the people in the industry—if they think their assets are not in good hands, if they think we might misuse those assets, if they think we might put our interests ahead of their interests, or if they think we might lie, cheat, and steal to get ahead—then that fragile public trust will be shattered and the game will be over. People will take their money away from the intangible assets, and from the investment managers, and put it in physical assets, and the economy will collapse.

That scenario may be overly dramatic, but it is within the realm of possibility. We must maintain public trust. Without it, our profession is history.

Without it, the modern capitalistic system that has developed and been so fruitful will disappear.

Investment managers can maintain public trust by being ethical and by being perceived as being ethical, by people thinking their money is in good hands. These achievements are easier said than done, however, because the investment business is a hostile environment for maintaining public trust. The environment holds several threats to the ethics of the people within the industry.

One threat to ethical behavior in the industry is that the business deals with lots and lots of money. People in the business get used to seeing many zeroes, and they begin to talk about millions of dollars as if those amounts were insignificant. Then, some find it easy to say, "Well, I am dealing with millions here, millions there. How about some going home with me?"

The second threat to the ethics of the people in the business is that the industry is very competitive. Everybody wants to get his or her picture on the cover of *Institutional Investor*. Everybody wants to be the biggest, the most successful, the richest money manager, consultant, plan sponsor, whatever. They want their competitors' clients. Some will do almost anything to be at the top of the competitive pyramid.

The third threat, one that is directly related to the competitive pressures of the business, is the nature of the people in investment management. The people who are in the money business are typically very success oriented. They have been successful all their lives; they were usually good students, overachievers; and they are type-A personalities. They are people who are used to winning and define themselves in terms of winning. Therefore, they put a lot of pressure on themselves to take the extra steps, do whatever is necessary, to win. Often doing what is necessary means simply working hard, working late, traveling hard, and studying hard, but sometimes people do not stop with those legitimate ways to win. They go over the line to illegitimate ways to win.

People who come into the financial analyst profession are basically "good" people, however. They have sound ethical backgrounds. (Those who do not have such backgrounds turn to other professions, like crime, in which they can get money fast without ethical principles.) But these basically good people enter a very hostile environment where they are under a great deal of pressure.

The threats to ethical principles are real in the financial services industry, as recent experiences in Texas banking can confirm. In the early 1980s, as oil money started flowing and the Texas banks started booming, some bankers began to conceive of ways to increase the money they could make that involved just a little step over to the dark side. They took that step, and nobody said anything to them, nothing bad happened, and they made a lot of money. Then they took another step, and again nobody said anything to them. Indeed, their pictures were on the front pages of the newspapers as great civic leaders, and they made lots of money.

Then, as the middle of the 1980s approached, they started taking big steps, but again, nobody said anything about it, and they continued making lots of money. Somebody finally said something, however, and the empires the bankers had been building came crashing down. Suddenly, they were criminals. Their lives and their organizations were ruined—all because they were overtaken by greed, because they succumbed to the temptation.

What happened to these bankers is that the environment became hostile to integrity; the rules were not enforced, and nobody reminded them of the responsibilities they had in dealing with other people's money. In their environment, one thing led to another; small baby steps led to more baby steps, which led to bigger steps, and the next thing they knew, the steps were into federal prison. Remember, I am not describing career criminals. They were not "bad" people. But the environment was very dangerous. It was full of risks; they arose continually.

Everybody in this business knows that opportunities to be unethical arise every day, and we can all think of many dishonest maneuvers that could probably be successfully pulled off. Moreover, you do not have to be very smart to figure out ways to cheat

in this industry. So, the nature of the environment is hostile to ethical behavior, but the business depends totally and completely and fundamentally on public trust. How to deal with this dilemma is the challenge AIMR's forerunners set out to meet by instituting a code and standards of conduct.

AIMR's Code of Ethics

The dangerous environment and the need for public trust emerged long before the 1980s. The dilemma has always been part of the business. At various times in the 1920s, for example, the investment community got carried away with itself, got out of line, and threats to public trust abounded. The passage of the Securities Exchange Act and the creation of the SEC in the 1930s were attempts to prevent excesses from happening again.

The 1950s were a time of buoyant markets, a time when lots of people got involved in investing, and a time when mutual funds started to take off. Unfortunately, many investment professionals took advantage of the new investors in the markets and the funds. As a result, as we went into the 1960s, many folks were mad at the investment world because they believed they had been ripped off. And they had been. A movement surged around the country for legislation to increase regulation of the investment markets generally and the financial analyst profession especially.

In an attempt to preempt the ongoing legislative initiatives, a group of professional financial analysts got together in the mid-1970s to develop a self-regulatory program of professional conduct. This program, jointly sponsored by the Financial Analysts Federation and the then newly formed Institute of Chartered Financial Analysts—together, now AIMR—consisted of a Code of Ethics and a statement of Standards of Professional Conduct. The code and standards, with examples of inappropriate behavior, are now published in a handbook.[1] The standards are written for the practicing investment professional and intended to be easy to understand and apply in our day-to-day work.

In the code and standards, AIMR is trying to deal with public expectations. The intention is to tell the public: You can expect this kind of behavior of every analyst every day. AIMR is trying to reinforce public expectations that we are an ethical business, that we will treat people fairly, and that we will treat them honestly. To carry out that intention, AIMR strives for rules that are realistic and reasonable, that every

---

[1]See Appendix A for the code and standards. The handbook is *Standards of Practice Handbook*, 6th ed. (Charlottesville, Va.: Association for Investment Management and Research, 1992).

analyst can follow every day, and that are directed toward the common end of maintaining public trust.

Because the AIMR Code of Ethics is the cornerstone for the standards of conduct, the code's key elements are important in understanding what is expected of the ethical financial analyst.

■ *Conduct yourself with integrity and dignity and act in an ethical manner in all dealings.* This first element basically means that the financial analyst will try to be a good person. The statement contains nothing really unique about financial analysts. Other professions—engineers, accountants, and lawyers, for example—have similar statements in their ethical codes.

■ *Perform financial analysis, and encourage others to do likewise, in a professional and ethical manner that reflects credit on the profession.* This statement adds the idea that merely being good in your own mind is not enough. The analyst's actions are to *reflect* credit; the public should *perceive* the analyst as being good. Moreover, the analyst must encourage others to act ethically and professionally.

When the public sees one financial analyst go bad, that hurts us all. The adages about interdependence are true: No financial analyst is an island. Ask not for whom the bells tolls; it tolls for thee. We are our brothers' and sisters' keepers. If one does something unethical and diminishes public trust, we all suffer. Thus, this second statement underscores something unique about financial analysts, which is that we are all in this together.

■ *Act with competence and strive to maintain and improve competence in yourself and others.* Competence is an ethical issue; it is part of public trust. When people give us their money, they not only expect us not to steal from them, they expect us to manage their funds competently. They do not expect us to be ignorant. We must be able to preserve their funds, and manage the risk, and do all the other things that a prudent and competent financial analyst does.

The second part of this statement—the specific stress on maintaining and improving competence—indicates that competency is dynamic. To have known the theories, tools, and practices of the investment management discipline once—to pass the CFA exam, for example—is not enough. The analyst must keep abreast of the changing investment market. Change abounds. New instruments come into use; new ways of doing things develop. There is globalization. The analyst who does not stay current—and, therefore, competent—is not ethical. So, the goal of being ethical imposes a continuing obligation to maintain and improve competency.

■ *Use proper care and exercise independent professional judgment.* This statement gets to the heart of being an ethical financial analyst. It specifies exercising *care* and *independent* judgment. Being competent is not enough. Because the market changes, the analyst must be careful, do the homework, exercise care with each decision and communication. A financial analyst who says, "Oh, the current style is to do this" or "My plan sponsor would like for me to do this with my votes" is not an ethical financial analyst. An ethical financial analyst does his or her homework, does the research.

In addition, a financial analyst who is competent and does the research but tells clients what they want to hear or bends to pressure is not an ethical analyst. The ethical analyst will look the client in the eye and tell the client what her or his opinion is—the good, the bad, and the ugly. You have got to do the work, *and* exercise independent judgment, *and* communicate independent judgment.

This fourth element completes the ultimate aim of the code: for financial analysts to have and be perceived as having dignity, integrity, and competence; to reflect credit on the profession; to care for the ethical behavior of other people in the profession; to perform professional duties with due diligence; and to exercise independent judgment. Perception of these characteristics is what we need if we are going to maintain public trust.

Ethical Dilemmas in the Financial Services Industry

Stanley Sporkin
U.S. District Judge
U.S. District Court for the District of Columbia

High ethical standards in the investment management industry are paramount if the United States is to maintain its worldwide lead in financial services. For that purpose, two areas in great need of reform in the industry are the commission compensation system for broker/dealers and the way in which investment managers conduct their personal investing activities.

Few professions are more fraught with conflicts of interest than the financial services industry. To talk about ethics in the industry, however, and to preach for better ethics are easy. To bring about ethical reform is a different story. This presentation will give an overview of ethical dilemmas in the areas of compensation and investing for one's own account, and will make some suggestions for reform.

Compensation

The entire compensation base of the typical broker/dealer firm is geared to producing commissions by generating purchases and sales of securities. The ethical dilemma posed by this compensation system is truly insoluble.

Good ethics are best achieved when the method of compensation is consistent and compatible with the services being purchased. This proposition is universal; it affects all walks of life. For example, the best and most objective accounting advice is obtained when a client retains an outside accounting firm to review the financial records of a prospective merger partner. The truth of this proposition can be found by comparing the accounting report prepared by an objective accounting firm with the routine accounting report filed by the target's long-standing accounting firm. If Company A wants to take over Company B, A will send in its accountants to look at the books and records, and the accountants will then file a report with Company A. Someone comparing that report with the annual certified reports filed by Company B may think the two accounting firms do not even talk the same language. The accounting firm hired by Company A will have been given the go-ahead to find the tough information because that is in the best interests of Company A.

For another example, compare the due diligence conducted in connection with a firm-commitment underwriting with that performed in connection with a best-efforts underwriting.

In the money management arena, the most ethical conduct usually takes place when the compensation incentives are the least tied to generating income for the money management organization. A look at those organizations deemed the most ethical in the financial services business community will confirm this point.

What is the solution? Use of fixed salaries is not the only sound and ethical method for compensating people in the investment industry. Indeed, a strict salary-only method of compensation also has its downside. Salaried workers in service industries are not the most productive people. They tend to turn into bureaucrats, and bureaucrats—even though they are employed in the private sector—are still bureaucrats.

No easy answer to the compensation dilemma exists because a combination of the following is needed First, before the question of compensation can be approached, a professional, licensed (with respect to all aspects of the securities and investment management business) cadre should be established. Licensing must be based on a combination of ethical and intellectual achievements under the auspices of a private licensing authority that has demonstrated credibility to both its private-sector and governmental overseers. Obtaining the license in the investment and money management fields must be an important achievement for practitioners in the sense that losing that license for nonperformance is a real possibility. In addition, an effective system of private and governmental oversight must exist to punish those who violate the established norms—both ethical and legal norms.

Finally, all systems of compensation must be appropriately balanced to minimize incentives to churn, make improper allocations, or be bureaucratic.

Personal Investment Activities

Another area that must be addressed is the way in which portfolio managers and investment advisors conduct their personal investment activities to avoid conflict with actions that they take on behalf of their clients. When other people's money is being managed, the manager owes those people the highest level of trust and fair dealing. The public is rightly appalled when it learns that some fund manager has engaged in front running, misallocation of purchased securities, buying and selling securities contrary to advice given or action taken, or other nefarious practices.

A recent misallocation case brought by the SEC is particularly troubling. The bucket shop is supposed to have gone out with the enactment of the Securities Exchange Act of 1934. In the SEC case, the problem concerned an allocation when buying a block of stock in the market. The management firm was servicing three or four different organizations, including one account that was the investment fund for the firm's employees. This account was apparently of primary interest to the money managers making the decisions.

The problem in this case stems from a money manager simultaneously managing her or his own investment trust and also public investment trusts. The issues in this care are: How should the allocations be made? Who should get the first allocation on the block of stock? Who gets the lower price? In other words, how does this manager make the allocations when buying big blocks of securities? How can that be done according to the rules?

The ruling in this SEC case states that a money manager cannot trade for any organization in which the manager has an interest, either directly or indirectly, and that rule really is an absolute prohibition. The only thing the manager could do in order to manage both types of accounts is go to the SEC and get an exemption. The problem of conflict of interest in this situation is real. If this case is not an aberra-

tion, then money managers face serious issues. These kinds of practices must be eliminated.

In handling their own investments, money managers must not only refrain from engaging in practices that pose a conflict of interest with a client, they must refrain from conduct that gives the *appearance* of a conflict of interest. This problem can be attacked in several ways.

The cleanest most draconian method would be for money managers or advisors to place their portfolios in blind trusts or engage others to manage their accounts. Although many would call this proposal overkill and unprecedented, the blind trust is the requirement for high government officials.

A second, less onerous, suggestion would require money managers or investment advisors to report their investment holdings to their employers, who would be required to examine the holdings to ensure that no improprieties were occurring. If the money manager or advisor were a single proprietor, the examination function would have to be carried out by an independent individual, such as a Certified Public Accountant. The responsibilities of this individual would be to examine and report on the submitted transactions.

A third suggestion would require that disclosures of personal investment decisions be made to the money manager's clients and, possibly, to the SEC.

A fourth proposal would involve setting up a fair and appropriate system for making allocations among accounts. When a money manager has an interest, that manager can under no circumstances be placed in a preferred position.

The point of all these suggestions is that money management and financial advice are highly sensitive activities. High ethical standards require that they be conducted fairly, in utmost good faith, and free of real or perceivedconflict of interest.

Conclusion

In this day and age, when the United States has been losing its premier position in industry after industry, it must retain its edge in financial services. The U.S. financial services industry remains the best in the world, but it will retain that position only if the system continues to perform in the excellent manner that it has in the past. The premier status will be lost if the industry is perceived to be other than fair and honest.

Adhering to high ethical standards will keep the U.S. financial services industry on top. Therefore, those who are committed to its continued success must be diligent in ferreting out and punishing the inside trader, the churner, the bucketer, the manipulator, and their ilk.

Question and Answer Session

Stanley Sporkin

Question: How would you extend your proposed solutions to money manager conflicts of interest to sell-side analysts?

Sporkin: To avoid problems, have a third party manage their accounts. Some say this approach is impractical, but what they mean is that they do not want to do it, or they want to control their own investments. It is a tough approach, but those in a position of trust must do something to eliminate conflicts of interest because, if they don't, others will always be second-guessing whatever they do. Now, what I mentioned are the ways big organizations can deal with the problem. The solution is more difficult when small organizations are involved.

Question: One concern if independent managers take over the management of broker/dealer accounts is that clients who want to know how broker/dealers are managing for their own accounts will not be able to see that performance. Would you comment?

Sporkin: The ethical problem relates to whose objectives are served first when the objectives differ. Without unlimited resources and unlimited bank accounts, the client cannot be buying and selling at the same time the manager is. Moreover, the client's goals and objectives may well be different from the manager's. For example, the man-

ager's personal objectives might well be to lighten up on equities at a particular time—in order to buy a house, for instance—when the client should be fully invested. Nothing is wrong with the money manager's actions, but if the client needs to be invested, the manager has the problem of explaining why he or she is taking actions that are inconsistent with actions taken for the client. That is the dilemma, and that is the ethical problem.

In government service, the solution used to be that someone coming in had to sell everything. The tax consequences were incredible. So the blind trust was offered as a lesser evil. The blind trust is a tough solution, but it has been found to be workable with newly appointed government officials.

Of course, one solution would be for people who go into the money management business to invest their own money somewhere else. They could put their money in debt instruments or some other type of non-market-sensitive investment.

Question: You have had a lot of experience with self-regulating organizations (SROs); how do you react to the criticism that they are like the fox guarding the chicken coop?

Sporkin: The SROs experienced some problems early in their existence, which they have resolved. I have a lot of faith in both the Na-

tional Association of Securities Dealers (NASD) and the NYSE, and for very specific reasons. The leaders of the NASD and the NYSE are fine, smart individuals who neither function as mere figureheads nor whitewash problems. The head of enforcement at the NYSE, Dave Doherty, and the head of the NASD enforcement program, Richard Ketchum, will not tolerate any monkey business. So, they provide real self-regulation.

The problem lies in how quickly the self-regulatory enforcement processes can work. I doubt that the enforcement processes, after the information is found, are smooth. In addition, having members themselves sit in judgment on other members' conduct may not be the right way to deal with major securities law violations.

What I would suggest is that the SROs use professional hearing examiners to develop the litigation record. Then, after the hearing examiners reach an initial decision and recommendation, they should turn the case over to the business people if an appeal is pursued. A full record will have been developed by an independent individual not affiliated in any sense with the business itself.

The SROs are developing good information and have good systems. They simply need an independent professional group of people in the first instances to adjudicate the cases developed.

The Role of Ethics in the U.S. Capital Markets

J. Carter Beese, Jr.
Commissioner
U.S. Securities and Exchange Commission

Major roles in the long-term continued success of the U.S. capital markets will be played by individual ethics, effective self-policing, and efficient regulation. Major challenges are being made to the self-policing and regulatory systems, however, from new technology, new investment instruments, and increased market access. Because the industry is built on trust, high personal ethical standards must meet these challenges until self-regulation and government regulation catch up to market changes. For the industry, specific problems exist in sales practices, supervisory standards, and suitability/investor education—particularly in regard to mutual funds.

In 1790, Thomas Jefferson said, "I have but one system of ethics, for men and for nations: to be grateful, to be faithful to all engagements and under all circumstances, to be open and generous, promoting in the long run even the interests of both." As usual, Thomas Jefferson was right on target.

An understanding of ethics and of the role it plays in the securities markets must focus on the long term. At their core, the markets consist of millions of individuals making conscious decisions about how to invest their capital. These decisions necessarily involve a large element of trust; otherwise, investors would not make others the custodians of their hopes and dreams—the hopes and dreams embodied in their hard-earned life savings.

To maintain this trust and continue to receive this vote of confidence from individual investors, Wall Street must recognize the advantage of building relationships that benefit all parties for an extended period. Following the events of the 1980s, however, some of the public view Wall Street simply as a "den of thieves," a bastion of greed that provides little of value to the productive capacity of America. This view is simply not true. Although Wall Street certainly suffers from the same human failings as other institutions, Wall Street is an invaluable source of strength to the United States.

The primary function of securities markets is to facilitate the efficient allocation of resources in the economy. In this task, Wall Street has no peer. The U.S. capital markets are without question the clean-est, fairest, and deepest markets in the world. All participants in the markets can take pride in this accomplishment.

Fundamental changes are sweeping the markets, however. The markets are near all-time highs, and capital is moving freely across borders in record volumes at the stroke of a computer key. In fact, advances in technology have led some experts to predict that people's abilities to compute and to communicate will increase by a factor of 100 during the next ten years. Moreover, from Shanghai to Budapest to New Delhi, market reforms are taking hold and creating new demand for capital.

The practice of corporate finance is also undergoing sweeping transformation. In today's markets, to use the terms "stocks" and "bonds" is almost anachronistic. Today's complex financial instruments are better defined in terms of cash flow and volatility characteristics.

The combination of new technology, new investment instruments, and increased market access provides investors with more opportunities than ever before, including the opportunities in an estimated $150 billion in privatizations going on around the globe. The combination will also lead to fundamental changes in how markets, both in the United States and abroad, operate. It may, given the increased opportunities for "regulatory arbitrage" and increased technological capabilities to circumvent regulation synthetically, lead to changes in the way regulation operates.

Challenges to the Success of the U.S. Capital Markets

Activities in three arenas will determine the continued success of the U.S. capital markets: ethics, self-policing, and efficient regulation. Each area is confronting practitioners with new challenges and responsibilities as they navigate the shifting tides of today's global markets. The success of the U.S. capital markets in meeting these challenges will determine whether those markets will maintain their comparative advantage in the years ahead and whether the industry will maintain a long-term relationship with investors that operates to everyone's advantage.

Personal Ethics

The first three lines of defense in the oversight of the U.S. capital markets are individual, firmwide, and industrywide ethical standards. At the level of the individual, ethics means different things to different people, but in general, ethics is about personal values. It's about staying true to one's beliefs and feeling good about oneself. In many ways, a person's ethics define the person more than any other trait: Like physical characteristics, ethics are ultimately visible; unlike physical characteristics, ethics involve conscious choices by individuals about themselves.

The choices people make have consequences—often irreversible. Unlike some mistakes individuals make in their lives and business careers, mistakes of character can determine a person's whole future. Many in business and in government have been lured by the siren song of easy money, only to end up on the rocks of despair. Ethical lapses ruin careers, tarnish firm reputations, and diminish public confidence in the marketplace. Good ethics is good business if one intends to be around for the long term in our markets.

Self-Policing

The second theme to the continued success of the capital markets is self-policing, or industrywide ethics. Unlike banks, securities firms do not operate under the watchful eye of an army of 22,000 regulators. In the U.S. securities markets, regulators rely extensively on the concept that firms have an enlightened self-interest in maintaining the integrity of the marketplace. This self-interest leads market participants to police voluntarily those that operate at the margin. Failure to provide this policing function will erode public confidence in the industry and operate to the disadvantage of all market participants.

Some prime examples of effective self-policing exist. Many of the largest securities firms, for example, have discontinued the practice of making political contributions in order to influence the selection of their firm as an underwriter. With the help of a bit of moral suasion from Arthur Levitt, chairman of the SEC, and an assist from Frank Zarb of Primerica, these firms sent the message that public confidence in the integrity of the marketplace is paramount. The actions of these firms should serve as a model for all participants in the municipal bond market: "Pay to play" must stop, whether through a voluntary code of conduct or through a Municipal Securities Rulemaking Board proposal.

Municipal market participants must also probe new ways of increasing transparency in the market. In a completely transparent market, market participants have equal and immediate access to all quotations and to reports of prices and volumes. Transparency is important in the markets because it gives investors confidence that they are playing on a level field. In addition, the virtually instantaneous information on quotes and the details of completed transactions that market transparency provides allow investors to judge the quality of services they receive from brokers.

Transparency in the municipal securities market today is simply inadequate. Currently, municipal market participants—investors and dealers—lack access to indications of buying and selling interest for most municipal securities. To protect the integrity and continued success of this market, market participants should take the lead in addressing this shortcoming. The municipal markets must find ways to make real-time trade, quotation, and other market-related information available to all participants.

In addition to market transparency, self-policing concerns involve sales practices, supervisory standards, and suitability. In connection with sales practices, the *Los Angeles Times* carried a series of articles in 1992 that highlighted the issue of disciplining rogue brokers. The question was: How many "bites at the apple" should a rogue broker be allowed before being barred from the industry? This series prompted an internal staff investigation at the SEC, which is nearing completion, and raised the interest of some on Capitol Hill. House Energy and Commerce Committee Chairman John D. Dingell (D, Mich.) wrote the SEC indicating a desire to hold hearings on the subject with the purpose of possibly introducing legislation to adopt a "three strikes and you're out" policy for rogue brokers. None of us wants to see rogue brokers in the business; neither do we want to resort to legislation to achieve the goal of barring them.

The subject of broker and supervisory standards and compensation is also receiving scrutiny today. Some have called for a rethinking of the way in which brokers are compensated. Arguing that the current commission structure creates an inherent conflict of interest, these critics advocate an asset-based compensation method. Similar concerns have been raised with regard to the compensation of branch managers with supervisory responsibility. For example, when firms compensate branch managers largely on the basis of the volume of business conducted by brokers in the branch, the managers have a potential disincentive to supervise the branch brokers vigorously. As in the case of rogue brokers, the industry needs to address these concerns before they receive heightened regulatory or legislative attention.

A final area of self-policing that warrants discussion is investor education, particularly as it relates to suitability of investment vehicles. In the last three-to-four years, people in the United States who have traditionally been savers have become first-time investors. Unwilling to live with the anemic 2–3 percent returns available on bank certificates of deposit, more and more Americans have turned to Wall Street. The vehicle of choice for these new investors is mutual funds, and individual mutual fund shareholders now total over 38 million people.

Many of these investors are unfamiliar with the risks attending their marketable securities. Formerly, these investors were holding government-insured instruments; now, they find themselves chasing yields in a market with no federal safety net. According to a recent survey conducted by the SEC, 36 percent of the respondents thought that mutual funds purchased from a stockbroker were federally insured. Clearly, this perception must change.

The return of the small investor to Wall Street is a tremendous vote of confidence, but these investors can, and will, take their money and leave at the first sign of a bear market. Market professionals thus have a vested interest in trying to educate new investors about the risks inherent in owning marketable securities and the advantages of having a long-term investment horizon.

Regulation

The third arena in which the continued success of the U.S. capital markets is being decided is efficient regulation. When ethics and self-policing do not adequately promote investor protection and public confidence, the SEC has an obligation to advance cost-effective regulation to achieve those goals. In fact, in many respects, the need for SEC regulatory action represents a failure of the personal ethics and self-policing aspects of the markets.

Three examples of SEC action, or proposed action, will illustrate how the SEC tries to ensure the integrity of the securities markets—insider-trading prohibitions, restrictions on payment for order flow, and the treatment of derivative products.

▪ *Insider trading.* One of the fundamental needs of successful capital markets is that investors believe insiders are not taking advantage of them. The United States has a long tradition of prosecuting insider trading, and this stance has contributed to the success and vitality of U.S. markets. In some countries, insider trading is not viewed as a crime but as an acceptable business practice. In Europe, for example, the belief is common that some investors have access to confidential information and profit from it. This belief is a major reason why comparatively few Europeans own stock. In the United States, 35 percent of adults own stock; only 7 percent own stock in Germany, 14 percent in France, and 20 percent in Britain. As these figures indicate, the perceived fairness of the U.S. markets serves as a significant competitive advantage in market depth and liquidity.

▪ *Payment for order flow.* Proposed SEC regulations regarding "inducements"—in particular, the practice of payment for order flow—are also designed to promote market fairness. The issue of inducements deeply divides the securities industry and has been the subject of extensive debate and analysis. Opponents of payment for order flow liken this practice to a payoff; proponents consider it a legitimate business practice in a highly competitive market.

Recently, the SEC published for comment a proposal to require a broker/dealer to include on the confirmation of each transaction whether payment for order flow or other inducements were received in connection with the transaction. The proposed rule strikes a balance between the competing viewpoints about inducements and does so in a manner that is wholly consistent with the core principles of the federal securities laws by basing the solution on the concept of disclosure. Requiring disclosure steers clear of picking "winners" and "losers" in the debate but ensures that investors will have the information necessary to make informed decisions for themselves. Ultimately, if investors determine that payment for order flow is an unfair practice, savvy market participants will use their refusal to pay for order flow to their competitive advantage.

The payment-for-order-flow release also contains language directing the SEC staff to report back promptly on the need for enhanced disclosure by investment advisers in the area of soft-dollar arrangements. In many respects, soft dollars and payment for order flow are two sides of the same coin. Although the two practices certainly have technical differences, they both represent payment of cash and noncash inducements for allocating business among market participants.

■ *Derivatives.* Without question, one of the dominant forces in the markets today is the explosive growth in the use of derivative products. Warning that derivatives will be the "next savings & loan crisis," some have called for severe restrictions on activities involving derivatives. The industry cannot navigate the road ahead, however, by looking exclusively in the rearview mirror. Although lessons can certainly be learned from prior experiences, including the S&L crisis, cops are already on the beat with regard to derivatives.

SEC oversight of derivatives activities revolves around four basic themes: risk assessment, capital, accounting, and coordination. Of these, good accounting is the underpinning—of good risk management, good regulatory oversight, and continued public confidence in the markets.

To the extent that settlement values under derivatives contracts are largely contingent, which is often the case throughout the life of a derivatives contract, current accounting standards do not require settlement values to be reflected on a firm's balance sheet. As a result, the financial statements of entities with OTC derivatives on their books far in excess of their capital are, for all intents and purposes, opaque. For the first time in recent memory, simply reading a firm's balance sheet does not necessarily give the reader a clear understanding of the firm's business or health.

The rapid growth of the derivatives market and the introduction into the market of complex new products and strategies has left the accounting profession behind. At present, generally accepted accounting principles simply do not comprehensively address the manner in which public companies must account for and disclose their derivatives activities. Only some footnote disclosures and mention in the management discussion and analysis are presently required. The SEC and the Financial Accounting Standards Board (FASB), which is currently considering a quick study to address concerns about derivatives, must attend to this area.

The securities industry, however, should not wait for regulatory action. Investors need assurances that derivatives are not a house of cards assembled by Wall Street for the sole benefit of Wall Street. By voluntarily adopting enhanced accounting standards, as proposed in the Group of Thirty report on derivatives,[1] the industry can bolster transparency in the derivatives markets and reassure the investing public.

Conclusion

The growth of the derivatives market is part of and highlights the current general challenge to traditional geographical and jurisdictional boundaries by new products and cross-border electronic networks. International electronic networks have spawned such markets as Forex, OTC derivatives, and Globex and are ushering in a new world in finance. Standards of doing business are being increasingly developed by the markets rather than by the regulators. The increased stress these trends place on regulators dictates that ethics and self-policing assume a larger role than regulation in maintaining the clean markets investors demand. Investors have more choices than ever before, and they will choose alternative repositories for their money if they perceive a market to be unfair.

In a sense, therefore, this new world is really merely a return to the way business used to be conducted. When the founders of Wall Street met under the buttonwood trees 200 years ago, they did not have an army of lawyers and regulators to dictate business practices. They relied on enlightened self-interest, a common code of conduct, and a handshake.

Ralph Waldo Emerson once said that "the only reward for virtue is virtue," but virtue is also good business. The markets are built on a foundation of trust. Trust is what attracts issuers and, perhaps most importantly, investors to the markets. For the industry, maintaining that trust is tantamount to maintaining the participants' livelihood. For the nation, maintaining that trust is vital to economic growth and prosperity.

---

[1]*Derivatives: Practices and Principles* (July 1993).

Question and Answer Session

J. Carter Beese, Jr.

Question: How much pressure is building up on Capitol Hill to regulate mutual funds?

Beese: The pressure to do something is enormous. Congress is clearly focused on these funds, and hearings are taking place almost monthly on this subject.

The concern about the flow of funds from banks into mutual funds is particularly great. The belief is widespread in Congress, and is somewhat confirmed by the recent SEC survey, that investors have large misperceptions as to the safety of mutual funds and as to what is behind these marketable securities, particularly when the securities are purchased directly from the banks themselves. The misperception is that these instruments are insured by the banks the way bank deposits are insured.

Congress is putting enormous pressure on the bank regulators. The big question is whether or not bank mutual funds will come under SEC jurisdiction or will stay under the jurisdiction of bank supervisors. The bank regulators have a vested interest in keeping supervisory responsibility for these assets, which have been disintermediated out of their immediate base. They are pressing hard to keep the assets under their supervision and have recently promulgated rules that somewhat mirror the SEC's rules with regard to supervision of mutual funds.

The SEC thinks the rules are insufficient to provide adequate investor protection. The SEC also believes that merely because certain mutual funds are housed in a bank rather than a securities firm or somewhere else is no reason

they should be considered separate and distinct from other mutual funds, including being subject to the enforcement process, which is clearly different in a bank environment from what it is in a securities environment. The SEC's position is that, if someone is murdered in a bank lobby, it is not the bank regulator who investigates the crime.

Question: Is the SEC or Congress concerned about the adequacy of inspection of mutual funds, and do you support the call for a self-regulatory organization (SRO) for mutual funds?

Beese: Clearly, mutual fund inspection is somewhat inadequate. Since 1983, mutual funds have more than quadrupled in size, and the SEC inspection staff has barely increased because of federal budgetary concerns that limit allocations to certain functions of the SEC. We have about 142 inspectors of mutual funds for a $2 trillion industry. We do not need for mutual funds the 22,000 people that bank regulators have, because bank regulators have duties other than inspections, but we probably need a couple hundred more inspectors to maintain the ratio the SEC had in 1980.

Ironically, the SEC took more than $80 million of fees from the mutual fund industry in 1992 and allocated back to the mutual fund industry, in a sense, only $18 million. From filing fees and fines, we are a profitable government agency, but to date, we have not been able to use even the direct fees that we get from an industry to regulate that industry directly. We are working hard to move to-

ward self-funding, however, and the chances of obtaining it are greater now than ever before.

At the moment, the SEC is able to inspect annually only the 100 largest mutual funds. That number captures about 80 percent of the assets in the mutual fund industry, but because potential abuses are as likely or more likely to occur in the small funds— the new funds, the fringe funds— than they are in the largest funds, we are worried about the adequacy of our inspection program.

If the SEC cannot obtain increased funding from Congress, one proposal that has been made is to create an SRO among mutual fund companies. The SROs that have worked well in this country, however, such as the NYSE and the NASD, work well because they are regulating primarily interactions between members of the SRO—that is, between market participants, between dealers—not regulating primarily entities that have their dealings directly with the public rather than with each other. The one example of an SRO formed to try and regulate entities that deal directly with the public is in the United Kingdom [the Securities Investment Board], and it has not worked well.

In a sense, we have an SRO already in place, the boards of directors of mutual funds, and do not need another layer of regulation. We may need to emphasize that these boards take a hard look at sales practices in mutual funds, however, and allocation issues among funds, such as the allocation of soft dollars. Also, the general counsels of mutual funds should be doing the tough internal audits that an SRO might perform.

Question: Is Congress concerned about the levels of fees and loads of mutual fund products?

Beese: Some in Congress believe that fee levels and load levels of mutual funds (and other products that are hot topics these days, such as wrap accounts) will be taken care of by market forces. Competitive pressures continue to bring fees down. Concern about the level of wrap fees still exists, however, although fee levels today are probably significantly lower than they were a year ago because of competitor pressures in the marketplace. We need to let market forces go to work before we try and regulate these fees.

The SEC's No. 1 tool, in use and in effectiveness, is disclosure, so that the marketplace can sort it out, but sometimes a ceiling is appropriate. So, the SEC has instituted fee ceilings in some cases. In 1992, the SEC imposed a cap of 8 percent on the aggregate load one can be charged for a 12(b)(1) fee.

The SEC is also concerned about loads that can creep up on an investor over the years. This issue is certainly an area of concern in light of the proliferation of new and different types of mutual funds and different ways to buy mutual funds.

Question: What is the state of international cooperation among regulators, particularly regarding insider-trading issues?

Beese: We have made huge advances in cooperation among regulators on insider trading in the past 10–15 years. Until today, those who started an insider-trading scheme of any significance in the United States were stupid if they did not operate out-side the U.S. national borders. From the standpoint of fairness, the good news today is that the United States has effective agreements concerning insider trading with a number of countries. The biggest advance came when we achieved effective agreements with Switzerland in about 1987. That breakthrough really opened the floodgates for a host of other markets, and the SEC now has about 30 "memoranda of understanding" between countries specifying cooperation on insider trading.

Worldwide securities regulators are well placed to negotiate these types of international agreements and to communicate among themselves. A lot of domestic competitive pressures exist *not* to communicate in some industries, such as banking. On the securities front, however, the state of communications is fairly open, and the industry has a strong international organization, the International Organization of Securities Commissions. IOSCO meets formally on an annual basis and informally almost every month.

Question: Is the SEC going to require greater disclosure of the use of soft dollars?

Beese: The SEC is under a lot of pressure from numerous industry groups and Congress to increase requirements for disclosure of soft dollars, but like the other questions we have been discussing, the issue of soft dollars is not an easy one to handle. Congressman Edward J. Markey (D, Mass.) and the House Subcommittee on Telecommunications and Finance, among others, held hearings during 1993 concerning soft-dollar practices. Increased disclosure may, therefore, come from the SEC or by legislation.

The issue of soft dollars is part of the whole system of induce-ments that exists in the industry, as is payment for order flow and, one step further, such practices as internalization of order flow at major securities firms. Internalization is simply another way of payment for order flow; one firm is simply capturing that spread itself rather than getting it rebated from some other firm. We have to take a look at the whole issue of inducements.

The issue of soft dollars is particularly tough because of the question of where to draw the line. The issue has thus generated strong lobbying on both sides.

On one side, some of the major securities firms that do not use soft dollars are saying they have lost all their easy order flow—order flow for the IBM trades and the General Motors trades—and are left with only the tough trades that require the firms to put capital at risk. Therefore, the use of soft dollars has significantly changed the cost basis of their doing business and put them at a disadvantage.

The soft-dollar users say, "If you are going to have increased disclosure for how our soft dollars are used as commissions, then we want increased disclosure of commissions by those full-line firms. We want you to go to the Morgan Stanleys and Goldman, Sachs of the world and tell them that, when they are paid a commission, they must disclose how much of that commission was for positioning of trades, how much was for research, and how much was for sales practices. If we have to unbundle our soft-dollar information, we want the other direct commissions to be unbundled."

That issue is tough, and the SEC is still in the middle of it. The easiest answer, and best first answer, is to require greater disclosure and let the market sort out some of the practices in strong sunshine, which is likely to be the outcome in the first six months of 1994.

Question: What is the status of the proposal by Congressman Dingell to do away with quarterly reporting?

Beese: The proposal is probably somewhere between dormant and dead. The rationale for it was good; the fact is that the quarterly reporting requirement may impose an excessive cost on some companies, particularly small companies and some foreign issuers that do not report on a quarterly basis in their own markets. So, in essence, the requirement may keep some companies out of the marketplace. It was rational to take a look at the cost–benefit trade-off of quarterly reporting, but the proposal is not under consideration at this time.

Question: Is the SEC interested in corporations' accounting for pension fund liabilities?

Beese: The SEC is one of several federal agencies that clearly have a jurisdictional interest in pension funds, and the SEC's interest in pension funds is growing dramatically, not only because of the types of performance assumptions that accrue to investors through a disclosure regime, but also because pension funds today are more likely to resemble defined-contribution plans than defined-benefit plans. The U.S. Department of Labor, the Internal Revenue Service, and the SEC are concerned with pension plans. When the issue is defined-contribution plans, however, such as 401(k) plans, the issue is increasingly within the jurisdiction of the SEC, because it is an issue of individual investors choosing their own investments for their own retirement.

As the situation is now, the disclosure requirements for a product bought through a 401(k) are not the same as those for that same product bought in the open market. A fund bought through a 401(k) is not required to deliver a prospectus or make other disclosures. So the SEC is working on several aspects of the retirement programs. The Division of Investment Management, for example, has proposed that a prospectus be delivered if a fund or stock is bought on an offering through a 401(k). The cost of this proposal is high, however, so we are searching for a more cost-effective way to inform buyers. The one-page prospectus we have proposed for use primarily in advertising might be useful, perhaps in a standardized form, to an employee who has 14 different choices of mutual funds in a 401(k) plan. Such materials might help narrow down the choices to three or four, and the employee could call an 800 number for full prospectuses for the final choices.

The member of a defined-contribution plan deserves as much information and education as, maybe even more than, those buying investments in the open market. In the next 10–20 years, people are going to wake up to the retirement situation in the same way they did to the need to start saving for a child's college education from the day the child is born; that realization resulted from the inflation years of the 1970s. They are going to realize that the investment decisions they make in their defined-contribution plans will determine the quality of the last third of their lives. After a generation of people who do not have enough on which to retire, who learn that no corporate safety net exists, and who discover that the government safety net (i.e., social secu-

rity) is little more than food stamps for the elderly, people will figure out that they must save 10 percent or more of their salaries from their first day of work in order to enjoy a satisfactory retirement. Anybody who is not contributing greatly to a defined-contribution plan today is borrowing against a decent life style later.

For those lucky enough still to be covered by some type of defined-benefit plan, two movements are developing. One is that benefits are continuing to be cut— not only because of changes in interest rate assumptions but also because of FAS No. 106. When FAS No. 106 was put into place in December 1992, 22 companies simply canceled their health care plans for retired employees. People had a rude awakening to the fact that some retirement plans are not rights but perks and they can be changed.

The second movement is for companies that still have pension plans to reduce the benefits significantly. Therefore, to have a satisfactory retirement life style, most employees will have to augment income from their retirement plans with monies from their own defined-contribution plans.

A major concern should be that defined-contribution plans are invested terribly. Defined-contribution plans tend to be stagnant and invested in so-called safe investments. Since about 1990, the 100 largest defined-contribution plans in the United States have averaged 70–80 percent in guaranteed income contracts and money market funds. In contrast, the 1,000 largest actively managed pension funds of corporations have 55–60 percent of their investments in equities (the level for the past three years) and practice continual asset reallocations.

Public Perception of the Investment Industry: Trends and Counteractions

Scott L. Lummer, CFA
Managing Director, Consulting Services Group
Ibbotson Associates

Unfavorable perceptions about the investment management industry persist, partly because of a lack of ethical education in business school curriculums and in companies. AIMR's Professional Conduct Program assists in dispelling these perceptions, but investment management companies themselves need to improve ethical education and ongoing management through providing a formal foundation in and frequent reminders about the company's ethical guidelines, through training, enforcement, counseling, and leading by example.

This presentation focuses on four aspects of public perceptions of the investment industry. The first is whether any trends are noticeable in the public's perception of ethics violations in the industry. The second aspect is what is being done to create ethical values in the industry, especially with respect to including ethics in business school curriculums. The third is how the industry garnered its negative public perception, and the presentation will close with ideas about how the investment profession—the overall industry and individual businesses—can counteract the current unfavorable perceptions.

Trends in Public Perception

The public's perception of ethics in the investment industry differs depending on whether "the public" is a plan sponsor, an individual investor, or the press in general. Statistical evidence suggests a fundamental difference between the media's coverage of ethical issues in the industry a dozen years ago and the coverage today. **Table 1** is based on an examination of the heading "Ethics" in the *New York Times* index. The index contains several categories of ethics reporting, which are summarized in the table. In 1981, ethics in the investment industry accounted for 0.3 percent of the total ethics reporting; in 1991, that category accounted for 5.8 percent.

Table 1 also reveals what the top news subjects with respect to ethics were in 1981 and 1991. In 1981, about 1,000 reports of violations related to politics;

every other topic pales in comparison. Politics was followed by business (nonfinance), sports, medicine, investments, and finance (noninvestment). In 1991, politics still led the pack, although its percentage of the total had gone down; it was followed by medicine, finance, and investments.

These data do indeed show an increase in reporting on ethical concerns in the finance and investment categories. The number of articles on investment ethics increased from 3 in 1981 to 73 in 1991. The number of ethics articles concerning noninvestment finance, which refers predominantly to banking, increased from 1 to 160. These figures are evidence of heightened attention to finance and investment ethics: If the percentage growth is examined as if the press reports were an investment, a typical investment chart would show that someone who had a dollar invested in 1981 in "investment ethics" would be a fairly wealthy person by 1991 with the money appreciating at this rate.

The number of articles on ethics in medicine is not really comparable because a report in the investment area would typically be discussing a violation, thus a problem known to involve ethics, whereas in the medical area, the topic would be whether something *is* an ethical problem. A recent issue of *Time* magazine, for example, had two reports on ethical concerns. One was in the investments area and focused on problems in the mutual fund industry, and the other was in the medical area and focused on cloning. The mutual fund article discussed an appar-

Table 1. Ethics Data from the *New York Times* Index

Category	1981		1991		Change	
	Number of Articles	Percent of Total	Number of Articles	Percent of Total	Number of Articles	Percent of Total
Investments	3	0.3	73	5.8	70	5.5
Finance (noninvestment)	1	0.1	160	12.7	159	12.6
Business (nonfinance)	122	11.1	56	4.4	–66	–6.6
Politics	749	67.8	636	50.4	–113	–17.4
Medicine	62	5.6	101	8.0	39	2.4
Lawyers	13	1.2	55	4.4	42	3.2
Science	38	3.4	27	2.1	–11	–1.3
Sports	64	5.8	74T	5.9	10	0.1
Education	16	1.4	64	5.1	48	3.6
Religion	36	3.3	15	1.2	–21	–2.1
Total	1,104	100.0	1,261	100.0		

Source: Derek Sasveld, Ibbotson Associates.

ent ethical violation. The cloning article focused on the ethical debate regarding whether cloning should be allowed.

The number of reports on sports ethics did not change much in the ten years. It is a sad commentary on what is important to the public, although perhaps the situation is to the benefit of the investment profession, that there is no more concern with investment ethics than with such things as whether a University of Alabama linebacker is getting overpaid during his summer job.

Creating Ethical Values

College curriculums are placing more attention on ethics training today than they did in the past. However, not all academics are enthusiastic about this increased focus. At a conference on business curriculum in the mid-1980s, a well-known finance professor made some crusty comments about ethics teaching in the classroom. When a member of the audience asked him about what his university did with respect to teaching ethics, everyone presumed that he would say, "Nothing." He sarcastically responded, however, that the school believed strongly in ethics: "We put a case in front of our students about two partners running a dry cleaning store. One day, one of the partners who is a little bit more preachy than the other one leaves the partner who is not as, perhaps, well founded morally manning the store alone. A woman comes in, drops off a coat, and leaves. As the partner is preparing the coat, he finds $300 tucked away in one of the pockets. This presents an ethical dilemma, and we raise that dilemma to the students. The dilemma is, of course, should the dry cleaner split the money with his partner."

That story is the kind of cynical comment on ethics teaching in business schools that goes around from time to time. Similar stories abound. What creates some of the cynicism behind that story may be the frustration of the job involved in "teaching" ethics. We learn ethics from three places—home, school, and work. Now, consider the relative number of hours the learner is in contact with each source. A parent gets a few hours a week during approximately an 18-year period to instill some type of ethical foundation. In the workplace, an employer has people for forty hours a week for 52 weeks a year. A typical professor has students only for two and one-half hours a week over a 4-month period. Moreover, only a small portion of that time can be devoted to ethical concerns.

The impact of ethics training in the classroom cannot possibly equal what can happen both before students show up at a university and after they leave the university. The teacher has a minute fraction of the time the parent and employer have to accomplish ethics training. Very little, relatively speaking, can be accomplished in the classroom. Universities cannot be expected to impart an ethical view if no one else has laid or will lay the foundation.

The university can, however, do some things. Ethics can be taught in four ways within business curriculums. First, elective courses on general ethics can be made available to students. Second, an elective course dealing specifically with business ethics can be offered. Most major business schools have such an elective; they usually do not staff it with a business professor, however, but with an ethics professor whom they pay to teach business ethics. This approach can create problems in applying ethics to actual business situations.

A third way to teach ethics is through a required course or long-term module on business ethics. A three- or four-week module devoted to ethics is not a lot of time, however, to focus on the topic.

The fourth method can be to require that several sessions of each course be devoted to the ethical concerns within that discipline. A number of institutions are using this fourth approach, but it requires that several professors become comfortable discussing ethical dilemmas, and faculty often resist this type of challenge.

How ethics should be taught is an important consideration. One alternative is a normative approach—that is, laying out rules distinguishing between right and wrong. An example is AIMR's standards. Children are given a normative ethical training when they are growing up, but universities provide little of that kind of training; almost none is provided in business curriculums. For example, I have yet to pick up an investments textbook that lists the AIMR standards. They should be there, but they are not. Neither are references to the Performance Presentation Standards.

The second alternative is the positive approach, which is the more commonly used method. This method deals with ethical decision making. In contrast to the normative approach's "here are the rules for what is right and wrong," the positive approach explores dilemmas that have unclear resolutions, such as when reporting violations is appropriate and whom to talk to about violations. Whereas universities are probably guilty of ignoring the normative approach, businesses are probably guilty of ignoring the positive approach when they conduct ethical training.

Roots of the Public's Negative Perceptions

Several factors have contributed to the public's negative perceptions of investment professionals. Clearly, some of the perception is a result of the desire of reporters to have a story. The huge financial successes of some individuals in the 1980s bred suspicion. Reports that Michael Milken's activities *might* be questionable were circulating before any solid evidence came out about his potential insider-trading activity. Then, when revelations did occur, the press indulged in a bit of sensationalism. The press apparently subscribed to the old adage that one bad apple can spoil the whole barrel, and reporters continued to describe violations via big sensational stories that damned the whole financial industry.

This tendency undoubtedly contributed to the increase from 3 reports of violations in the 1981 data to 73 in the 1991 data. The industry professionals were probably not that much less ethical in 1991 than they were in 1981, but a lot more attention has certainly been paid to their every move. These aspects indicate that the increased attention is caused not by widespread ethical decay but, instead, by poor public relations.

Another root of the negative perceptions is the industry's apparent lack of training in ethics. What are investment companies doing early in their employees' careers to expose them to ethical issues, either in a positive or a normative way? If the companies are providing this kind of ethics education, they are not often talking about it publicly. Perhaps some normative training is going on, such as regulatory concerns, but little focus is evident on such issues as what employees should do when faced with ambiguous situations. Most firms simply do not emphasize ethics training.

Firms also usually practice little management of ethics. The readings in the CFA curriculum make clear, however, that ethical outcomes depend on managerial concern. Creating an ethical culture is not a simple matter of hiring good people; good people can and do make bad choices. The process must be managed so as to tilt good people toward making good choices.

Counteracting Unfavorable Perceptions

The investment industry is taking some steps to counteract the unfavorable perceptions it is facing, but it needs to do more. At the industry level, AIMR does a great deal to focus on the problem. The major effort is AIMR's Professional Conduct Program, which members are required to abide by. In addition, AIMR provides a myriad of educational materials directed toward ethical behavior, including publications, conferences, and the ethics curriculum in the CFA program. Hiring professionals who participate in the Professional Conduct Program or have studied the ethics curriculum for the CFA exams does not, however, absolve companies in the industry of their duty to deal responsibly with the ethical training and ethical behavior of their employees.

At the company level, the issues of continuing education and management are important. Companies need to examine how well trained their employees are in following the company's guidelines. Companies cannot rely on the guidelines simply being provided; they need to ask whether their employees know what they should be doing. They need to make an effort to be sure—through questionnaires or other means—that employees know what to do when confronted by a wide variety of ethical dilemmas. Do they know where to turn when there is not a clear resolution to the situation? If they suspect a violation, do they know what should be done, and are they willing to do it? If the answer to these questions is no, the company has a training problem that must be addressed.

The ongoing management of ethics is not difficult if companies will devote enough energy to the task. First, companies need to make sure that employees are told from the beginning what ethical guidelines they should be following. Managers should state and enforce ethical standards and ensure that employees stay up to speed on ethical issues that concern the company.

Another key to counteracting unfavorable public perceptions at the company level is leadership. The adage "don't manage, lead" may be truer in ethics than in any other aspect of management. And a primary way in which managers lead, particularly at the middle-management level, is by example. Think of how many signals you, as employees, pick up from your managers and follow. Think of the many little things that, as managers, you do that you can then see your employees emulating.

Providing leadership in ethics is most important for new employees. They are like sponges when they first walk in the company's front door, so that is the time really to influence them—with a formal foundation in the company's ethical guidelines, with counseling, with training, and by example. Establishing an ethical foundation early in employees' careers and following up with frequent reminders of company policy are critical in avoiding and solving problems that could otherwise lead to ethical crises.

Public Perception of the Investment Industry: Trends and Challenges

Gary G. Lynch
Partner
Davis Polk & Wardwell

The public's perception of integrity in the investment industry has dropped noticeably since the securities scandals of the 1980s. The industry is now challenged to explain the increasingly complex markets and securities products to the public and Congress, to ensure (and document) that product information has been effectively communicated to clients, and to establish the suitability of products for clients.

This presentation focuses on my subjective impressions of an era that ended with the passing of the 1980s and the advent of the 1990s but the effects of which linger today. My theme is that the public's perception of the investment industry underwent significant and dramatic change in the 1980s. The support for this view comes from my experiences at the SEC from 1976 to 1989 and in private law practice.

Changed Perceptions and Their Effects

Securities regulation at the federal level began in the 1930s with the Securities Act of 1933 and the Securities Exchange Act of 1934, which created the SEC. At that time, Congress held hearings about abuses in the securities markets—in particular, market manipulation. The SEC's performance was rarely in the nation's spotlights, however, and the SEC garnered little public attention until the decade of the 1970s. At that time, the SEC focused public attention on foreign payments and bribes by U.S. companies. While the "foreign payment" era brought about notable and laudable changes in international business ethics, these matters, in my view, did not really go to the heart of integrity in the U.S. securities markets.

The U.S. approach to securities regulation underwent a sea change in the 1980s because of major cases that revealed profoundly disturbing abuses occurring in the markets at that time—the Dennis Levine, Ivan Boesky, and Michael Milken cases. These cases severely stained the securities markets in the eyes of the public and of Congress. As a result, the penalty structure for the U.S. regulation of the

securities markets was radically altered.

The events that precipitated this change began rather suddenly with the investigation of the Levine case in 1986. The SEC knew that it was a major case—$12 million in insider-trading profits dwarfed any case before it—but the commission was totally unprepared for the press attention that focused on the case. We were shocked by the interest and overwhelmed with requests for interviews. Day after day, new stories appeared in various publications around the country; committee after committee on Capitol Hill decided it had an interest in this matter. The committees would then hold hearings, and the hearings, in turn, would lead to more press stories. The scandal simply fed on itself. I knew the situation was out of control when *People* magazine requested a profile on me. I respectfully declined.

The next major case focused on Ivan Boesky. His photo appeared in practically every publication in the United States during a two-month period in 1986, with the caption "Greed is good." Obviously, the public was interested in this issue; so Congress became interested. After all, hearings gave members of Congress the opportunity to criticize the awful things occurring on Wall Street that were working to the detriment of the country, and a member's comments would likely produce a valuable sound bite for the hometown newscast. So, this case also fed on itself, and more legislation passed. The Boesky case settled at $100 million, which was truly unbelievable to the SEC staff, particularly when the largest previous settlement had been the Levine case, only six months earlier, at $12 million.

Changes in Penalties

The SEC was criticized for coming down too lightly on Boesky, which was hard for the SEC staff to comprehend because the settlement dwarfed anything that had gone before it. As a result of the criticism, Congress started to ask why the country had these types of problems. The outcome was that the power of the SEC was increased from the power to penalize people for insider-trading violations to the power to penalize for *any* violation of the securities laws.

As a result of the Levine, Boesky, and Milken cases, the SEC has the power today to levy a penalty in any matter brought before it. Today, a regular feature of every settlement is the payment of monies by someone who gets caught in the SEC's enforcement net.

As a result of this change, the regulatory environment is much tougher today than in the past. In a recent case, for example, an employee of a major investment advisory firm was charged with failing to fill out order tickets promptly that allocated trades among managed accounts. The penalty in this case was $50,000 and three months out of the business. If the same case had occurred in the mid-1980s, it probably would have raised little regulatory interest. Today, however, not only will a case be made of such actions, but the resolution can temporarily expel someone from the investment business and cost that person a substantial fine.

A Focus on Ethics

The public's attention is much more focused on investment management ethics now than it was in 1980, and the press has had a lot to do with this heightened awareness. Stories on the big cases do not appear only on the business page; they are front-page news in every newspaper across the country.

During the 1987–88 period, at the height of the big cases, the public clearly had a very negative view of Wall Street ethics, and they thought of Wall Street as composed of Ivan Boeskys and Michael Milkens. Obviously, this perception was warped. The SEC tried to clarify to the world that the cases represented a relatively small segment of the securities community, but the public did not buy that assertion. Nor did Congress, which is why the penalty power of the SEC was radically increased.

The systemic securities violation cases like Boesky's and Milken's reinforce a long-standing populist view of Wall Street held by many in the country. This view is that people in the securities industry make enormous amounts of money and they make it by what Main Street views as merely shuffling paper—not building things or growing

things. There is a view—one that stems, at least in part, from envy—that for these people to be making so much money, they must be doing something illegal. Obviously, such a view is not grounded in fact, but it does exist.

Challenges for the Future

The industry is not going to lose the taint of the 1980 scandals overnight. We probably should not anticipate that professionals in the investment community will be rated in public polls the number one most ethical group in the country in the near future. Indeed, that high rating may not ever be attained because of the populist perceptions about Wall Street and what it takes to make money on Wall Street. One can only hope that the taint of the 1980s dissipates somewhat, however, as time passes.

One of the biggest problems facing the securities industry today is the increasing complexity of the markets. This complexity raises questions about how to explain the markets and securities products to customers, to the SEC, and to Congress. In the mid-1980s, most of the world clearly did not understand what the scandals were all about. The public understood insider trading, at least to some extent, and Congress understood insider trading, but the public and Congress did not fully understand the violations alleged against Drexel Burnham and Milken.

Therefore, one of the biggest challenges for the future will be educating the public and Congress about innovative investment products and about how the securities industry operates. Imagine a congressional hearing of the future focused on mortgage-backed securities, for example, in which inverse floaters and IOs and POs are discussed. Neither the public nor Congress is going to understand when we talk about interest-only or principal-only strips or inverse floaters.

An important issue for industry participants in the future—assuming a participant *is* ethical and wants to do the right thing—is self-protection and protection of one's firm. The most important tools for achieving that protection are communicating and making certain that customers understand what they are buying in the first place. The documents should explain the instruments being traded in understandable terms in plain English.

Of course, the public does not attach ethical issues to selling mortgage-backed securities or derivatives or any other instruments until the market turns down. When the market turns down, that is when ethical issues are raised. Then, the questions will likely be, "Why was this product sold to the person, entities, or municipalities that bought it? Was it suitable for them in the first place?"

Cases dealing with the issue of suitability will increase in the future. Mortgage-backed securities, for example, have become the subject of complaints. Everything about these instruments was fine as long as the market was profitable. When the market turned and the investments became unprofitable, everything became not so fine. Then, an ethical issue was raised: Were people sold suitable investments? Therefore, an important responsibility of all investment advisors is to make as certain as they can, given the nature of these markets and the products that are traded in these markets, that their customers understand what they are buying and selling.

Question and Answer Session

Scott L. Lummer, CFA
Gary G. Lynch

Question: How can organizations and individuals working with firms pursue self-regulation effectively in the future in light of the increasingly complex financial services field?

Lynch: Having standards that people understand is important. Most people in this industry want to do the right thing, but what the right thing is, is not always clear. The ethical issues that I see are issues that have no clear answers, such as the resolution of a conflict between a firm and a customer when no clear, articulated standards on the issue exist.

One problem people are having is staying current on all the regulations put forth by the SEC, the self-regulating organizations (SROs), and state regulatory bodies around the country. Not only is the federal regulatory environment getting tougher than it has been, but so are the state regulators. In addition, the transactions being processed are increasingly complex. The result is that people are not able to keep up with all the requirements. No firm of any size can comply with the laws perfectly every day.

The regulators need to develop a better understanding of the complexity of this business and the difficult decisions that come up every day. Although I recognize that this recommendation is not likely to be followed, one specific improvement in the system would be to eliminate state regulations for transactions in SEC-registered securities and centralize regulation of the securities markets at the federal level.

Question: Do you think Representative John D. Dingell's (D, Mich.) suggested legislation to allow the SEC to revoke licenses of rogue brokers with significant disciplinary histories is a good proposal? Is an ethical issue involved in deciding when a person should be thrown out of the business?

Lynch: The SEC already has the ability to suspend or bar someone from the industry. If the SEC can demonstrate that a banker has violated the securities law, it does not hesitate to institute a proceeding and seek appropriate sanctions.

Question: How do young people in the investment management field view ethical issues? Is ethics an area of high priority in their minds as they begin their careers?

Lummer: I don't think young people in the industry place a high priority on ethical issues, but they are not without ethical standards. I found Gary Trudeau's recent cartoon series on Michael Milken distressing not because of the attack on Milken but because the cartoons showed the business students cheering Milken on; they implied an aura of moral bankruptcy in business schools. I do not get such a sense of moral bankruptcy from my experiences on college campuses.

When it comes to ethics, students are probably no different now than they were a generation ago. Students then and now are often naive. They want to do the right thing, but they are not greatly focused on what the right thing is. I get the same impressions today from the new employees we are hiring as I did a couple of years ago when I was on the college campus.

Question: Does the SEC's enforcement agenda differ in any way from what would be the optimum agenda for the SEC? Do areas of regulatory and legal frustration exist?

Lynch: The SEC tries to react to problems it perceives in the industry. Its perception of the problems may sometimes lag a little bit behind the development of those problems, but essentially, the commission does a pretty good job of scoping out the problems and addressing them by pursuing cases that relate to those problems.

One problem area that could have been addressed more forcefully than it was is the penny-stock market. When I was at the SEC, I thought more resources should have been directed to that area. Segments of this market—particularly the Denver and Salt Lake City segments—do not exhibit the same level of ethics as the rest of the industry.

I believe the SEC's emphasis is somewhat misdirected in one current area of priority—the municipal bond market. The commission's focus is on investigating what it considers to be past abuses in the industry. I think the focus should be on defining the standards of conduct in the industry. If the SEC doesn't want firms to make political contributions to get business, then that should be the standard of conduct for the future. I see little purpose in using enforcement resources to investigate whether people made political contributions for business purposes in the past. Clearly, they did. If political contributions are an abuse, the Municipal Securities Rulemaking Board should pass a rule or Congress should pass legislation to make sure the abuse cannot happen in the future.

Question: Are private SROs such as AIMR and its professional conduct enforcement program beneficial to the markets and the SEC?

Lynch: SROs like AIMR provide a useful contribution in that they focus the attention of groups within the industry on issues of ethical standards. The industry benefits greatly from getting people together to talk about ethical issues that come up and how to resolve them.

Question: Shouldn't individuals accept personal responsibility for their investment decisions? Would less regulation make people more careful with their money?

Lummer: The answer depends on the type of regulation, but I think some regulation is necessary to instill confidence in the markets. Investors have a responsibility to know the general nature of the type of investment in which they are getting involved.

Investment advisors have a responsibility to point out the characteristics of various investment vehicles—for example, the characteristic that high-yield funds have a fair amount of risk and will decline in value if a credit crunch occurs.

Lynch: An unfortunate perception among a relatively large percentage of the population is that investment firms are somehow guarantors of investments. If things turn down, if people suffer a loss, they believe someone has defrauded them. They believe someone gave them poor advice in the first instance. They then come back to the firm that sold them the investment, basically seeking a guarantee from that firm.

Frankly, I think this perception is encouraged by the popular press and by plaintiffs' lawyers who bring class-action suits and arbitrations at the drop of a hat. A common occurrence if a public company has a bad quarter is that a lawyer files an action alleging that a fraud has occurred. So a class-action suit is filed, and the company spends $5 million defending itself, all of which comes out of the coffers of the company and hurts the current shareholders. This trend has to be reversed.

Question: Every boom seems to carry the seed of a bust or a scandal. In light of today's boom, what areas of ethical behavior should be of particular concern in the next several years?

Lummer: One potential problem is the extensive use of deriva-

tives with respect to fixed-income mutual funds. People who have been paying attention to mutual funds have known about the problem for a while. It has also attracted some press attention, but certainly not to the extent that it will if, for example, interest rates spike up, bond fund values start coming down, and a couple of the derivative products that have exacerbated the risk of interest rates explode. If some bond funds start to be really dragged down, we will see a lot of press reaction. The best policy for a mutual fund to take is full disclosure of what it is doing from the beginning so that the investors will understand the risk characteristics of the fund.

Lynch: Another potential problem is the use of mortgage-backed derivatives in mutual funds. These instruments are very risky, and investors in these funds may not be aware of the risk. Similarly, some of the emerging market funds are risky. If those markets turn down, people will begin to question whether investors should have had relatively high percentages of their portfolios invested in emerging markets.

Disclosure will help head off some of these problems, but disclosure alone is not sufficient. Investment advisors must also take responsibility for making sure their clients—particularly the individual investor—hold balanced portfolios that can be defended later if a market turns bad. This responsibility involves restraint on the part of advisors.

Applying Ethics in the Real World

William E. Avera, CFA
President
Fincap, Inc.

The AIMR Professional Conduct Program consists of a code of personal ethics, standards for ethical conduct, and an enforcement program. The code and standards provide a safety net to help investment professionals make the hard choices they may confront. The AIMR enforcement process gives credibility to the program; it works through regional peer review, self- and peer reporting, confidentiality, and professional staffing. Interpretation of the standards is an ongoing process, and this presentation discusses the specific questions most often asked about application of the standards.

When financial analysts set out to apply ethics in their day-to-day business, they face the challenge of translating concepts about ideal behavior into actual behavior. Sometimes this challenge is difficult indeed, and AIMR can provide important assistance. The AIMR Code of Ethics and Standards of Professional Conduct form a framework in which to make decisions about ethical behavior.[1] In addition, AIMR publications and staff can provide guidance in applying specific concepts in the real world. This presentation summarizes AIMR's Professional Conduct Program and discusses some of most frequently asked questions about applications of the Standards of Professional Conduct.

AIMR Professional Conduct Program

All AIMR members, including holders of the CFA designation and CFA candidates, are required to participate in AIMR's program for professional responsibility and are required to sign initial and annual statements relating to their professional conduct.

The initial impression some people have of AIMR's professional responsibility program is sometimes negative, because most people in the investment management profession believe the world has enough regulation. People do not take kindly to the idea that AIMR is another level of regulation. AIMR is not, however, an enforcement body in the way the SEC is; it cannot put anybody out of the business or extract funds from people.

The standards are not another level of regula-

tion; rather, they are a safety net AIMR gives its members, a safety net to help them be ethical. The self-regulatory program is a friend to AIMR members, not an enemy. The standards remind members who may go down the wrong road to pull back. The safety comes from the reminder that, if they do something that brings discredit upon the profession, they may be found out by regulators and by their peers, and bad things will then happen to them. For some, their CFA charters may be revoked.

AIMR is a self-regulatory organization. It is not related to the government or Congress, which is an advantage because neither Congress nor government regulators know the profession the way its members do. In addition, AIMR can be international in scope to reflect the fact that it represents a global profession; it is not restricted, in the way a governmental regulator is, to the United States or to Canada or to any other specific country.

The essential elements of AIMR's self-regulatory program of professional conduct are the Code of Ethics, the Standards of Professional Conduct, and the enforcement Rules of Procedure. Perhaps the most important, and difficult, task of self-regulation is to define clearly what constitutes good behavior and what constitutes bad behavior. AIMR met this challenge by establishing the code and the standards, which are presented in Appendix A and are published in a handbook that provides commentary and interpretation of the standards.[2] Together, the code and standards contribute four statements of core val-

---

[1]See Appendix A.

[2]*Standards of Practice Handbook*, 6th ed. (Charlottesville, Va.: Association for Investment Management and Research, 1992).

ues and nine specific steps for realizing those values.

The values and steps were not handed to the members on a mountain written in concrete. They were forged by practicing financial analysts serving on the Professional Ethics and Responsibility Committee. The code and standards are not rigid; they are constantly under review by PERC.

Enforcement lends credibility to and is an important part of AIMR's Professional Conduct Program. The enforcement aspect has five major elements. First, it is based on peer review, which is conducted by the Professional Conduct Committee. That is, the people working, living, and bleeding in the community are ultimately responsible for making self-regulation work.

Second, it is regional; so people in an analyst's area are the ones investigating that analyst's behavior and, if necessary, the ones involved in a hearing.

The third element of the self-enforcement system is an active, competent, professional staff in Charlottesville that makes the system work. The staff assists the Professional Conduct Committee with investigations, follows up complaints and inquiries by members and nonmembers, and communicates with members. If a story appears in the press involving a member who may have gotten into trouble, the staff keeps close tabs on the incident.

The fourth key element of the enforcement system is confidentiality. If an investigation is carried out and nothing is found, neither the member's name nor the circumstances ever appear in public. The process carefully protects the identity and the privacy of AIMR members. A member who goes through the process and is found to have done something wrong, however, may face a public sanction.

The final element of the system is self-reporting. All members must annually file a professional conduct statement in which they indicate whether or not they have been involved in an investigation, a legal problem, or a regulatory action or whether their professional or business conduct has been the subject of complaint. Most violations are revealed by these reports, and the AIMR professional staff follows up to ensure that appropriate action is taken.

In addition to self-reporting, the program is very dependent on peer reporting—members reporting when they have observed a questionable ethical action. If a problem is found, the members have a responsibility to each other and to the public to identify and deal with it. The staffing and confidentiality guidelines assure members that if no problem is found, the confidentiality of all will be maintained.

Although enforcement is not the most pleasant side of self-regulation, it is crucial: Credibility with the relevant public, the media, and the regulators necessitates that everybody know an enforcement system exists. The AIMR program shows the public that our profession does have an enforcement procedure, that we try to take care of our own problems. Since 1990, the professional conduct program has processed more than 1,000 matters and currently has about 300 pending. Nearly 150 sanctions have been imposed since 1990, including 118 suspensions of membership and/or CFA designation.

Of course, the enforcement process is not foolproof. It cannot stop the really dedicated bad actors from going to the dark side. The important purpose of these "teeth" is to have a credible system in place for disciplinary action so members will have one more reason to stay on the ethical side of the line and so the public will know that we do not tolerate unethical behavior by our members.

In summary, the Professional Conduct Program is a way to hold the profession together as it attempts to maintain a fragile public trust. The AIMR regulatory enforcement process works through regional peer review, self- and peer reporting, confidentiality, and professional staffing.

Education and Awareness

An important aspect of the Professional Conduct Program and the system of self-regulation is that they be dynamic, that they change when necessary and improve. The program must *continue* to work and maintain credibility inside and outside the profession. Suggestions from members are encouraged because all members have a stake in the system and its credibility.

Part of the staff's responsibility for promoting awareness of the Standards of Professional Conduct and part of the continuing education of members about the standards and enforcement procedures is to answer the many questions they are asked. The following questions deal with frequently raised issues.

▪ *How should initial public offerings (IPOs) be allocated?* This issue is particularly current because so many IPOs are "hot issues" that fewer shares are available than investors wish to purchase. Several standards relate to this issue. First, Standard IV says that an investment professional should give priority to customers. So, customers should get the first crack at any IPOs available to an investment manager.

In allocating IPOs among customers, Standard III G comes into effect; it states that the investment professional will treat all customers fairly, which means not systematically favoring some customers and disfavoring others. Standard III G does not say exactly what "fair" is because fair depends on the circumstances.

With the allocation issue, as with many others, investment professionals need to remember that, in practical circumstances, some issues are simply hard to resolve. Standards can give guidance, but they cannot dictate the appropriate course of action for all situations. In IPO allocations, first, try to be fair. Then, carefully establish and document a procedure for making the allocations. Sometimes an investment manager can allocate some of the issue to every account, but often, as a practical matter, the manager will have too many accounts for that approach to make sense. The new issue must then be allocated to some accounts before others. Sometimes this decision is clarified because the accounts have different objectives; the IPO might not be appropriate or suitable for some accounts. The investment professional is going to have to make judgments, but the standards require that those judgments not systematically favor or disfavor particular clients.

Standard III A says that everything the investment professional does must have a reasonable basis; therefore, because one of the things investment managers do is allocate IPOs, they need a reasonable basis for their actions. Standard III A also says that a reasonable basis cannot exist only in one's head; when ethical financial analysts do something, they document it. The best protection is to have a reasonable procedure and to have it in writing.

■ *Can information be distributed during the "waiting period" for an IPO?* SEC regulations restrict the distribution of written materials other than the preliminary prospectus (commonly called the "red herring" because the required disclaimers on its cover are printed in red) during the registration period. Oral communications and clarifications are permitted. If a firm distributes any written materials during the waiting period, the materials must be of a general nature, not specific to the IPO.

■ *Can investment in a personal account be contrary to recommendations and actions for clients?* Standards III A, B, and C require that any recommendation or action for a client have a reasonable basis and consider the circumstances of the client. An analyst could invest personal funds in a manner that would be unsuitable for the analyst's clients. In such a circumstance, the analyst should be sure that any potential conflict arising from this contrary investment strategy is disclosed (Standard V) and that none of the analyst's transactions has an adverse impact on clients (Standard IV). Finally, the analyst must also take care to maintain both the reality and appearance of independence and objectivity (Standard VII B).

■ *How long should one wait before taking action in a personal account?* The answer is that there is no universal rule with a certain number of hours or days; the timing depends on the circumstances. Many firms have rules that at least 48 hours must elapse between these trades; others require seven days or more.

Standard IV and various securities laws require investment professionals to take care of their clients before they take care of themselves. In addition, the investment professional's actions must appear to be reasonable to the public. For example, clients must be given a reasonable opportunity to be positioned so that their investment manager will not be in front of them—that is, will not be front running. In general, financial analysts should remember the rule: The client always comes first. The analyst, the analyst's firm, the analyst's interests are subservient to the client.

The analyst's best protection, again, is to have a *written procedure.* It can clarify that the analyst applied a consistent policy—for example, did not wait one hour one time and three days the next time unless certain specified conditions were met.

Investment professionals also need to be concerned about how a situation might appear. For example, if an investment professional purchases a security for a client and then very soon buys it for her or his own account at the same or a lower price, the appearance might be that a deal has been made with the broker or the executor to link the transactions.

A related issue arises when an investment manager is also an investor in a portfolio—for example, is managing a portfolio for a mutual fund and owns shares of the mutual fund. If the manager's ownership of the mutual fund is a very small part of the mutual fund, and in turn, the manager's personal investment in the mutual fund is a relatively small part of the manager's personal wealth, then that mutual fund is treated as a client. Remember, however, the Standard III G responsibilities, namely, that the mutual fund with the manager's money in it cannot be treated any differently from a similarly situated fund without the manager's money in it.

In summary, investment professionals may invest in the funds they manage, but they should make sure that they do not nurture those funds more than other funds. Under Standard IV, the manager's investment should be disclosed to the manager's employer and clients.

Indeed, the investment professional's saving grace, protection, and "purification" is disclosure. Disclosure is always good policy because it gives the investment manager's employers, his or her clients, the opportunity to evaluate for themselves where a risk of unethical behavior exists.

■ *When is a gift too valuable to accept?* A primary principle of the profession's ethical standards is that analysts' opinions cannot be bought and sold. No matter what an investment professional's strength of character, when that person accepts a valuable gift, her or his judgments may be affected.

Moreover, people who see an investment professional accepting the gift might perceive that person to be selling his or her opinion, which is a violation of Standard VII B: Use particular care and good judgment to achieve and maintain independence and objectivity. Also, the people giving the gift may believe that acceptance of it means they will receive some future benefit. Those people then believe they have purchased the opinion of a financial analyst.

Thus, investment professionals need to be very careful with gifts. Gifts should be nominal, and as with other standards, the financial analyst's best protection is a written procedure that has some dollar number. The AIMR handbook suggests limiting accepted gifts to a value of $50–$100.

This principle often requires hard choices. It may even offend a person who offers a gift. The benefit of the principle—sustaining the profession's credibility—is greater, however, than the disadvantages. The greater value lies in being sure that one has done the right thing and knowing that one is an upstanding member of the profession and has done nothing to undermine public trust.

■ *Are referral fees acceptable, and how should they be disclosed*? Because referral fees are an area of potential abuse, the SEC and other regulatory bodies have placed restrictions on such fees. For example, ERISA prohibits referral fees by fiduciaries. Before entering into any referral fee arrangement, an analyst would be well advised to seek competent and independent legal advice. Under Standard VI B, however, AIMR members are clearly obliged to disclose all referral-fee arrangements, in writing, to present and potential clients.

■ *What are the limitations on reporting the investment performance of managers when they worked for previous employers*? The AIMR Performance Presentation Standards (Standard III F) limit performance results to the firm, so the historical record of an individual cannot be linked to the record of a new affiliation or newly formed firm.[3] However, the individual's performance in a previous affiliation can be communicated as supplemental information, with the proper disclosures. The SEC guidelines on performance reporting similarly limit the use of performance data from a previous firm unless it is disclosed in a way that does not mislead. One of the key issues in disclosing performance with a previous organization is to make sure that other individuals were not partly responsible for that performance.

Conclusion

The challenge of our profession is that good ethics are essential to maintaining public trust but our day-to-day business involves many temptations and difficult choices. For this reason, we need all the help we can get. AIMR offers this help by providing in its code and standards a vision of the ethical financial analyst and specific guidance for required and prohibited behavior. In addition, the AIMR handbook describes the application of the standards and suggests procedures to maintain compliance. The AIMR professional conduct staff is available to respond to questions and educate members. Even with the support of AIMR's Professional Conduct Program and of peers and supervisors, however, the responsibility for ethics lies with the individual analyst, who must make hard and courageous choices.

---

[3]The Performance Presentation Standards are given in Appendix B.

Interpretation and Implementation of Ethical Standards: The Client

Judith D. Freyer, CFA
Vice President, Investments, and Treasurer
The Board of Pensions of the Presbyterian Church (USA)

Philosophical concepts of ethics exhibit a tension between morality imposed by external controls and internally imposed morality. Investment analysts' responses to questions about ethical beliefs and behavior suggest that most people combine the philosophical extremes. Fear of laws *and* moral and religious beliefs are believed to be the most important deterrents to unethical actions.

Pension plan sponsors often have a different perspective on the investment management industry and its ethics. Plan sponsors represent the final buy-side entity, the consumers and end users of many of the products that Wall Street develops, engineers, and markets. One of the things that plan sponsors quickly learn is the old Latin phrase *"caveat emptor,"* and buyers of Wall Street's products need to have it engraved on the door over their offices. As vendors of innovative products and sellers of performance dreams meet with us, we must constantly remind ourselves, *"Caveat emptor."* The meaning for buyers is to watch closely and understand clearly what we are buying.

With changes in educational standards and required languages, and with the globalization of world economies and marketplaces, to define what ethics is in our world in the 1990s is difficult even for holders of a CFA charter. Other people and cultures may have very different ethical standards from Americans, and understanding what ethical norms are appropriate in the United States compared with what is appropriate in Malaysia, Singapore, or Brazil can be challenging and often frustrating.

The dictionary defines "ethics" as a noun meaning morals, morality, or rules of conduct—certainly nonthreatening definitions. The dictionary also, however, refers the reader to the word "duty." Duty has two basic definitions. The first says that duty or ethics is a moral obligation, a liability, accountability, onus, responsibility, or bounden duty. We can feel those words pushing down on our shoulders, and we get smaller and smaller as we now think about our

"liability" and "responsibility." These synonyms for duty are all external controls upon a decision maker and upon ethical behavior. The second definition of duty, however, is different. In addition to morality, duty or ethics is also defined as the Ten Commandments, conscientiousness, an inward monitor, a sense of obligation, or that still, small voice within a person delineating right and wrong. This definition implies an *internal* control mechanism: the still, small voice, the little angel that sits on our shoulders who tells us what is right.

This discussion of philosophical concepts of ethics will focus on the tension between morality imposed by external controls and morality imposed from within. It will also stay within the bounds of Western tradition, basically Judeo-Christian ethics. Even with this narrow focus, however, vast differences exist in perceptions of ethics, of what is right and what is wrong, and of the efficacy of internal versus external controls on ethical behavior.

If you assume the philosophy of Jesus or Buddha, for example, you will believe that virtue is love, that one resists evil by returning good and turning the other cheek, and that people are basically good. You expect people to be able to live within a democratic structure with few rules and to have the internal discipline and self-control to monitor themselves.

This philosophy differs radically from the approach proposed by Machiavelli or Nietsche, in which virtue is equated with power, and adherents believe that inequity and inequality will persist throughout the land so evil must be resisted with force. You believe people are basically lazy, stupid, and in need of strong hierarchical structures and laws to keep them in line.

These diametrically opposed philosophies lead to significant philosophical, legal, and moral differences. One focuses on internally generated mores; the other on externally enforced discipline. Internal versus external. Historically, dominant control mechanisms have been one or the other. The external emphasis, however, is rarely satisfactory: Where societal or professional norms are inadequate, laws, regulation, and external control will be ineffective; where ethical norms and morals are widely adopted, laws will prove to be redundant.

It was in the middle of the 18th century, just about 30 years after the Presbyterian Church (USA) pension fund was founded, that the German philosopher Immanuel Kant prescribed what is known as his categorical imperative: "Act as if the maxim of thy action were to become by thy will a Universal Law of Nature."[1] Kant advised us that, when we act, we must bear in mind that the world is not as it is, but that in our actions we help to create it. We are also told, "So act as to treat humanity, whether in thine own person or in that of any other, in every case as an end withal, and never as means only."[2]

Note that the central tenet of the categorical imperative is that moral law is within, is the still, small voice of the person acting. Kant implies that our laws and our CFA Code of Conduct will be inadequate for those who do not possess a moral law within and cannot hear the still, small voice. Is this implication true today?

John Casey, writing in the 1980s, reminds us in his book *Ethics in the Financial Marketplace* of the importance of having strong internal controls and disciplines *and* working within a framework of laws.[3] He suggests that being ethical requires us to be honest with ourselves about our own limited wisdom, our inability to act in a fully unbiased, disinterested way, and the amount of time we can reasonably spend analyzing and weighing alternatives in typical day-to-day situations. What Casey suggests is that, if we do not have that small, inner voice, and if we do not have the moral law within, we will go from day to day unable to evaluate the impact of our actions. In this case, we will not relate the cause and effect of our actions: One little indiscretion can lead to another, and we will go from the little white lie to the large black lie, and to picking which prison we

want to be in. It also means that, if investment professionals do not have the moral discipline within, they will equivocate on tough issues or end up being paralyzed by their own indecision. The magnitude of their tasks and the enormity of their fiduciary responsibility will lead them to make no decisions at all. That is not what investment professionals are paid to do. We are paid, and usually very well paid, to use our own judgment and make the difficult decisions.

Survey of Investment Professionals

In 1992, the Research Foundation of the Institute of Chartered Financial Analysts published a survey on ethics in which some of the findings illuminate how the external disciplines—codes of law—and the internal disciplines really work in the financial marketplace.[4] The survey population was randomly drawn from 3,600 members of AIMR who identified themselves as investment analysts (out of a total membership of 21,500). Questionnaires were sent to about 900 analysts and generated about 400 usable responses. The majority of the analysts, 75 percent, were men; 48 percent were in the age bracket of 25–35 years; and 55 percent had been in the investment profession for fewer than 9 years.

One of the questions asked these analysts what they thought were the appropriate sources of ethical training—their ideal or "best world" sources. **Table 1** contains the respondents' answers. These financial analysts believed that the single most important source of ethical training is senior management—that is, the example of those above them. Second and almost equal in importance is home environment.

The second-tier ideal sources of ethical training were reported to be programs provided by employers and professional organizations. Schools and religious education are given the lowest ratings by this particular group of analysts. In summary, direct personal example, whether in the home or on the job, parent or boss, is believed to provide the most appropriate source of ethical training.

The question addressed in **Table 2** also concerned ethics training; this time, the question focused on the *effectiveness* of sources of ethics training. Home environment was clearly identified as the most effective source, with senior management and professional organizations of secondary importance. Training by employers moved down in the effectiveness rating. This outcome may reflect the facts that high expectations are generally set for training pro-

---

[1]*Fundamental Principles of the Metaphysic of Morals*, T.K. Abbott, trans. (Prometheus Books, 1785):49.

[2]*Fundamental Principles of the Metaphysic of Morals*:58.

[3]New York: Scudder, Stevens & Clark, 1988.

---

[4]E. Theodore Veit and Michael R. Murphy, *Ethics in the Investment Profession: A Survey* (Charlottesville, Va.).

Table 1. Opinions about Appropriate Sources of Ethics Training
(percent of respondents, except as noted)

Source	None (1)	Small Amount (2)	Moderate Amount (3)	Substantial Amount (4)	Weighted Average of Ratings
Senior management (by example)	0.0%	7.5%	40.3%	52.3%	3.45[a]
Home environment	1.3	8.0	41.4	49.4	3.39[a]
Employing firm (training programs)	2.8	19.1	49.2	28.9	3.04[b]
Professional organizations	3.8	23.2	49.7	23.2	2.92[b]
School or college	4.5	44.4	44.1	7.0	2.54[c]
Religious education	20.4	25.3	33.9	20.4	2.54c

Source: Veit and Murphy, *Ethics in the Investment Profession.*

[a, b, c]Sources with matching letters are not significantly different from each other at the 5 percent level.

Table 2. Opinions about Effectiveness of Various Sources of Ethics Training
(percent of respondents, except as noted)

Source	Not Effective (1)	Slightly Effective (2)	Moderately Effective (3)	Very Effective (4)	Weighted Average of Ratings
Home environment	1.8%	5.0%	18.4%	74.8%	3.66
Senior management (by example)	12.1	28.9	34.4	24.6	2.92
Professional organizations	6.0	23.8	43.4	26.8	2.91
Religious education	20.7	21.2	29.4	28.6	2.66
School or college	19.1	41.5	29.1	10.3	2.31[a]
Employing firm (training programs)	22.4	34.4	32.7	10.6	2.31[a]

Source: Veit and Murphy, *Ethics in the Investment Profession.*

[a]Not significantly different at the 5 percent level.

grams and that those expectations are not always fulfilled.

The survey dealt specifically with the question of what prevents us from being unethical—a fear of the law or the still, small voice within. Is the prevention provided by respect for ourselves and others or concern over losing our jobs? **Table 3** provides the surveyed analysts' evaluations of the importance of various deterrents to unethical behavior. Fear of the law surpassed the still, small voice, although moral and religious beliefs ranked second in importance. A published code of ethics was ranked last; more than 61 percent of respondents believed such codes are not at all or are only slightly important.

The analysts were also asked to indicate how frequently they believed, based on their own experi-

Table 3. Importance of Various Deterrents to Unethical Behavior
(percent of respondents, except as noted)

Deterrent	Not Important (1)	Slightly Important (2)	Moderately Important (3)	Very Important (4)	Weighted Average of Ratings
Concern about sanctions from the SEC or state or provincial agencies	2.5%	14.9%	43.1%	39.5%	3.20
Moral or religious beliefs	9.0	20.4	25.4	45.2	3.07
Concern that family or friends will find out	7.3	28.9	34.7	29.1	2.86
Concern about sanctions from self-regulatory organizations	12.6	34.7	33.4	19.3	2.60
Having a published code of ethics	21.0	40.2	25.8	13.1	2.31

Source: Veit and Murphy, *Ethics in the Investment Profession.*

ences and observations, certain ethical or legal violations occur. **Table 4** shows that the respondents reported failure to use due diligence and thoroughness in making reports the most frequent violation observed; 66 percent of analysts had observed these lapses periodically or frequently. Front running placed lower in frequency than communicating on inside information and not dealing fairly with all clients. Failure to disclose conflicts of interest ranked last in violations observed; nevertheless, more than 31 percent of respondents believed it happens frequently or periodically.

Table 4. Perceived Frequency of Various Ethical or Legal Violations
(percent of respondents, except as noted)

Violation	Never (1)	Rarely (2)	Periodically (3)	Frequently (4)	Weighted-Average Frequency[a]
Failure to use diligence and thoroughness in making recommendations	7.4%	26.1%	48.8%	17.6%	2.77
Writing reports that support predetermined conclusions	11.9	32.5	39.9	15.7	2.60[a]
Communicating inside information	11.9	33.2	39.1	15.7	2.59[a]
Trading based on inside information	17.0	35.0	35.3	12.7	2.44[b]
Not dealing fairly with all clients when taking investment action	18.7	38.9	32.5	10.0	2.34[b,c]
Plagiarizing another's work	17.3	45.7	31.6	5.4	2.25[c]
Misrepresenting a firm's past or expected future performance	19.5	43.3	31.8	5.4	2.23[c]
Front running (making personal trades before client trades)	25.8	38.9	27.1	8.2	2.18
Failure to disclose conflicts of interest to clients and/or employer	23.6	44.9	26.4	5.1	2.13

Source: Veit and Murphy, *Ethics in the Investment Profession.*

[a, b, c]Violations with matching letters are not significantly different from each other at the 5 percent level.

Table 5. Personal Observation of Unethical Behavior

Item	Number	Percent
In the past 12 months, an employee of the firm has acted in an unethical manner:		
Yes	95	24.1%
No	300	75.9
Total	395	100.0
If yes, respondent's action:[a]		
Made the activity known to a superior or other person in the chain of command	39	41.1
Took no action	34	35.8
Discussed it with the person who made the infraction	30	31.6
Made the activity known to the ethics compliance officer	11	11.6
Total	114	

Source: Veit and Murphy, *Ethics in the Investment Profession.*

[a]Respondents could indicate more than one action. Percentages are of the 95 individuals indicating they had witnessed unethical behavior.

In a related question, the survey asked the analysts to comment on their personal observations of unethical behavior in the last 12 months. **Table 5** indicates that almost a quarter of the respondents knew of situations in which colleagues or fellow employees had acted in an unethical manner during that time. The majority of those analysts who knew of such behavior took some form of action.

Conclusion

What does the survey reveal about these financial analysts' philosophical approach to ethics? Do we follow the ethics of Jesus and Buddha, Machiavelli and Nietsche, or Kant and Casey? Does *caveat emptor* need to remain the Rosetta stone of the investment profession?

Fear of the law, as well as moral and religious beliefs, are believed to be more important deterrents to unethical actions than codes of ethics. Moreover, the respondents believed that the home environment is the most important source of training for ethical behavior and that senior management leadership and company training programs should provide better guidance than they currently do.

In the conflict between ethics and profits, and in the task of improving public perception of those in the investment industry, the AIMR Code of Ethics and Standards of Professional Conduct provide a framework for ethical conduct that combines external and internal controls—that is, legal, regulatory, professional, and moral norms. The code and standards provide us with the means to apply the Golden Rule, respond to that small voice within, and make ethics the most important part of our daily lives. The code and standards also provide the means by which senior managers can effectively exemplify moral conduct.

Interpretation and Implementation of Ethical Standards: The Sell Side

O. Ray Vass
First Vice President and Director of Compliance and Regulatory Policy
Merrill Lynch, Pierce, Fenner & Smith

The compliance and ethics function in a broker/dealer firm must deal with rules of conduct that rely on interpretation and ethical judgment that go beyond legal constraints. Such firms need to clarify not only their standards but also their interpretations. One large broker/dealer firm's policies are built around three primary concepts designed for the long-term benefit of the firm: the customer's interest must come first; good compliance is good business; and no one's bottom line is more important than the reputation of the firm.

In recent years, the securities industry has faced increasing negative publicity about its lack of ethics. I reject the idea that participants in the industry have no ethics. Our industry has many bright, innovative, and often aggressive people, the great majority of whom are as ethical and honest as those in any business in this country. The industry is one, however, with inherent and severe conflicts and temptations. It is also an industry that is perceived to operate in the public interest, and accordingly, it is highly regulated.

Brokers, analysts, and financial managers have tremendous freedom of action in how they conduct business, but they are also subject to extensive regulation, well-established ethical standards, and sharp scrutiny. In addition to regulation at both the federal and state levels, the industry is subject to an extensive system of self-regulation. Moreover, the industry is unique as a business in that the National Association of Securities Dealers (NASD), the NYSE, and other exchanges serve not only as its major marketplaces but also as regulators.

Ethical Standards in the Industry

A simple definition of ethics would be: acting in a way that is right rather than merely legal. It is a higher standard than legality, but in most instances, if we simply do what is right, we will also avoid running afoul of legal or regulatory requirements.

The Veit–Murphy Research Foundation study indicated that analysts' primary motivations for ethical behavior are fear of the consequences, or sanctions in the event of ethical lapses, and moral or religious beliefs.[1] Another motivation—and one that is not emphasized enough—is self-interest. Self-interest, in the enlightened sense, means that it is in the industry participants' own interests, to their long-term benefit, to conduct their business in an ethical manner. This motivation encompasses, of course, the fear of consequences, of negative publicity, and of regulatory sanctions.

Ethical concerns in the securities industry are not new. Securities firms, regulatory bodies, and self-regulatory organizations have focused on ethical issues at least for the last three decades. In the early 1960s, brokerage firms began developing large internal staffs of attorneys and compliance people to control and manage the firm's business properly. A wide range of compliance rules were developed to provide guidance regarding the judgments and choices that brokers make in their everyday dealings with customers.

Many of these rules imposed inexact requirements to govern sales practices and to establish standards for ethical conduct. Consider, for example, some of the fundamental rules and underlying concepts that have been basic to securities industry

---

[1]E. Theodore Veit and Michael R. Murphy, *Ethics in the Investment Profession: A Survey* (Charlottesville, Va.: The Research Foundation of The Institute of Chartered Financial Analysts, 1992). See also Table 3, p. 41, in Ms. Freyer's presentation.

regulation: the "know your customer" rule, the suitability standard, requirements as to a "reasonable basis" for recommendations (applicable to both analysts and brokers), the embodiment of "just and equitable principles of trade" in formal regulations, and the designation of a significant portion of the NASD's regulations as "Rules of Fair Practice" (a title suggestive in itself of an ethical context).

Until the mid- to late 1970s, the emphasis was on the retail side of the business because of the perception that regulation was needed to protect the public or individual retail customer. In the 1980s, the emphasis shifted, and both firms and regulators now devote considerable resources to encouraging and enforcing ethical behavior in the capital markets—in trading and investment banking, for example—and to the behavior of analysts.

In summary, ethics in the securities industry is an old subject but one that is getting a healthy new emphasis—through media attention, college courses, and seminars.

Compliance Programs

The compliance function in a large broker/dealer deals primarily with conduct and sales practices. In most cases, the concepts and rules of conduct are not exact, and often, they are not easily measured. Many are subject to a great deal of interpretation and involve a significant amount of judgment. The reason is that the subject of ethics involves many gray areas; issues are not often black and white.

Companies do not need written policies on the straightforward ethical rules, such as "Employees shall not steal." Companies do need to state their policies regarding interpretation of the industry standards of conduct and do need to educate employees on applying those policies in their conduct.

The approach of Merrill Lynch, Pierce, Fenner & Smith can serve as an example of stated policies for a compliance program and the philosophy underlying the policies. Merrill Lynch policies in regard to ethical behavior can be summarized in three slogans:

- The customer's interest must come first.
- Good compliance is good business.
- No one's bottom line is more important

than the reputation of the firm.

The first slogan dates back to the days of the firm's founder, Charles E. Merrill. The latter two clearly fall into the category of pursuing the firm's long-term self-interest. They reflect the belief that the firm will be most successful and will attract the most public trust and business if it follows these concepts.

Merrill Lynch also promotes its belief in ROI—return on integrity. We think return on integrity is as real a factor in success as return on equity. This attitude also stems from the enlightened pursuit of self-interest.

As an example of dissemination of information and the establishment of expectations, Merrill Lynch's *Guidelines for Business Conduct*, which outlines broad-based ethical standards, is distributed to every new employee for review and written acknowledgement of its receipt. In addition, the guidelines are periodically disseminated to all employees for review and reinforcement. Various, more extensive, policy and procedures manuals that apply to different segments of the business articulate many of the same points. The importance of the firm's reputation and ethical conduct is also periodically emphasized through memos or articles in internal publications.

As an example of the application of technology to supporting ethical behavior, combined with information dissemination, Merrill Lynch also has a system called EARS (Employee Account Review System). This highly automated system is intended to facilitate monitoring of employee securities transactions by line supervisors and surveillance from a compliance perspective. We conduct an annual survey to verify that the system has tracked all employee and related accounts, and we use the annual survey as a vehicle to disseminate summaries of key policies on fundamental issues such as inside information. All employees must acknowledge that they have read and understood the summations.

Finally, Merrill Lynch has found that the most important element of a compliance program is the support of senior management and its insistence on ethical conduct as part of the culture of the company.

Question and Answer Session

Judith D. Freyer, CFA
O. Ray Vass

Question: Does Merrill Lynch implicitly or explicitly endorse or require adherence to AIMR's Code of Ethics and Standards of Professional Conduct for all personnel? If the company makes exceptions, for whom and why?

Vass: Virtually all of the principles in the AIMR standards are incorporated into our Research Division Compliance Manual and other policy manuals, although not all of the AIMR standards are applicable to all our employees. The principles relating to the preparation of reports and recommendations, for example, do not apply to most of our employees. On the other hand, the principles relating to conflicts and basic honesty and ethics are applicable to all employees.

Question: How does a broker equitably allocate hot new issues?

Vass: Allocating new issues is a difficult task, and individual brokers are probably never quite comfortable that they have been able to allocate hot new issues equitably. The supply for any given broker is very limited; hence, brokers often end up parceling out small amounts on the retail side.

The key regulatory concept in this case is, of course, the NASD Free-Riding and Withholding Interpretations, which prohibit hot-issue allocations to securities firm employees or persons in a position to direct brokerage business in return for such allocations (such as bank trust officers or other institutional portfolio managers). Merrill Lynch tries to adhere rigidly to those interpretations. Merrill Lynch also has certain internal guidelines for allocating new issues. For example, we discourage—not prohibit, but discourage—the allocation of a new issue to a new account.

Question: May an investment manager buy a bond based solely on its Standard & Poor's or Moody's rating, or must the manager hire an analyst or research service to rate the bond? Should a portfolio manager have a file on every bond in the portfolio?

Freyer: An institutional manager should always do additional research prior to trading a bond. At a minimum, the manager should be familiar with the legal covenants of the bond and should assess its quality.

Although a file on each bond is not a requirement, maintaining one is clearly in the manager's best interest.

Vass: People obviously trade bonds based primarily on their published ratings, but the practice is, generally, more acceptable for the more traditional bonds. Managers have a greater reason to document their decisions when they buy and sell the higher risk, more esoteric bonds.

Question: To what extent does a money manager who has been hired to manage one segment of a portfolio, such as equities, have an obligation to assure that the client's portfolio has not been over- or underallocated to that segment? When can the money manager defer to the asset allocation decisions of others?

Freyer: Speaking from the perspective of an institutional client, asset-class managers are not expected to make asset allocation recommendations or decisions. The plan sponsor retains the responsibility for asset allocation. On the other hand, small pension funds that give one or two managers balanced portfolios to manage *would* expect the manager to make asset allocation decisions—usually, within guidelines.

At the retail level, the answer is probably different, because the broker is typically asked to provide asset allocation advice.

Vass: The retail environment is changing somewhat. In the past, brokers could operate on the assumption that the wealthier clients were also the more sophisticated investors and thus needed less advice and protection. That assumption may not prevail, however, as some recent litigation shows. Some cases have suggested that brokers have a duty to prevent a client from committing so-called financial suicide. If an asset-class manager observes something that clearly does not seem to be in the interest of the client, then I think that manager has an ethical responsibility to say something to the client. The courts today also seem to be starting to impose some legal responsibility.

Compliance Guidelines: Introduction

Michael S. Caccese
Senior Vice President and General Counsel
Association for Investment Management and Research

The two most effective steps in combating ethical violations are the creation of and adherence to an appropriate compliance program and Chinese Wall procedures. Specific criteria are outlined here for the design and operation of both programs. In their compliance efforts, firms need to be particularly aware of the responsibility and personal liability of direct and indirect supervisors.

This presentation briefly outlines the security firm's need for a compliance program, what such a program entails, and the special role of a compliance officer. The final section is an overview of Chinese Wall procedures.

Need for a Compliance Program

Deteriorating ethics within the investment industry since the mid-1980s are evidenced by the increasing number of reported violations of securities regulations. For example, in a three-week period in the fall of 1993, the *Wall Street Journal* reported on four cases involving investment advisor conduct. The first case concerned misleading advertising material. The *WSJ* description of the case (October 14, 1993) stated that an investment advisor, Stephen Leeb, made a splash when his newsletter publisher advertised that his stock market system would have reaped a gain of 390,000 percent—yes, that is right—since 1980. The publisher offered $10,000 to the first person finding a better performer. The publisher lost the bet twice, having to pay out $20,000, and the SEC is now investigating this advertising practice.

The second case, reported in the *WSJ* on October 21, 1993, concerned a violation of the Investment Company Act prohibition of unfavorable trades between affiliates. The case involved a portfolio manager's misallocation of trades between Kemper Financial Services mutual funds and the Kemper pension plan. The result was that Kemper, in addition to the substantial bad press, had to pay $10 million in fines and $300,000 in civil penalties.

The third case involved an advisor's disregard for the suitability of an investment for its clients. On October 22, a *WSJ* article described the SEC's settlement with Prudential Bache Limited Partnership. The settlement totaled over $3.5 million, the second largest settlement in SEC history following the Drexel Burnham settlement.

Finally, on November 3, the *WSJ* reported that the National Association of Securities Dealers (NASD) Equitable Life Assurance Society failed to supervise adequately two registered representatives for the sale of variable life insurance products. Equitable also failed to supervise properly certain registered representatives in selling limited partnership private placements. The result was a $1.4 million fine imposed by the NASD and a required review of Equitable's supervisory procedures by an independent consultant.

These cases exhibit violations of the basic ethical principles of

- suitability,
- fiduciary responsibility,
- truthful performance representation, and
- fair treatment of all customers and not providing an advantage to one to the detriment of others.

The actions described in these cases also show, in light of the negative publicity, a fundamental disregard for the principle that good ethics make good business.

One way for firms to combat these types of ethical problems is to implement effective compliance programs.

Pros and Cons of a Compliance Program

Although firms are not legally required to have a

formal compliance program, firms are responsible under the Securities Exchange Act of 1934 for the proper supervision of their employees. Briefly, a failure to supervise properly has occurred when an individual or a firm "failed reasonably to supervise with a view to preventing violations . . . another person who commits such a violation, if such other person is subject to his supervision."[1] Formal compliance programs are the most effective way of meeting firms' legal requirements to supervise their employees and their responsibility to guide employee behavior.

Compliance programs provide certain other benefits. They foster an ethical culture within the firm; they deter crime, negative publicity, and misconduct; and if followed, a compliance program can mitigate penalties for violations through what is called an affirmative defense.

In an affirmative defense, the key issue from the SEC's standpoint is whether supervisory failure contributed to or made the violation possible. That failure could occur either at the firm level or at the compliance officer level. At the firm level, no failure to supervise will exist if the firm has established compliance procedures, if a system is in place for applying the procedures, and if the system can be reasonably expected to prevent and detect a violation. In other words, if you have an effective program that is up to industry standards, you have an affirmative defense at the level of the firm's responsibility.

On the negative side, once a compliance program is in place, adherence becomes mandatory. The firm cannot establish a program and then put it in a drawer and forget about it. Another drawback is that the program discloses negative information. One of the requirements of a compliance program is keeping records of how it has been enforced, so when a regulator does an inspection, the road map to the negative information is right there. The regulator can use this map to assess whether the firm has appropriately followed stated compliance procedures.

An Effective Compliance Program

To be effective as an affirmative defense, a compliance program must meet five essential requirements: First, the program must be in place prior to the violation. It does not help if the program is established after the fact.

Second, the program must be geared to anticipate the activities most likely to result in the misconduct in the particular firm. Thus, the program must reflect the business of the firm. The program cannot

be designed to anticipate all potential violations.

The degree of formality of the program must also be appropriate for the size and culture of the firm. Small firms—three-, four-, or five-person shops, for example—can apply a less formal program than, say, a major brokerage house that has multiple lines of business and many offices.

The program must meet, and preferably exceed, the minimum industry standards for professional conduct. Those are the standards the regulators and the courts will use as a basis for judging whether the firm has an effective compliance program.

Finally, the program must be followed. Participants must be informed of the program, and it must be continually updated.

Program Development

Developing an effective compliance program entails six steps:

▪ *Obtain board and CEO support.* The program must have the support of the senior management of the firm or it will not be effective.

▪ *Review the firm's business activities and regulatory environment.* The compliance program must be tied to the firm's specific business activities and the applicable regulations. Firms in the brokerage or securities industry have certain minimum legal requirements with which to comply.

▪ *Review competitors' programs.* The compliance program must meet minimum industry standards to pass the fundamental test of appropriate scope applied by regulators. A review of competitors' programs can provide valuable information in meeting this requirement.

▪ *Draft the program.* The program must be drafted by someone who is knowledgeable about both the firm and the applicable regulations and laws. Firms should thus seek outside expertise when internal expertise is not available. The program should include designation of a compliance officer; a statement on the scope of the program; and statements of permissible conduct, procedures for reporting violations, and enforcement actions. Finally, the written procedures must be understandable by all employees; the authors should avoid "legalese" and other hard-to-understand writing styles.

▪ *Implement the program.* Careful implementation of the program is important to its success and effectiveness. When you implement the program, take the time to do it right. Be thorough. Make sure people know what the program is. Make sure they understand it, and be prepared constantly to remind them of the program and what their responsibilities are.

▪ *Keep the program current.* Compliance pro-

---

[1]Securities Exchange Act of 1934, Sections 15(b)(4)(E) and 15(b)(6).

grams are not static. They must be modified and refined to reflect changes in the firm, the industry, and the environment.

The Compliance Officer

At the compliance supervisory level, the law states that no failure to supervise will exist if the compliance officer "reasonably discharged the duties and obligations incumbent upon him by reason of his firm's procedures" and if he or she had no reasonable basis for believing that those procedures were not being followed.

The SEC considers someone a compliance officer who has the responsibility, ability, or authority (1) to affect behavior and (2) to respond to the misconduct. If one of these two factors is missing, the person is not a compliance officer. A compliance officer may be held personally liable for a violation that occurs.

A compliance officer has a duty to identify a wrongdoing and promptly conduct an inquiry; respond to the wrongdoing and limit the activities of the alleged violator or institute procedures to prevent ongoing violations; and verify that recommendations are implemented. Compliance officers cannot put their heads in the sand and look the other way.

The two types of compliance officers are direct supervisors and indirect supervisors. A direct supervisor has the authority and ability to influence the conduct of others. These individuals are hierarchal supervisors; they can fire, hire, and determine compensation. In the case of a violation, the legal questions are whether the individual was a direct supervisor of the violator and whether the supervisor acted reasonably in discharging her or his duty.

The indirect supervisor, sometimes called a statutory supervisor, is not a hierarchal supervisor but is in a position of responsibility in the firm for supervising professional conduct. People who could be considered indirect supervisors are senior managers, people active in the compliance function, and general counsels. If you are in one of these positions, you should determine whether you can be considered an indirect supervisor.

What confers membership in this category is difficult to define, but the SEC has provided some guidance about who is a compliance officer through several proceedings, including *Salomon Brothers, Tennenbaum,* and *Huff.*

In the *Salomon Brothers (in the Matter of John H. Guttfreund and Others)* case, senior officers at Salomon Brothers became aware that the head government trader had submitted bogus bids in the government securities market. The officers did not remove the head trader from his position, however, nor did

they investigate to determine whether this violation was a single act or a pattern of conduct. In addition, it took them more than three months to inform the regulators.

The SEC determined that the general counsel was an indirect supervisor and was thus liable for the acts of the head trader. Although the general counsel did not have direct supervisory responsibility for any of the activities of the head trader, he had the ability to direct the firm's response and had in the past been relied on by the firm to make recommendations on violations of the compliance program and to make sure that those recommendations were implemented. In this situation, the general counsel gave advice but initiated no follow-through and did not make any concerted effort to determine whether there was follow-through.

The guiding principle from *Salomon* is that a person becomes a statutory or indirect supervisor when he or she has the "requisite degree of responsibility, ability or authority to affect conduct of the employee whose behavior is at issue." The key words are "ability" and "authority to affect conduct." In *Salomon,* the general counsel had that ability. He could have removed the head trader from his position or, at a minimum, started an investigation or inquiry to determine whether this action was one act or a pattern, and if a single act, recommended different controls to make sure the same type of illegal conduct could not occur again in the future.

The guiding principle from the *Tennenbaum* case is that line employees are not the only ones who can be compliance officers;[2] the SEC stated that, once trading authority is granted, the person who granted that authority also has the ongoing responsibility to ensure that the authority is being appropriately used and is not being abused.

Arthur James Huff: Administrative Proceeding File #3-6700, March 28, 1991, provides an example of someone who detects a problem but does not have power over the violator's conduct and is not, therefore, considered to be an indirect supervisor or compliance officer.[3] In the *Huff* case, the SEC ruled that Huff was not an indirect supervisor. Huff acted

---

[2] In *Michael E. Tennenbaum: Administrative Proceedings File #3-5797, January 19, 1982,* the SEC took the position that a general partner at Bear, Stearns was an indirect supervisor and, therefore, was liable for the actions of a salesman engaged in excessive trading. The general partner was not the salesman's direct supervisor, but he had sole authority to permit options trading.

[3] In 1991, Arthur J. Huff was a senior options principal who was new to his position. He identified significant customer losses by the key producer within the organization and recommended to his supervisor that the salesperson be terminated. The supervisor took no action. Huff, as the senior options principal, did not have the authority at that time to terminate this individual.

responsibly within the bounds of his authority; that is, he found out an error had been made, he went to the immediate supervisor, and he made a recommendation that the individual be terminated. Huff was not considered a supervisor because he did not have the power to control the violator's conduct. The ruling specifically stated that *control* is the essence of supervision.

Chinese Wall Procedures

Chinese Wall procedures are procedures within a firm that restrict the flow of confidential information to those who "need to know" in order to perform their duties effectively. Chinese Walls exist to avoid insider-trading violations by removing the opportunity for individuals to trade on material nonpublic information. Chinese Walls are very similar to compliance procedures; in fact, they are part of the compliance procedures in many firms.

The Chinese Wall structure has two parts. First, the Wall entails a physical separation of the part of the organization that receives inside information from the rest of the organization, especially the portion of the securities firm that does its own trading. In some firms, however, because of space constraints, this separation may not be practical. The second element is a written policy that specifically states the trading restrictions used by the firm to prevent insider trading.

The Chinese Wall must be structured to fit the nature of the firm; no two systems are alike. A Chinese Wall policy must contain six minimum elements, which can form the basis for a compliance manual on insider trading:

First, the firm must take substantial control of intra- and interdepartmental communications. Most firms meet this requirement by establishing a clearance area within the firm, either in the legal department or the compliance department. It acts as a clearinghouse whereby if the people behind the Chinese Wall believe they need to share confidential information with somebody on the other side, they go to this clearinghouse to determine this necessity and how much information is to be shared. If the sharing is necessary, the clearance area helps the person who needs to see the information "look over the Wall" into the area that has the information.

Second, the firm needs to review employee trades and document the review. This review is typically carried out through "watch" and "restricted" securities lists. On a watch list, the securities firm lists companies about which the firm has material or confidential information. Only the compliance or clearance department and employees behind the Chinese Wall know what is on this list, and the clearance area monitors the trading activities of people within the securities firm to see whether they are trading these securities and will also compare the trades with prospectues, news reports, and other market-related information. A restricted list is similar to a watch list except that it is made public throughout the securities firm. Some firms start with a watch list, and when they reach a certain level of activity in a company—for example, handling an investment banking deal—they move the securities of the companies participating in the deal to the restricted list.

Third, the firm must have written and widely disseminated Chinese Wall procedures so that all employees are familiar with them. The firm must also continously educate its employees about the procedures. Historically, some firms have laid out Chinese Wall procedures piecemeal in numerous documents distributed periodically to employees. An important requirement of Chinese Wall procedures today is that those procedures be stated in one document so that everybody has one source for an explanation of the policies.

Fourth, the firm needs to maintain a record of any enforcement action related to the Chinese Wall procedures. If an error or violation occurs, the firm should "memorialize" it—that is, make sure the file is complete, particularly as to the action taken.

Fifth, the firm should place controls on trading while processing material nonpublic information. These controls need to include a restriction on proprietary trading in any securities on the restricted list. The lack of such controls creates a high burden for the firm if it needs to verify that it is not trading on inside or confidential information. In addition, if the firm trades a security on the watch list, the firm should make sure it has written documentation to establish that its trades were not based on confidential information.

Conclusion

As you can see, maintaining a current compliance manual is imperative for securities firms, and compliance officers must know who they are and be knowledgeable about their responsibilities. If a firm possesses inside information, it should maintain and disseminate to its employees, in one document, clear and appropriate Chinese Wall procedures.

Compliance Guidelines: The Securities Firm

Paul G. Haaga, Jr.
Senior Vice President
Capital Research and Management Company

Two important aspects of investment companies' compliance efforts are insider-trading policies and personal securities transactions. These aspects are used here to illustrate one company's documentation of its code of conduct and compliance program. Because of its importance in carrying out an effective compliance program, a firm should pay particular attention to its compliance department: picking the right people, maintaining the right environment, involving the compliance head with the business and the top management with compliance, publishing manageable manuals, correcting the false ideas that infect an organization from time to time, and using people skills.

All companies should have written documentation of their codes of conduct and applicable compliance procedures. This presentation uses the program and guidelines of the Capital Group companies (CG), which include Capital Research and Management Company, the sponsor of the American Funds, to outline the key elements of a code and compliance program. The insider-trading guidelines and reporting requirements for personal securities transactions in CG's *A Handbook for Associates* are used to illustrate the company's policies and compliance processes. The company code of conduct covers numerous areas, such as outside employment, acceptance of gifts, etc., but this presentation focuses on insider trading and personal securities transactions. For reference, the firm's code of conduct is presented in **Exhibit 1**.

Insider-Trading Policy

The section on insider-trading policy in the handbook begins with a statement and description of applicable laws and regulations and then discusses the company's policy and compliance procedures.

The Law of Insider Trading

The law concerning insider trading prohibits trading by a company "insider" while in possession of material nonpublic information; trading by a "noninsider" while in possession of material nonpublic information when the information was either disclosed in violation of an insider's duty to keep it confidential or was misappropriated; or in either case, passing along material nonpublic information to permit someone else to trade.

Company insiders include the company's officers, directors, and associates, as well as its accountants, lawyers, investment bankers, bank lending officers, and any other persons with a special or confidential relationship that would be expected to bring them in contact with material nonpublic information about the company. Generally, investment analysts are not insiders unless, of course, they are doing some investment-banking-type work for a company. Then, the analyst could be considered a temporary insider.

Note that for a violation of the insider-trading law to exist, material nonpublic information must be involved. These terms are defined as follows: *Nonpublic* information is often described as any information about a company, or the market for the company's shares, that has not been generally disclosed to the marketplace. *Material* information is material that, if disclosed, would be likely to affect the price of the company's shares significantly or would be considered important by reasonable investors in determining whether to trade in those shares. A good test of the materiality of the information is to consider whether the share price would be likely to change significantly, up or down, if the information were made public.

Insiders have an absolute duty under the law either to abstain from trading or to disclose to the public the material information. An additional test of illegality applies to noninsiders: In addition to

Exhibit 1. The Capital Group Code of Conduct

All of us within the Capital organization are responsible for maintaining the very highest ethical standards when conducting business. In keeping with these standards, we must never allow our own interests to be placed ahead of our shareholders' and clients' interests.

Over the years we have earned a reputation for the highest integrity. Regardless of lesser standards that may be followed through business or community custom, we must observe exemplary standards of honesty and integrity. If you have trouble interpreting laws or regulations, ask CG's Legal and Compliance Department for advice.

If you know of any violation of our Code of Conduct, you have a responsibility to report it. Deviations from controls or procedures that safeguard the company, including the assets of shareholders and clients, should also be reported.

Source: The Capital Group, *A Handbook for Associates*.

being in possession of material nonpublic information, to be in noncompliance, they must also know or should have known that the information was either misappropriated or was disclosed by an insider in breach of a duty. Generally, a breach of duty occurs only if the insider personally benefits, directly or indirectly, from the trade or disclosure. The basis for the additional test applicable to noninsiders is the antifraud nature of these rules.

AIMR Standards

Our handbook specifically points out that the AIMR Standards of Professional Conduct in a case of insider trading, which standards we endorse for our employees, require action beyond abstaining from trading. Under the AIMR standards, if a breach of duty occurs in the disclosure of material nonpublic information, an analyst is required to take reasonable steps to obtain public dissemination of that information. That is, if an analyst receives information in a breach, he or she must go beyond merely placing a trading halt on the firm's securities. The analyst must take a further affirmative step, namely, go back to the company and try to get it to disseminate the information.

Insider-Trading Compliance Program

The Insider-Trading Sanctions Act of 1988 places an affirmative duty on investment advisors and broker/dealers to have a compliance program reasonably designed to prevent insider trading. This provision can be violated even without an insider trade or tips taking place. Congress enacted the law after finding that, despite highly publicized insider-trading cases in 1986 and 1987, some of the major Wall Street firms had no formal written policies for preventing insider trading. The firms apparently expected people to read the papers and know what not to do.

Running an insider-trading compliance program has several aspects. First, the program should focus on the employees who are most likely to come into contact with material nonpublic information. In

most investment management companies, research analysts are the ones who will be talking to the companies and who will be coming in contact with material nonpublic information. So, even though all employees—including mail-room staff and receptionists—should be trained in professional conduct and compliance, the program should focus on the activities of analysts.

Second, having several people in the organization who can answer questions about insider trading is important. Six of our employees have conducted insider-trading classes and can thus answer questions as they arise. Even a small organization should have several people able to answer the questions, because the questions tend to require very rapid response times.

Third, if an insider-trading problem is identified, the company must have a mechanism for ceasing trading in that security. Our mechanism is to use the investment control departments, through which all trades for clients or employees must pass for compliance review and which serve, therefore, as an effective mechanism for halting all transactions. For example, the departments screen trades to make sure that a portfolio does not exceed a 5 percent limit in each security.

Another key to running an insider-trading program is to reinforce education. Discussion or education sessions tend to generate even more questions about possible insider-trading situations. If even a few months elapse without a reminder, however, the number of questions tends to decline. People need to be reminded. They want to comply, but they are busy and need to be reminded of the existence of the issue. Every few months, we try to reserve five minutes at a general investment meeting to remind people about insider-trading issues.

In addition to reminding people about insider trading, an important element of a program is commending associates, particularly the younger, newer ones, for bringing a potential insider-trading problem or scenario to management's attention. Usually when an analyst raises a question, the situation ends up not involving an insider-trading problem, but we are glad the analyst has raised the issues. Analysts must be encouraged from time to time to continue bringing forward these questions, or the "not a problem" responses might discourage them from ever asking the questions.

One last point regarding insider trading: The world seems to be evolving toward what is called relationship investing, which essentially involves a long-term commitment to supporting a company and possibly being involved with its management. At the least, such relationships increase the likelihood of coming into contact with material nonpublic information. At the extreme, they could make institutional investors "insiders" of a large number of companies.

Reporting of Personal Securities Transactions

Investment management companies have various procedures for monitoring personal securities transactions in an attempt to prevent conflicts of interest. A recent survey of brokerage firms' policies on personal securities transactions by their employees found, not surprisingly, that the policies range all over the place.[1] Policies may include mandatory holding periods, preclearance requirements, absolute prohibitions on investing in investment banking clients, and so forth. Most, if not all, brokerage firms require that any personal accounts be maintained internally with that company.

Our procedures involve both a reporting obligation and preclearance for personal securities transactions. Employees who have any contact with transactions, which is about one-third of the total staff, are required to file a quarterly report, the form and policies for which are in **Exhibit 2**, on their personal securities transactions.

In addition, all personal transactions except the trades not subject to the policy (as listed in Exhibit 2) must be precleared through the Investment Control Department. Personal transactions requiring preclearance and reporting include accounts of family members residing with the employee, including trust or partnerships over which the employee or family member exercises investment discretion or voting power.

If clearance is granted, it is generally good for five trading days (including the day of requesting clearance). Any transaction in stocks that are being considered for purchase or sale by the mutual funds or other clients is prohibited.

We also have an Exceptions Committee, which has been called the "No-Exceptions Committee" be-

cause it so rarely grants exceptions to the policy. In fact, the only exceptions have been for people who wanted to sell a security, never for purchases.

Role of a Compliance Department

Establishing a compliance department is an important part of the investment management firm's overall compliance program. Selecting the right people for the compliance department is probably 20 percent of the challenge. Good compliance people need internal motivation. Their contribution cannot be measured by sales or accounts going up in value, and nobody ever thanks them for all the things that did *not* go wrong. They are people who must be internally motivated.

The other 80 percent of the challenge relates to what the company does with the compliance people once they are there. Some tips for creating and maintaining an effective compliance department follow.

Environment

Create the right environment to educate and motivate people. I prefer to use the term "educate" rather than "train." Training is what you do with circus animals. Education is teaching people not just to perform a function but to understand what they are doing and maybe even to get a little ahead of what they are doing by suggesting improvements in procedures or responding flexibly and appropriately to unanticipated situations.

Being a compliance officer can be lonely; often, there is only one compliance officer per facility. The loneliness is not because compliance officers feel isolated from the organization or because they are not valued but because they are surrounded by people who are not doing what they are doing. We help overcome that loneliness by gathering these officers together about twice a year at compliance retreats, where they can spend a couple of days with people who do the same work. This type of get-together goes a long way not only toward communicating and informing but also toward motivating these people.

Involvement

Keep the compliance people involved in the business of the company. Compliance should not be a dead-end or isolated job; if it is, you will not attract the best people to it. Compliance officers should have some business functions in addition to their compliance responsibilities. For example, make them officers of a fund, or get them involved in SEC filings, board meetings, or so on. Keep in mind that dual responsibilities can create additional problems, however, such as complications related to multiple

[1] *Investment Dealer's Digest* (November 15, 1993).

Exhibit 2. Quarterly Report of Personal Security Transactions

Trade Date	Quantity	Price	Purchase	Sale	Rating (if bond)	Security	Broker, Dealer, or Bank through Whom Effected

Prepared for Quarter Ended:_____

_____   _____

(Please *print* or *type* your name)   (Please sign)

You are required to report certain securities transactions made during the quarter. You must file a report (even if there were no transactions) within 10 days from the end of each calendar quarter. These reports are, of course, held in confidence.

Read these instructions before completing the report:

1.   If you had no reportable transactions, state "none" on the form.

2.   You must report all transactions or options on securities in an account over which you (or an immediate family member residing with you) exercised voting power or investment discretion (these should also have been precleared) *except*:

   - Mutual (i.e., open-end) fund shares (whether or not of The American Funds Group)
   - Shares of CG stock
   - Money market instruments
   - Direct obligations of the United States or of a U.S. government agency or instrumentality
   - Commodities
   - Options or futures on broad-based stock indexes (e.g., the S&P 500)
   - Gifts or bequests of securities (of course, if these securities are later sold, the preclearance and reporting requirements could apply)
   - Transactions in accounts over which neither you nor an immediate family member residing with you has any direct or indirect influence or control

3.   You must report (but need not have precleared):

   - Transactions in debt instruments rated A or above by at least one national rating service
   - Sales pursuant to tender offers for *all* outstanding shares
   - Sales pursuant to tender offers for small (less than 100 shares) holdings
   - Dividend reinvestment plan purchases

Reminder: All purchases or sales of securities or options on securities of any kind must be precleared with the secretaries of *both* The Capital Group's and Capital Research and Management Company's investment committees except as noted above.

Source: The Capital Group Audit Committee.

supervisors. One way we attempt to handle those types of problems is through dual compensation reviews.

Manageable Manuals

Do not rely excessively on manuals. Written manuals are great, but when I think of these huge manuals, I think of the old Donald Duck comics in which Huey, Dewey, and Louie had the *Junior Wood-chuck's Handbook*. No matter what situation they were in, they could turn to some page in the Handbook and it told them exactly what to do. If you can write a compliance manual that is that detailed, then everybody except the person who wrote the manual is overpaid. A good manual is necessary, but do not try to do everything in it. You will make mistakes and discourage flexible responses to changing situations.

Moreover, if compliance people wander around with their noses in the manual, they are going to miss things, and they are not going to be effective. They are also going to have a terrible job and not want to do it very long.

Demythify

I have found that if procedures are not adequately communicated to people, they will make up myths to fill in the gaps in their understanding. For example, people will say they thought the rules for personal securities transactions allowed them to buy options on securities so long as they did not buy the securities. Where did they get that idea? The compliance department needs to have people out there in the company— connected people—meeting with others and finding out what the myths are. Then, the department has to deal with the myths.

Management Involvement

Involving the compliance department head di-rectly in company management is important. It shows that the compliance function is valued and allows the people in the compliance function to keep abreast of company information. A spot on the management committee is ideal, because then the compliance head truly knows what is going on and he or she can have an impact. Direct involvement in company management must be measured, however, or the compliance head will end up doing so many things that it could take his or her attention away from the compliance function.

Conclusion

I would like to leave you with one last suggestion for an approach that I have found invaluable in running a compliance department (or any other department for that matter). It is to take a lot of parenting courses. Employees are not children, of course, but most of the principles of effective parenting are the same ones that make someone effective in running a compliance area. For example, in neither case can you say, "Do what I say, not what I do," because people and children learn from and emulate what you are doing and how you are acting much more than what you are saying.

Another area of similarity is in motivating people for rewards that may seem quite distant and abstract. Compliance involves no immediate feedback or rewards, just as education has few immediate rewards for children. You cannot go to your child in prekindergarten and say, "You have to do this so you will get into Harvard." That reward is too remote. The challenge is the same with compliance people: You must find a way to persuade them that what they do has intrinsic value, that it has value even though people do not stop by their offices each evening and say, "Thanks for another day in which the company did not blow itself up!"

Compliance Guidelines: Designing a Program

Lori A. Tansey
Senior Consultant
Ethics Resource Center

Compliance/ethics programs can prevent firms from violating the law and serve as a mitigating factor if violations do occur. Before instituting a compliance or ethics program, however, companies need to establish the goals for the program and investigate current systems, attitudes, and behavior. Constant management vigilance is needed to make the program work.

A recent article in a major business ethics publication sums up the subject of this presentation. The title of the article is "Sentencing Guidelines: Are Corporations Being 'Snookered'?" and a sidebar reads, "The people who are targets of ethics marketers often do not know what they need, what they are buying, or how to evaluate it."[1] In order to help firms know what they need and how to evaluate it, this presentation will begin with a brief discussion of the U.S. Sentencing Guidelines, then focus on how to develop an effective ethics or ethics/compliance program to meet the SG criteria. Factors to consider in evaluating such a program will also be discussed. The presentation will close with results from Ethics Resource Center (ERC) surveys that demonstrate the importance of certain elements in an ethics/compliance program.

Implications of U.S. Sentencing Guidelines

The SG became law in November 1991 and basically accomplished two things. First, they dramatically increased the fines and penalties for corporations convicted of misconduct. In fact, some reports estimate about a fortyfold increase over the preguideline period in the fines and penalties that can now be levied against corporations. Second, the guidelines provided five mitigating factors—that is, five proactive steps and positive actions corporations can take to mitigate any penalties and fines levied against them if convicted.

The mitigating factors include such steps as voluntarily reporting the offense and cooperating with the federal or regulatory investigations that ensue.

[1] *Ethikos*, vol. 6, no. 6 (May/June 1993).

The third and, perhaps, most important mitigating factor is having an effective program "to deter and detect violations of the law." The guidelines specifically stipulate the following seven fundamental elements that determine whether an ethics or compliance program will, in fact, be considered effective:

▪ *Standards and procedures for employees and agents.* This element would basically be the corporation's code of conduct, code of ethics, and other articulated policies and procedures.

▪ *A high-level employee designated to ensure compliance.* Some corporations have a "compliance officer" and others have an "ethics officer," but the duties are often much the same.

▪ *Discretionary authority not delegated to known or likely offenders.* This element can create some difficulty; how are corporations to know exactly who may be a likely offender? The most obvious approach is to investigate individuals' backgrounds by contacting previous employers. Given today's fears of lawsuits, however, prospective employees' former employers will rarely provide any significant information about a person's character or integrity.

▪ *Effective communication of standards.* The guidelines specifically mention training. Merely promulgating standards is not sufficient; educating employees about the standards is required.

▪ *Monitoring and auditing systems.* The most frequent methods in which organizations monitor compliance are through internal financial and compliance audits and through security organizations. Another increasingly common approach is board-level ethics committees charged with overseeing the integrity of the operations of the firm.

Ethics hot lines have also been established by

organizations. They not only provide guidance to employees who have questions about ethics but also function as a confidential or anonymous channel through which employees can report misconduct.

■ *Consistent and appropriate disciplinary mechanisms.* This element increases the importance of having a high-level ethics/compliance officer, because that person, by serving as the focal point to which all disciplinary actions of a compliance or ethics nature are reported, can help ensure consistency in the firm's disciplinary actions. The ethics officer can then develop written documentation that consistent disciplinary action has been taken when misconduct has occurred.

■ *Continual program improvement.* No ethics or compliance program is guaranteed to be 100 percent fail-safe. Therefore, corporations must have processes in place that, when misconduct occurs, will help prevent further similar offenses. Again, by structuring an organization for ethics/compliance officers to monitor complaints or misconduct and by having the steps established to address those concerns after a problem has occurred, the organization demonstrates continual improvement.

Measuring the Effectiveness of a Corporate Ethics Program

If a firm is to tackle the challenge of establishing an ethics program and then measuring its effectiveness, the firm must first understand the three primary causes of misconduct.

First, misconduct, unintentional misconduct, can occur out of ignorance. Somebody just did not know the rules. The offender did not understand, for example, the subtleties of what constitutes insider information or material information. Ignorance is usually the easiest cause to correct and is, in fact, the least common reason that corporations and individuals get in trouble.

Second, misconduct can result from greed. People know what they are doing is wrong but they do it anyway out of personal greed. For example, they engage in insider trading because they will profit dramatically from it, or they knowingly misrepresent products and services to a client to meet their sales quotas and get their bonuses.

Third, misconduct can result from individuals' desires for the corporation to succeed. People of ordinarily good character may believe the best way to help their company succeed is by doing something they know to be wrong. For example, people may circumvent Chinese Walls, not necessarily because they will personally benefit (often, they do *not* personally benefit), but because they think it will help

the firm. It will help the company win, compete better, be more successful.

Three factors help determine a compliance/ethics program's effectiveness in guarding against misconduct stemming from these three causes: identifying the objectives of the program, establishing what needs to be evaluated or measured, and determining the tools and methods needed for the measuring.

Program Objectives

The first and most critical task when measuring the effectiveness of a corporate ethics program is to determine the program's objectives, which may include the following:

■ *Foster congruence between management values and employee values.* People should be pulling in the same direction. Unfortunately, often they are not.

■ *Increase the clarity of company ethical standards.* This goal should not be pursued to the ridiculous point that people overdefine the standards. A more effective approach usually is to focus on communicating the general value systems within the organization.

An example of a company that accomplished this focus with some success is Johnson & Johnson after the Tylenol poisoning crisis in the 1980s. When seven people died from the ingestion of Tylenol, J&J implemented what was, in effect, a $100 million product recall, despite the fact that the "experts" believed the company would be tainting the Tylenol brand name, that the recall was in some way admitting responsibility. Indeed, J&J's stock took a hit after the recall, but the decision turned out to be one of the great crisis-management success stories in American business. Public approval of how the company handled that crisis reached more than 90 percent; consumers showed their confidence by repurchasing the product; and the company quickly regained its leadership share in Tylenol's highly competitive marketplace.

Johnson & Johnson's chairman and CEO, Jim Burke, said later that the recall was not a single $100 million decision. As he described what happened, "There were dozens of people that had to make hundreds of decisions. They had to make them on the fly. They could not even get through to my office." It was a field-based recall; sales people and marketing managers around the country (eventually, around the world) went into the pharmacies, the drug stores, the grocery stores, the hospitals and pulled the product on their own responsibility. He added, "They made those decisions unerringly correctly because they knew what we believed."[2]

---

[2] Ethics Resource Center, *Management Ethics: A View from the Top* (1986).

Burke stressed the company's credo, which emphasizes that J&J's *primary* responsibilities are to the mothers, fathers, children, doctors, nurses, and patients who use Johnson & Johnson products. That statement is an unambiguous commitment to product quality and safety. Only two years prior to the Tylenol poisoning, the credo had been reevaluated and recommunicated to the organization. In a crisis situation, those actions turned out to be very prudent—from both a business standpoint and an ethical standpoint.

▪ *Make company ethical standards relevant to ethical risks.* Almost every company and major corporation in the United States has a code of ethics, but these codes often lack relevancy. For example, we all know that an important function of a company in a competitive environment is gathering competitive intelligence. So, a relevant issue for a code of conduct—particularly for people in sales and marketing, whose day-to-day responsibilities include going out and getting that kind of information—is the appropriate circumstances and ways in which employees can seek out and use information of a proprietary nature about competitors. Only a handful of codes, however, contain any meaningful guidelines on how intelligence gathering can be accomplished within the ethical standards of the corporation.

A corporate ethics program should ensure that employees understand the risks they face in their day-to-day responsibilities and then make sure that the standards apply to those risks.

▪ *Improve the value of ethics training.* ERC surveys typically show that a third of respondents believe their companies' ethics training is hardly or not at all effective. Therefore, a reasonable objective for many ethics/compliance programs is to improve education about ethics.

▪ *Increase employee awareness of the proper role of the ethics office.* Ethics offices are not well advertised or communicated with respect to their purposes, but this situation must be changed if employees are expected to use them.

▪ *Increase the effectiveness of the ethics office.* To accomplish this goal for an ethics program, companies must first *measure* the effectiveness of the program and ethics office, which is the subject of the next section.

What Should Be Measured

Several areas should be examined when measuring the effectiveness of an ethics program, including company and employee values, congruence between the company's values and its operating systems, and employee attitudes, knowledge, and observations of misconduct.

▪ *Congruence between the company's stated values and its operating values, and between management's and employees' values.* These words appear somewhere in most company value statements: ethics, quality, customer or client first, and customer/client service. When one looks at the incentive systems of the companies, however, these terms stand out: profitability, cost cutting, sales quotas. Thus, people soon learn that what is hanging on the wall—the written values statement—may not actually be the principal drivers and motivators in the company. Achieving congruence of such necessary operating values as profitability and performance achievement with the ethical values of the corporation (and achieving a reasonable balance between them) is a challenge that companies need to understand and meet.

▪ *Adequacy of the support for ethical standards in the management systems.* In addition to lack of congruence with value statements, management systems can sometimes create unintended impediments to ethical behavior. An organization will be much more successful in establishing an ethical environment if it focuses on supporting the ethical standards with appropriate management systems rather than simply writing and rewriting the standards or code of ethics.

▪ *Attitudes about the commitment of management, peers, and subordinates to fairness and ethical business conduct.* Even when people understand the company's policies and values, negative attitudes—for example, management does not "walk the talk"—create cynicism, and the ethics effort is for naught. The corporation must send a clear signal that it is seriously committed to ethics. Therefore, understanding the current attitudes and in what ways those attitudes need to be strengthened or improved is another important aspect to measure.

▪ *Perceptions of ethical risks and vulnerabilities.* The company also needs to measure employees' current perceptions of what the ethical risks are in their daily work life. The company must then provide guidance in those areas through standards of conduct or employee training.

▪ *Employee knowledge of company standards.* Companies should try to eliminate misconduct that is committed out of ignorance. Therefore, employees' knowledge of the standards must be evaluated.

Equally important to eliminating ignorance, however, is to make sure employees can *apply* the standards in real situations. In particular, managers should be able to apply the principles even to situations that have ambiguities.

▪ *Attitudes about the integrity and effectiveness of the ethics office.* If people do not have confidence in the ethics office, they are not going to use it as an effective safeguard for the organization. Are people aware of the office? Do they trust the office? Do they believe it is effective?

    ■ *Experiences in reporting observed misconduct and reasons for not reporting misconduct.* The company needs to identify the circumstance in which people report misconduct and the reasons they often do not report it. Why are people not coming forward? Often, the reason is that people fear retribution for reporting incidences of misconduct.

Measurement Tools and Methods

    Several tools and methods are available for measuring the effectiveness of a corporate ethics program. The evaluators can analyze the code of ethics and the training materials—for example, articles and case studies—to ensure that they are up-to-date and relevant to current issues. In addition, a comparison of these materials with industry norms and model programs may be useful. Three methods of gathering information throughout the organization may also be of use:

    ■ *Interviews and focus groups.* Typically, interviews work better at the senior level and focus groups work better at the middle and lower levels. For example, a group of senior vice presidents may be guarded in discussions, but lower-level managers may feel empowered and encouraged among their peers.

    ■ *Management workshops on issue identification and action planning.* Using ongoing education efforts can help determine new or emerging ethical issues. Typically, successful workshops are those that give participants an opportunity to list the ethics issues about which they are concerned. Such information can be collected periodically and sent to the appropriate people within the organization so that trends can be spotted and areas of frequent or overlapping concern can be addressed.

    ■ *Written surveys.* Many different forms of written surveys are available, and the resulting data can be significant.

ERC Survey Results

    The ERC routinely conducts written surveys for clients to provide feedback on the effectiveness of their ethics programs. These surveys also provide the ERC with a great deal of data on ethical behavior and attitudes in U.S. businesses. This section reports some of the data from questionnaires fielded during the 1989–93 period. The percentages are based on responses of about 10,000 employees in many different industries, including aerospace, telecommunica-

tions, health care, and consumer products.

    ■ *Question: How useful is the code of ethics in guiding your business decisions and actions?* Responses to this question were as follows (note that, in all these questions, respondents could give more than one answer):

Very	15%
Fairly	29
Occasionally	43
Never	12
Haven't read the code	8

About 20 percent, one in five respondents, said either the code is never useful or they have not read the code. Almost half, 43 percent, believed the code is only occasionally useful, which reinforces the warning that corporations should not count on a code alone. Its usefulness is typically only as good as the management systems supporting it and the education programs designed to communicate it.

    ■ *Question: How useful is the ethics training course in clarifying company standards?*

Very	10%
Fairly	24
Somewhat	36
Hardly	17
Not at all	13
Haven't attended this course	15

Almost a third did not find their ethics training courses particularly useful, and 15 percent had not attended such a course. Thus, 45 percent of the employee population are not gaining value from their ethics education programs.

    Often, the problem is that the ethics training course is not pragmatically focused. Some ethics courses spend two hours on 20-step ethical decision-making models. No one remembers those 20 steps. No one uses the models. The more practical and more pragmatic the course—the incorporation of case studies, for example, of situations employees are likely to encounter on the job—the more useful employees will find the course.

    ■ *Question: Are you ever pressured to compromise the company's ethical standards in order to achieve business goals? If so, how often?*

No, never	37%
Yes, but very rarely	29
Yes, periodically (contracts, quarterly pressures)	22
Yes, fairly often	9
Yes, all the time	3

About a third admitted to at least periodic pressure to compromise the company's standards to achieve business goals.

    ■ *Question (a): Have you observed violations of company ethical standards during the past year?*

Yes, often	9%
Yes, occasionally	33
No, never	58

On average, about 42 percent said they had observed

some misconduct in violation of the standards in the course of ten years. That number seems to be fairly consistent across industries and company sizes.

■ *Question (b): If so, did you report your observations to management or an appropriate department?* Perhaps more interesting than the figures on observing misconduct is that, of the 42 percent who had observed misconduct, only slightly more than half (52 percent) indicated that they had made any attempt to report the misconduct.

An important aspect is that sometimes the observer has not witnessed actual misconduct but what *appears* to be misconduct. Companies need people to come forward in both situations, however, because the company must either correct the problem if there is one or clear up the misperception. If the observer does not come forward, he or she may brood over the supposed misconduct, and it may cause that person to question the company's commitment to ethics. These misperceptions can cause attitudes toward the company to become very negative.

■ *Question (c): If you didn't report, why not?* The most common reasons for not reporting were not trusting the company to keep the report confidential (51 percent) and fear of retribution from supervisors and co-workers (50 percent). Thus, companies should create ways in which people can bring forward concerns about misconduct anonymously and confidentially.

Another reason people gave for not reporting was that they did not want to be known as "snitches" (22 percent). People learn at an early age in our society that telling on other people is not nice, and we have all kinds of lovely names for folks who do tell—snitch, tattletale, squealer, fink. Not surprisingly, people grow up with a natural reluctance to report on other people. In a business environment, however, people must be encouraged to come forward, because bringing their concerns to light is, in fact, doing a service to the company.

Other responses to this question were as follow:

none of my business, 20 percent; didn't know who to contact, 14 percent; ethics office not accessible to me, 9 percent; and nobody else cares about ethical business conduct, 19 percent.

■ *Question (d): If you did report, what was the response?* For the 48 percent who did report observed misconduct, the corporate responses they received included: investigation launched, 24 percent; corrective action taken, 28 percent; management cover-up, 14 percent; investigation was inconclusive, 17 percent; I was a victim of retribution, 19 percent; and nothing happened, 36 percent, which was closely correlated with 27 percent who said they never heard the outcome.

The last two responses point out a problem with some ethics programs, namely, that the people who investigate the incident do not get back to the person who made the allegation. Sometimes, the reason is concern for legal liability or related problems in divulging sensitive information. Companies should inform the reporting individual, however, at least that the report was investigated and appropriate action was taken. That response will give the employee confidence that something happened in the system, and that individual is then more likely to come forward in the future.

The 19 percent who believed they had been a victim of retribution, that some form of retaliation was taken against them, correlates with some of the reasons the half of respondents who did not report gave as to why they did not report.

Conclusion

Corporations often hope that once a code of ethics is written, ethics education is conducted, and an ethics office is established, they can "check the ethics box" and move on to the next corporate initiative. Ethics, however, is an ongoing process. When the company ceases to manage to achieve it, they begin to lose it.

Question and Answer Session

Michael S. Caccese
Paul G. Haaga, Jr.
Lori A. Tansey

Question: What sanctions does The Capital Group impose if a covered person fails to preclear a personal securities transaction?

Haaga: The manual states simply that sanctions will be imposed up to and including dismissal. We do not attempt to define specific consequences for specific violations; a certain amount of flexibility is necessary because every situation will be different.

For example, most lapses occur when people who have been working for the company several years but have never engaged in a personal securities transaction forget that the rules require preclearance of a particular type of transaction. When they get the quarterly report form, they realize they should have precleared the trade. These cases present no reason to terminate people. If we were to discover a pattern of violations, however (and such a pattern is usually accompanied by a pattern of other types of ethical and compliance lapses), then obviously we would impose penalties up to and including termination.

Question: The Capital Group's personal securities transaction report (Exhibit 2 of Mr. Haaga's presentation) does not require commissions to be reported. How do you check that employees are not getting special favorable commissions from brokers?

Haaga: Actually, I would be more concerned about favorable prices or general access to hot issues than I would about commission rates per se. I also would focus most on the individuals who conduct company business with brokers (e.g., the trading department).

Question: Analysts and portfolio managers are frequently criticized for concern about quarterly results and the effect that concern has on stock price volatility. Have you ever suggested to a corporate pension fund officer or board that, although the company should focus on long-term investment goals, it should also pressure the money managers for short-term results?

Haaga: We always try to get people to focus on long-term results, but it is difficult. The *Los Angeles Times* publishes weekly the top ten and bottom ten funds based on four-week results; so, for example, gold funds are in the top or bottom category every single week! With newspapers spotlighting the short term, getting people to focus on long-term results is very hard, but we keep plugging away in all our publications and discussions.

Tansey: We have gone as far as suggesting to some clients that they do away with some of their quarterly meetings with analysts if those meetings are leading to severe pressure on short-term results in terms of forecasts and budgets.

Part of the complaint about pressure for short-term results, however, is passing the buck.

Certainly pressure is coming from the analysts, and from Wall Street, but a corporate officer gets paid a fairly significant amount of money to do the right job for the shareholders' interests—the shareholders' long-term interests. When we analyze it, the problem has basically to do with the senior executive compensation system. Those quarterly and annual financial targets put more pressure on many executives than does discreet pressure from Wall Street.

Question: Please elaborate on the physical separation of an organization for Chinese Wall procedures.

Caccese: The physical arrangements should not be conducive to sharing information by the people on one side of the Wall with people on the other side of the Wall. A firm should also make sure that it has protection in, for example, its computer systems. Areas to which some parts of the firm should not have access include the mergers & acquisitions and the arbitrage departments; they should each have separate files and should not be located next to each other.

Haaga: If an investigation establishes that some part of your organization possessed material nonpublic information, you will effectively, even if not legally, have the burden of proof that it was not shared. Physical separation is an important part of that proof. One problem many firms have with Chinese Walls, however, is that the people who are supposedly isolated still go to the same meetings and talk to each other every day.

Question: If a firm acts as a fiduciary to an ERISA client, can Chinese Walls be used effectively?

Haaga: The involvement of ERISA would not have any specific impact on effective use of the Chinese Wall; the rules and procedures would be the same. The presence of ERISA enforcement mechanisms and penalties, however, probably increases the importance on getting the Wall built correctly.

Question: Regarding personal transactions, what is your interpretation of mutual fund managers investing their own personal assets in the funds they manage when the funds are being allocated shares on the same basis as other accounts?

Haaga: We are not troubled by that situation in the usual case because the impact of any one stock pick on the results of a mutual fund is so diluted that it should not involve any conflict. A small-capitalization fund, for example, has 300 different positions, so one position is not going to affect it much. Also, with respect to compensation, most managers will make much more money by having all their clients perform well than they will by having an excellent stock in one particular account in which they have their personal assets.

Question: How does a global organization educate the people in the different offices and different countries about the rules and standards? Also, how does it monitor the insider-trading requirements in various countries?

Haaga: We have for years applied our personal securities transaction and insider-trading provisions worldwide, despite the fact that many of the countries in which we operate did not have insider-trading laws comparable to those in the United States. We also monitor other countries' laws and regulations to determine whether any country has adopted laws that are either different from or more rigorous than the SEC standards. Right now, however, we are comfortable that if we comply with the SEC standards, we are complying with every country's standards.

Question: People may not act exclusively in the interest of their own compensation, but at the same time they cannot be expected to act contrary to their personal interests. Do you look at an organization's compensation structure as a possible behavior factor?

Tansey: That kind of problem is exactly what the ERC has corporations examine. As I mentioned, the more insidious and the more troublesome form of misconduct is when the management systems within the organization somehow push people of good character—people who are pillars of their communities, good family people—over the line. Everyone has that breaking point. Compensation systems are one of the most critical systems; incen-

tive systems can create so much pressure on individuals or create such great incentives for individuals that they lead in the wrong directions.

Two other important systems are the performance-evaluation system and the goal-setting processes. How is performance review conducted? What areas of the employee's behavior are checked? An important factor to remember in goal setting is that, if goals are so aggressive that employees have little or no chance realistically of achieving them, people will end up cutting corners, taking shortcuts.

Haaga: One approach we found helpful in squaring up the ethical and the operating principles is simply lengthening the focus. For example, the Johnson & Johnson decision was a series of ethical decisions that had a short-run negative impact but a long-term positive impact. Couching the discussion about whether or not to do something in terms of the long term—"what is the impact ten years down the road?" instead of "what is the impact on this quarter's earnings?"—is truly a help in coming to the right decision.

Tansey: Again, incentive systems are involved, because most employees' incentive systems are built on an annual basis, not on a five-year or ten-year basis. One of the complaints about American business is that it is too short-sighted and does not look at the long-term implications of decisions.

Regulation and Ethical Standards around the World: Global Institutional Investors

Brian E. Hersey, CFA
Director, Investment Manager Research
Towers Perrin

Private pension funds are growing rapidly outside the United States, which has spotlighted the lack of worldwide ethical standards and regulations for investment management practices. AIMR standards could become the global model in the long term, and consultant firms in the industry could play a significant role in the development of global standards. Currently, however, many forces are working against global standards—among them, national cultural differences regarding risk and the failure of some international investment management firms themselves to uphold high standards.

The American poet Ogden Nash once said, "There is only one way to achieve happiness on this terrestrial ball, and that is either to have a clear conscience or none at all." Just as achieving happiness involves conflicting choices, so also does balancing self-interest and client interest in the financial world. The challenge for the profession is to do well and do good, to conduct the normal commerce of our industry while dealing ethically with one another.

With the increasing globalization of the investment management industry, the challenge of ensuring a fair and equitable basis for informed decision making has taken on an added dimension of complexity. This presentation focuses on global institutional investors—specifically, non-U.S. private pension plans—and its purpose is to provide a perspective on:

- what factors appear to be driving the growth of overseas pension assets and how local issues are affecting global competition for pension asset management;
- what the local practices of the investment management community are and how consistent with or different from the AIMR standards they are;
- how AIMR member organizations might be disadvantaged in competing for international institutional investment management assignments.

Growth of Overseas Pension Assets

The value of total private pension assets outside the United States is growing rapidly. The United States, with total pension assets of more than $2.5 trillion and growing at an annual rate of 6–8 percent, remains the dominant market in total dollar amounts invested. In comparison, continental Europe represents $360 billion (half from the Netherlands, $10 billion from Belgium, and most of the remainder from Switzerland and Germany), Australia represents $100 billion, Japan $260 billion, the United Kingdom $300 billion, Canada $130 billion, and Hong Kong $10–$15 billion. The growth rates of the pension assets abroad, however, are significantly greater than the growth rate in the United States. Australia is growing at 20 percent, Japan at 17–18 percent, and Europe at 16–17 percent.

The major catalysts for the growth in non-U.S. private pension assets are the overall maturing of plans abroad as a result of work-force aging and extensions of service definitions for determining benefits. Moreover, some governments are increasingly taking legislative actions to shift retirement burdens to the private sector in order to reduce liability burdens on social security systems. For example, Belgium, the United Kingdom, and Germany are shifting retirement plans to the extent the plans are funded.

In addition, countries are establishing minimum benefit requirements and indexing or partially indexing benefits to inflation. The Netherlands and Germany have introduced indexing, for example; Switzerland has established a minimum benefit requirement; and Spain and Italy will soon be introducing new pension laws. Similar discussions are under way in France. Australia has established a minimum pension benefit requiring employers to spend 5 percent of payroll per employee. This minimum level is targeted to increase to 9 percent by the year 2002.

Standards of Practice

Countries are at different stages of development in establishing standards of investment management practice, but the general trend is toward adopting practices that are very similar to those in the United States. Various approaches address investment policy issues within an asset/liability framework, create formal investment policy standards, establish appropriate benchmarks, adopt standards for measuring performance, and address investment structure in a sophisticated way—some, even to the point of focusing on the structure of fund management and the role of different managers within such a structure.

Notwithstanding the trends toward U.S. practices, many local impediments to universal standards of practice remain. Differences from U.S. practices and differences among countries outside the United States exist in government supervision, governance requirements, structure of the capital markets, tax

rules, legal restrictions on investments, legal structures for pension funds, the availability of reliable performance data, and cultural attitudes. For example, strong cultural biases in the Netherlands and Switzerland favor low levels of investment performance volatility (that is, risk is defined as the probability of achieving the actuarial assumption in the short term) even though pension benefit liabilities are long term in nature and the practice may lead to suboptimal investment structures. The Insurance Chamber that oversees investments in the Netherlands has directed plan sponsors to invest "solidly," and most plan sponsors interpret this directive to require significant allocations to fixed-income securities.

In Japan, the attitude toward performance is very different; performance is focused on investment income and realized capital gains. Plan sponsors are satisfied if the combination of these two return components produces a 6 percent annual return. This attitude significantly influences investment behavior, even though regulatory constraints on investments now allow much greater latitude in managing pension assets.

As shown in **Figure 1,** local regulatory constraints and traditional investment practices produce wide divergences among countries in typical asset allocation practices—particularly in the areas of equity/fixed-income allocations and international exposures.

Figure 1. Variations in Asset Allocation Practices

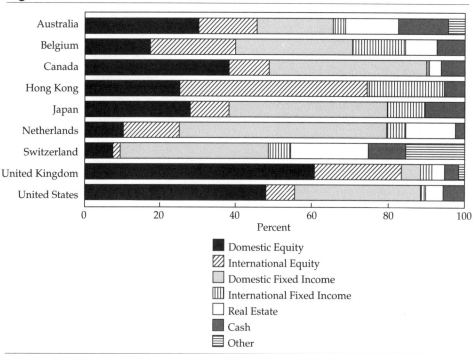

Source: Towers Perrin.

Standards in Pension Asset Management

A conceptual snapshot of the situation today in the globalization of pension asset management is in **Figure 2**, and **Figure 3** outlines the probable future. The major conclusion that can be drawn is that many markets are in the nascent stages of globalizing their pension-asset-management practices. This circumstance offers great opportunities to those who provide consulting services to pension funds, but it also greatly complicates the evaluation of service vendors by plan fiduciaries, particularly in localities where no single, unifying set of standards of conduct exists.

This point introduces the issue of how consistent with or different from the AIMR Standards of Professional Conduct the standards around the world are and whether organizations that adhere to the AIMR standards might be disadvantaged in competing in the international arena for institutional investment management assignments.

To the question "What are ethics, anyway?" John Casey suggests in his book *Ethics in the Financial Marketplace* that the answer involves a combination of elements: being pragmatic, being just, and being protective of an individual's rights.[1] A focus on these three concepts will lead to decisions that are both workable and fair. These concepts are embodied in the AIMR Code of Ethics and Standards of Professional Conduct, which provide a clear framework for conduct in balancing self-interest and client interest as our industry evolves.[2] In considering the global investment organizations, the Standards of Professional Conduct most logically at issue are

- use of material nonpublic information (Standard II C),
- standards for presenting performance (Standard III F),
- priority of transactions (Standard IV), and
- disclosure of conflicts (Standard V).

In addressing local investment practices vis-à-vis the AIMR standards, a helpful approach is to categorize the markets loosely in terms of the relative development of their pension industries, their regulatory authorities, and their emphases on an accepted set of ethical investment practices: fair representation, uniformity, and comparability of investment performance among vendors. Not surprisingly, the English-speaking countries—the United States, United Kingdom, Australia, and Canada, all with mature pension systems—are the most developed in these terms. Each has well-established and forceful regulatory agencies effectively overseeing securities trading in order to minimize abuses in insider trading, priority of transactions, and disclosure of conflicts. Furthermore, material ethical issues with respect to the investment management industry serving these markets are few because standards of conduct are well established.

An important development from the standpoint

---

[1] New York: Scudder, Stevens & Clark, 1988:20.

[2] See Appendix A.

Figure 2. Stages in the Globalization of Pension Asset Management, 1993

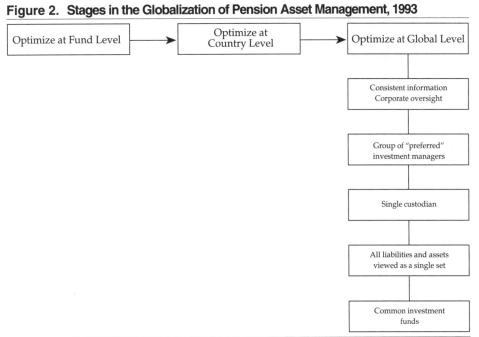

Source: Towers Perrin.

Figure 3. Direction of the Globalization of Pension Asset Management

```
┌─────────────────────┐     ┌─────────────────────┐     ┌─────────────────────┐
│ Optimize at Fund    │ ──▶ │ Optimize at         │ ──▶ │ Optimize at Global  │
│ Level               │     │ Country Level       │     │ Level               │
└─────────────────────┘     └─────────────────────┘     └─────────────────────┘
          │                           │                           │
┌─────────────────────┐     ┌─────────────────────┐     ┌─────────────────────┐
│ Focus on: governance,│     │ Consolidate reporting│     │ Produce consistent  │
│ target asset         │     │ Practice master      │     │ information across   │
│ allocation,          │     │ custody              │     │ countries           │
│ benchmarks,          │     │ Establish common     │     │ Share comparative   │
│ investment policy,   │     │ investment funds     │     │ information among    │
│ manager structure    │     │                      │     │ subsidiaries        │
│ and selection,       │     │                      │     │ Establish committee(s)│
│ manager mandates,    │     │                      │     │ with oversight      │
│ and performance      │     │                      │     │ responsibility at   │
│ assessment           │     │                      │     │ regional and        │
│                      │     │                      │     │ corporate levels    │
└─────────────────────┘     └─────────────────────┘     └─────────────────────┘
                                                                    │
                                                        ┌─────────────────────┐
                                                        │ Identify group of   │
                                                        │ "preferred"         │
                                                        │ investment managers │
                                                        │ world-wide; each    │
                                                        │ fund selects from   │
                                                        │ "preferred" list    │
                                                        │ where possible      │
                                                        └─────────────────────┘
                                                                    │
                                                        ┌─────────────────────┐
                                                        │ Select single       │
                                                        │ custodian at        │
                                                        │ regional and global │
                                                        │ levels              │
                                                        └─────────────────────┘
                                                                    │
                                                        ┌─────────────────────┐
                                                        │ View all liabilities│
                                                        │ and assets as       │
                                                        │ single set worldwide│
                                                        │ Pursue country-     │
                                                        │ specific strategies │
                                                        │ that optimize global│
                                                        │ strategy            │
                                                        └─────────────────────┘
                                                                    │
                                                        ┌─────────────────────┐
                                                        │ Establish common    │
                                                        │ investment funds    │
                                                        │ such as asset-class │
                                                        │ specific, region    │
                                                        │ specific, and global│
                                                        └─────────────────────┘
```

Source: Towers Perrin.

of standardizing practices globally is that an increasing number of international investment organizations are complying with AIMR standards in marketing their investment services outside the United States. The compliance is just beginning, however, because the pension plans are only beginning to make pension allocations to equities. AIMR member organizations are not likely to be disadvantaged, therefore, in competing for global investment business. Even in the absence of broad-based compliance with AIMR standards in many markets, AIMR members will not be at a disadvantage, because the major departures from AIMR standards in local markets typically occur in standards for performance presentation, and in this area, the differences between local practices and AIMR standards are not material.

The United Kingdom

In the United Kingdom, investment performance monitoring is largely controlled by two independent organizations. These organizations ensure accurate and uniform calculation of investment results because they audit and calculate performance results for a significant percentage of U.K. institutionally managed investment portfolios. Furthermore, by acting as totally independent auditors of investment results, they provide the mechanism for ensuring fair representation and full disclosure in investment managers' performance presentations. They also serve an important function in the creation of composites by determining what funds should be included in proper peer groups and then ensuring that composite records are reliable, relevant, and uniformly calculated.

The major sources of differences between United Kingdom performance presentation standards and AIMR standards lie in the following areas:

- absence of cash allocations in specialists' assignments (because of the prevalence of balanced-fund mandates in the United Kingdom), limited composite samples, and survivor issues for specialist assignments;
- use of medians versus weighted-average returns;
- selective compliance with AIMR standards (some organizations have adopted full compliance, but many others limit compliance to their SEC-registered entities); and
- absence of actual audited data.

Canada

The tradition in Canada is for consultants to provide the major audit function of investment management performance by calculating rates of return and constructing appropriate manager composites. Quarterly rates of return are typically provided by the managers, so audit control is less independent than in the United Kingdom. Although an increasing number of managers are beginning to comply with AIMR Performance Presentation Standards, few have actually reconstructed historical performance at this time.[3]

In addition, composite construction practices are far less rigorous than set forth in the AIMR standards, and clients must screen composites much more thoroughly to validate the comparability of performance. For example, domestic equity portfolios commonly contain significant allocations to U.S.-exchange-listed securities. Moreover, domestic fixed-income portfolios have occasionally made significant allocations to non-Canadian-dollar securities.

Australia

The funds management industry in Australia has worked hard in recent years to develop a set of standards for investment performance measurement. A representative group of fund managers, investment advisors, and external academicians established standards for performance measurement and attribution. These standards are less rigorous than the AIMR standards and, importantly, do not include the same requirements with regard to the provision of a consistent composite measure of performance. In most other respects, however, the

standards are comparable to industry standards in the United States.

An important shortcoming in Australia is the fact that not all fund managers choose to comply with the standards. Some managers have taken the step of actually producing their performance numbers consistently with the AIMR standards, but they are clearly in the minority.

Hong Kong

In contrast to the preceding established pension markets, Hong Kong's pension industry is in its infancy, and industry standards are just beginning to evolve. The Hong Kong pension market is not presently extensively regulated, and self-regulation practices are virtually nonexistent. Accordingly, such practices as insider trading, personal account trading, preferential treatment of accounts, and even front running are not uncommon. *Caveat emptor* is clearly the guiding principle for investors in Hong Kong.

No standard practices apply to performance measurement, and regular, independent reporting of the actual performance of investment portfolios is underdeveloped by U.S. standards. Managers typically calculate their own investment performance results, and the figures are monitored only by means of two surveys performed by local consultants. The surveys thus represent only computations of manager-submitted investment results.

No standard practices exist with respect to methodologies for actual performance calculation, creation of composites, or treatment of multiple-asset portfolios. Single portfolios are frequently used to represent a manager's past performance record, even in some instances in which that single portfolio is inappropriate in the context of the assignment being considered. In addition, investment track records often derive from a blending and linking of different portfolio results—frequently, from different investment mandates. The managers themselves selectively choose the portfolios to be monitored, and complete investment histories may be reconstructed when portfolios are substituted.

The major catalyst for a change in practices at present is Hong Kong's desire to attract the assets of U.S. and Australian pension funds, whose sponsors (and the consultants advising them) are likely to demand adherence to more rigorous standards.

Investment organizations fully complying with AIMR Performance Presentation Standards may be potentially disadvantaged relative to local investment organizations in competing for Hong Kong business in the following areas: First, a significant potential exists for competitors to misrepresent in-

---

[3]See Appendix B for the Performance Presentation Standards.

vestment results because of the absence of established standard practices for presenting those results. Second, local investment organizations may be able to charge significantly lower fees because broker rebating is standard practice.

Japan

Investment management of private pension funds is also at an early stage of development in Japan and continental Europe. As mentioned previously, in Japan, the concept of performance has been narrowly linked to a nominal return hurdle rate, such as 6 percent. Efforts are under way, however, to create a broader awareness of performance standards. The Pension Fund Association is taking a leading role in educating plan sponsors about such issues as market-value accounting and asset allocation.

Continental Europe

The predominant cultural tendency throughout continental Europe toward conservative investment practices has been reflected in a low tolerance for volatility and, therefore, a dependency on fixed-income securities. As pension allocations to equities increase, however, offshore investments will play an increasingly important role in investment structures, which will increase the need for reliable, uniform, and fair representation of investment results. For example, in the Netherlands, where pension funds have largely been insured or otherwise invested in-house and local managers traditionally run only balanced funds, some managers report only the income component of total returns. Clearly, the Netherlands, although one of the most developed markets in Europe, is just beginning to focus on investment performance standards. It will probably follow the model of the United Kingdom, the geographically closest developed market.

In Germany, the rapid development of Special Funds as an alternative to book reserve accounting will lead to an increasing emphasis on investment performance. As in the Netherlands, this development will provide an opportunity for significant advances in current practices.

In Switzerland, the traditions until recently have included little disclosure of investment practices and performance. Pension funds typically pay few or no fees because local investment organizations execute transactions in-house and derive revenues through this mechanism. The concept of best execution does not exist. Again, however, this situation is likely to change as plan sponsors gradually move away from their typical asset allocations of 90 percent to domestic fixed-income securities and real estate and 10 percent to equities.

Consultancy and Global Ethical Standards

Consultancy is the business of providing counsel to clients in the execution of their stewardship, governance, and fiduciary responsibilities. Consultants have played and should continue to play an important role in the globalization of pension asset management. In this role, consultants can be powerful agents for change in shaping industry practices—particularly in areas needing a high degree of uniformity, precision, and objectivity in information and data.

Yet, at a time when the need is great for consultants to take a leadership role in promoting consistent and ethical standards, the industry is fraught with nondisclosed relationships that can lead to the appearance, even if not the reality, of clouded objectivity. Many consulting firms and broker-related consultants function as multifaceted financial factories combining consulting, investment management (directly or indirectly through alliances), trading execution, and the selling of consulting services to investment organizations. Questions of objectivity and accountability must inevitably be raised, therefore, by plan sponsors—the clients who are ultimately the final arbiters of acceptable practices. After all, the consulting industry's only deliverable product is competence and trust, which derive ultimately from uncompromised objectivity. These qualities are almost impossible to measure, in the sense of a performance standard, and thus must be carefully guarded.

Now that the scope of consulting activities and revenue sources has blurred the traditional demarcation between consulting and investment management, perhaps a set of guidelines should be established enabling consulting organizations to disclose the range of their business activities, alliances, and revenue sources, particularly from investment organizations. Clients need to know this information in order to make informed and objective decisions about the services they may seek in carrying out their fiduciary responsibilities.

Conclusion

The financial services industry is becoming increasingly complex, which has led to the creation of financial factories that merge previously separate activities and operate globally in markets that are at vastly different stages of development. Not surprisingly, the industry is already full of information that, at the very least, requires disclosure. The future holds a major risk for the industry that business interests will subsume objectivity and accountability if the codification of ethical standards of conduct does not keep pace with the growing (often, undisclosed) sources of conflict.

As our business activities expand globally, the challenge to develop and implement uniform ethical practices and standards of conduct becomes immensely complex. The effort is necessary, however, if the industry is to maintain the fragile trust of clients.

At the moment, how the evolution in standards of practice worldwide will affect the development of uniform global ethical practices and standards of conduct is not clear. A single, unifying framework for conduct and ethical standards around the world may not be achievable in the near term, but such an objective is an important long-term goal.

Regulation and Ethical Standards around the World: Europe

David H. Beevers
President
Capital International Limited

Continental Europe has only begun the process of introducing rules for the operation of the securities business; the United Kingdom, although an old financial center, has a very new set of regulations. Both environments need relatively simple laws, within an uncomplicated framework, that are enforced by tough sanctions and reinforced by ethical standards. Cohesion on what the laws, regulations, and standards should be will not be easy, however, as differences are currently large and competition for practitioners' business may lead to undercutting standards in the future.

Regulations are in a state of flux throughout Europe as policymakers deal with national differences in history and attitudes and the need to fashion consistent laws and standards for the European Union. This presentation offers an overview of the regulatory status in the United Kingdom, with some recommendations for change. It also examines the proposed regulations for the European Union, differences between U.K. and continental Europe regarding regulation and ethics, and the challenge of improving ethical standards in Europe.

The United Kingdom

The United Kingdom has a long history of equity investment; it stretches well back into the 19th century. The current governing statute is the United Kingdom Financial Services Act, which became law in 1986 and came into effect in 1988. This legislation was the culmination of a lengthy debate on the regulation of financial markets.

The regulatory system introduced by the Financial Services Act was substantially that proposed by Professor L.C.B. Gower of London University. Because of this heritage, many were afraid that the law would depend too heavily on theory and too little on practicalities and would be too complex to be effective on a day-to-day basis. The system has been running for about five years now—long enough for some judgments on its effectiveness to be made—and it does seem to suffer from those defects.

The Financial Services Act created a two-tier system. The Securities and Investment Board, as the senior regulator, supervises the front-line delivery of regulation by bodies recognized by the SIB. These bodies, the self-regulating organizations (SROs), regulate their members and grant them the status of "authorized persons."

Current SROs are the following:

- Financial Intermediaries, Managers and Brokers Regulatory Association, whose members are independent intermediaries selling mainly insurance, unit trusts (mutual funds), and similar collective investment products;
- Investment Management Regulatory Organization, whose members primarily manage investment portfolios;
- The Life Association and Unit Trust Regulatory Organization, which regulates the marketing of life assurance, unit trust, and other collective investment schemes by firms that create those products and by associated marketing intermediaries;
- Securities and Futures Authority, which was formed by the merger of the Securities Association and the Association of Futures Brokers and Dealers on April 1, 1991; and
- Personal Investment Authority, an SRO now being established that will regulate

the investment business conducted by private investors—mainly, business related to packaged products.

The fields of these SROs overlap somewhat, so a participant in the industry could have several regulators. The system creates a lot of confusion without necessarily enhancing the quality of regulation. Each SRO has its own rule book, and a lot of work is thus needed by the financial services community to understand and comply with all the rules. Each SRO must also have its own staff to operate its system; maintaining the large staffs and services imposes a substantial cost on the regulators.

In addition, the second tier contains a number of other institutions involved in regulation:

- the Department of Trade and Industry, which deals with the enforcement of corporate legislation, also supervises insurance companies and prosecutes insider-dealing cases;
- the Bank of England, in addition to its role as a central bank, supervises all other banks operating in the United Kingdom;
- the London Stock Exchange (LSE), a Recognized Investment Exchange whose members trade U.K. government bonds and U.K. and international equity and bonds, provides settlement services and is the authority for listing securities in the United Kingdom;
- the London International Financial Futures Exchange and London Fox, both of which are Recognized Investment Exchanges, trade futures and options on soft commodities and agricultural products.

The result of the multitude of overlapping regulators and complexity of rules is that it is sometimes not clear who should deal with a particular problem or abuse.

Conflict over the Rules

Despite some mergers of SROs and attempts to simplify the rule books, the system remains complicated. The SIB's first book of rules was heavily criticized as being too legalistic and complex, and an attempt has been made to simplify the book. The current chairman of the SIB carried out a comprehensive review of the U.K. regulatory system and concluded that no legislative changes are needed but that details do need attention.

Others disagree. The group chief executive of the Prudential Corporation of the United Kingdom, for example, one of the largest institutional investors in the United Kingdom, believes that a clear distinction exists between ensuring adequate minimum standards of investor protection and seeking to improve standards beyond that minimum. He takes the view that a strong statutory base should establish the clearly enforceable standards. Failure to meet those standards would result in the wrongdoer being put out of business. Decisions about improving the standards and about ethics are not the province of the regulators or of the statutory system. The promotion of the higher standards should, in his view, be the preserve of voluntary trade associations such as AIMR.

The concept of self-regulation was originally established in the United Kingdom when the City of London, despite being a major financial center, consisted largely of a relatively small group of institutions whose histories and personnel were closely linked. Peer-group pressure could be relied on to ensure ethical standards in line with generally accepted moral standards. The sanctions imposed, although not normally obvious or legal, tended to be quite effective.

The United Kingdom certainly has an indifferent record in enforcing insider trading and related practices. The threat of effective punitive action has been notably missing. The whole industry was undoubtedly shocked in mid-November 1993 when Roger Levitt, who had run an organization that failed with about £35 million of deficiencies and a record of large embezzlement of client funds, was given 180 hours of "community service" (which probably means light gardening).

Self-regulation may have worked fine with a relatively small group of people who grew up together, worked in similar organizations, knew each other well, and were subject to fairly effective peer pressure. Now that London's financial world has become a much larger operation, with multinational organizations working in it, an answer to somebody's question about whether something is permitted or not is increasingly difficult to give. Without a legislative basis from which to work, answers tend to be fuzzy.

Ethical standards in the financial world change over time, just as they do in other walks of life. As a result, the standards of an earlier time may seem quite inappropriate now. Thus, one argument often advanced for self-regulation is that the regulators are experts in the industry and can respond quickly to changes and innovations in a way that statutory regulations cannot. I am personally rather skeptical of this argument. The United States is not lacking in change and innovation in the financial services industry, but the evidence is that the regulators there are able to deal quite as effectively with wrongdoers as their U.K. counterparts.

What Is Needed

The United Kingdom needs a statutory basis for its system of regulation, and it needs a much simpler system than the current one. In addition, however, emphasis needs to be placed on promoting higher standards. All of Europe needs to catch up with the standards in the United States.

For the time being, there is little prospect that any U.K. government will want to legislate to enforce higher standards, because other, more pressing issues need to be addressed. At the same time, there is a real danger that legislators are not sufficiently aware of the issues, so legislation could be introduced that responds only to some particular scandal and damages the whole financial services industry in the process.

Continental Europe

In Europe, the approaches to both regulation and ethical standards diverge widely. Although the title "European Union" and the concept of a "European community" suggest a reasonably cohesive organization, the terms are misleading. European countries have individual philosophical, linguistic, and other traditions that often divide the countries more than they unite them. Little common ground exists in countries' approaches to legislation, and less in their approaches to ethics.

The lack of cohesion within Europe can be seen in a number of areas. One example is the recent attempt in the Maestricht Treaty to make fairly detailed plans for, among other issues, monetary union. Governments in the member states disagree internally about monetary union and many other major issues, and the public reaction to the Maestricht Treaty in each state indicated a considerable amount of disillusionment and disagreement. Even a country as small as Britain contains widely divergent outlooks on many issues, and the linguistic and cultural differences within Europe are enormous.

Historically, the stock markets of the member states of the European Union (EU) have evolved along quite different lines. For example, the United Kingdom has (as does the United States) a long history of substantial equity ownership and the trading of equity securities. Many continental European countries, in contrast, have traditionally relied heavily on fixed-income instruments and on bank finance.

The continental approach has had two important results: First, where the public has been little involved in holding equities, the concept of protection of minority shareholders has tended not to advance. Second, as major providers of finance, the continental banks have had strong positions in the corporate sector, strong links with their customers, and detailed knowledge of their customers' operations. Frequently, they have representation on the boards or supervisory boards of their client companies. (The supervisory board has a nonexecutive role and supervises the activities of the board of directors, who have executive responsibility.) Detailed rules relating to, for example, insider trading have not evolved in these jurisdictions. Germany, for example, is only now on the point of introducing legislation that will make insider trading a criminal offence. Two examples, one from Germany and one from Switzerland, will illustrate differences between Continental Europe's approach and the approach in the United States.

Daimler Benz

In the 1970s, Daimler Benz was concerned about being taken over by Arab interests. It thus created a holding company, called Mercedes Holdings, that held a substantial block of shares of Daimler Benz. The shares of Mercedes Holdings were listed but normally traded at a discount of about 20 percent to a comparable holding in Daimler Benz.

In 1993, when Daimler Benz decided to obtain a listing in New York, the Mercedes Holdings company had to be dissolved. In March 1993, before this action was announced, the chairman of IG Metal (one of the key trade unions in Germany and a member of the supervisory board of Daimler Benz), bought a substantial number of shares of Mercedes Holdings. In April 1993, when the dissolution of Mercedes Holdings was announced, he made a substantial profit when the discount vanished.

Similar actions took place in 1986 and 1987 when Daimler Benz bought AEG and in 1992 when it bought Fokker. None of these activities was, or is, illegal under German law. The chairman of IG Metal did resign, but he did not break any law. Legislation to prohibit such activities in Germany has been promised and is expected to be published shortly.

Philip Morris's Takeover of Jakob Suchard

Klaus Jakob controlled 62 percent of the votes but only 30 percent of the capital of Jakob Suchard of Switzerland. He accomplished this level of control by means of a private holding company. Philip Morris bought Klaus Jakob's holding company at a price equal to 40 times Jakob Suchard's earnings and then offered public shareholders an equivalent to 19 times earnings. The result was that Klaus Jakob received a premium of about 120 percent for his controlling interest. He also bought back some of the assets of Jakob Suchard at a price that seemed low.

In the offer document, Philip Morris discouraged rejection of the offer by stating that the Suchard dividend was likely to be cut. The danger also existed that if only a few shares remained outstanding, the shares would be delisted, so trading in them would be very illiquid. As a result, most outside shareholders gave in and accepted.

A takeover code had been adopted in Switzerland only a few months before this deal, but it was voluntary. The Swiss Bourse Regulatory Commission said that the rule that a bid must treat all shareholders equally did not apply in this case. Philip Morris (having acquired Klaus Jakob's holding company) already had a voting majority in Suchard; therefore, Philip Morris did not have to make a public offer at all. In the end, no law or regulation had been broken, but the public shareholders did not think themselves well treated.

New Rules in Europe

The Investment Services Directive (ISD), which is to become effective in 1996, begins the process of introducing a framework of rules for the operation of the securities business in Europe. Banking and insurance-related directives are also becoming operative, but the ISD is the most important development for investment managers.

The ISD is designed to establish a single securities market within the EU. The objective is to provide a framework of authorization requirements and prudential rules to ensure a reasonable level of investor protection.

The ISD seeks to create a single European passport for nonbanking investment firms. Once authorized in one member state, a firm will be able to do business in all other member states. The ISD will also prohibit member states from requiring firms to set up locally incorporated subsidiaries in order to do business within that state. It will thus require the repeal of restrictive laws in, for example, Italy and Germany.

Although the ISD lays down minimum standards of authorization for the regulation of the financial services industry and general principles governing the prudential conduct of such business, it does not set these standards out in any detail; nor will the directive involve the supervision of firms within the EU. The member states will appoint organizations to carry out those tasks. The philosophical approach, drafting, and enforcement of the rules that will apply in each member state may thus differ widely.

Potential Problems in EU Regulation

Considerable rivalry exists among European countries to claim the title of financial center of Europe. At present, London clearly accounts for the bulk of the foreign exchange business and stock market transactions. For example, the daily turnover in foreign exchange transactions averages US$300 billion in London, and 92 percent of European cross-border equity trades are done on the LSE. Some 1,600 companies are listed on the LSE, compared with 484 in Paris, 426 on the various German stock exchanges (of which Frankfurt is the largest), and 218 in Milan.

The United Kingdom's relative economic weakness, however, its departure from the Exchange Rate Mechanism, and the well-documented doubts of the U.K. authorities about European monetary union and the European Monetary Institute have given cities such as Frankfurt and Paris a chance to stake their claims. The recent collapse of Taurus (the LSE's proposed automated transfer system) and continued reliance on an out-of-date settlement system have also weakened London's position.

Because of this competition, the regulations and enforcement arrangements that each member state will establish under the Financial Services Directive may reflect a competitive lowering of standards as countries try to attract business to their financial centers. Some financial centers may produce regulatory systems that practitioners will not welcome because the systems create difficulties in compliance and entail costs. If some other centers produce less demanding sets of rules (in relation to compliance difficulties and/or costs) in order to compete, the result will be devaluation of regulation, which will set a very unhealthy trend.

Conclusion

Significant changes are occurring in the financial world, whether because of new technology or because of new treaties and laws and the regulatory systems created under them. Investors are expanding their activities into markets that only a few years ago would not have been considered. In such an environment, a clear set of standards of conduct is essential.

The standards should be governed by the best interests of investors rather than the lowest common standard derived from either a laissez-faire approach or from competitive devaluation of regulation. This stricture may seem to be taking a rather high moral line, but it is, in fact, a very practical approach. Whenever good, prudent standards have been abandoned and a laissez-faire attitude has been accepted, in the end, the result has been a major scandal or disaster. Then, after many investors have suffered, tough new standards are finally imposed. While those standards are being established, investors frequently refuse to risk their resources, and corporations in need of funds as well as the financial services industry suffer.

Relatively simple rules within an uncomplicated framework are needed. These rules should be enforced by regulators wielding tough sanctions. Efforts should be made to ensure that the regulatory framework is always kept up to date.

The basic framework of laws should be reinforced by ethical standards that, because they are widely accepted, will become effectively mandatory; that is, no professional investor or financial institution should be able to act in disregard of reasonable and well-established standards of conduct.

This area is one in which AIMR can play a major role. These standards will change over time, and as with the legal framework, the ethical standards should thus be the subject of ongoing debate to upgrade them.

Europeans must agree what our standards are and ought to be before we can establish or enforce any code of conduct, but this agreement will be difficult to achieve. In some European countries, insider dealing is still not a crime; at the same time, some people in countries where it is a crime argue that no loss is suffered or harm done by insider dealing and, therefore, it should be decriminalized.

Finally, we must keep a constant pressure on the legal systems involved to see that appropriate changes are made to embody ethical standards in a legal framework where necessary.

Regulation and Ethical Standards around the World: Hong Kong

Ermanno Pascutto
Executive Director, Corporate Finance Division
Hong Kong Securities & Futures Commission

The large and rapidly growing Hong Kong market was virtually unregulated five years ago. After several years of work on a formidable agenda of reform, however, the market is generally in line with international standards of market regulation and practice. Moreover, the Securities & Futures Commission has significantly increased its enforcement activities since 1991. Of particular interest as regards ethical standards are the commission's "fit and proper" criteria and the nine general principles of the Hong Kong stock exchange's new Code of Conduct. Investment professionals are warned, however, that the regulatory and ethical frameworks have only recently been introduced, much is in preliminary, untested form, and standards reflect unique characteristics of Hong Kong's environment.

Investor interest in foreign equities reached new highs in the United States in 1993 and is expected to continue to increase in future years as investors diversify their equity portfolios in search of better returns. Net purchases of foreign equities in the second quarter of 1993 reached a quarterly record of $13.2 billion.[1] An effective and efficient regulatory environment that meets international standards will be a significant factor in investors' assessments of the risks and rewards of investing in a specific foreign market. In particular, because of the significance of Hong Kong's market, U.S. investors will want to know whether Hong Kong standards meet their requirements.

Therefore, this presentation will begin with some background information on the Hong Kong securities market and then discuss the role of the Securities & Futures Commission (SFC) in promoting a viable and efficient market for domestic and international investors. The presentation will then consider changes that have been made or are to come to the regulatory structure in Hong Kong, with emphasis on the corporate governance of listed companies and regulation of intermediaries.

The Hong Kong Securities Market

Hong Kong is an active center for securities trading; the 465 companies listed on the Stock Exchange of Hong Kong, Ltd. (SEHK), represent a total market capitalization of HK$2,358 billion (US$305 billion). Hong Kong is the second largest stock market in Asia, after Japan, in terms of market capitalization and the seventh largest market in the world. The SEHK reported an average daily turnover in 1993 of more than US$500 million; turnover in late 1993 was approximating US$1 billion a day.

Hong Kong's buoyant economy and proximity to China has resulted in rapid growth in the size of its market. Market capitalization grew by 450 percent from 1986 to 1993—from HK$419 billion (US$54 billion) to HK$2,358 billion (US$305 billion)—and the number of listed companies increased by over 80 percent from the 253 in 1986.

Intermediaries

More than 10,000 licensed brokers, dealers, and investment advisors currently operate in Hong Kong. The community of market practitioners in securities and commodities dealing and advising is distinctly international in flavor, with over 178 securities dealers and 48 commodities dealers controlled by overseas entities, including major financial insti-

---

[1] "Foreign Activity," The Securities Industry Association (October 1993).

tutions from the United Kingdom, the United States, Japan, and other developed countries. Estimates attribute 40–60 percent of the daily turnover on the SEHK to international institutional investors.

Fund Management

Hong Kong is the leading center for fund management in the region. More than 850 funds are authorized to be marketed to the investing public in Hong Kong. A large number of multinational fund management companies have their Asian headquarters in Hong Kong.

Hong Kong and China's Emerging Market[2]

Based on size and its 100-year history of securities trading, Hong Kong ranks as a developed market, but it is also a gateway to investment in China (the People's Republic of China or PRC), which is probably destined to become the largest emerging market in history. In a sense, therefore, Hong Kong may also become a major emerging stock market.

The Hong Kong market serves as an investment medium for a variety of PRC investments, of which the most significant are as follows:

▪ *Traditional Hong Kong-listed companies.* The Standard Chartered Bank estimates that more than 70 listed companies managed and controlled out of Hong Kong have at least 2/3 of their production based in the PRC and that the market capitalization of these firms is in excess of HK$60 billion. Most of these production facilities have emerged in the last few years, and many of the companies have only recently listed on the stock exchange.

▪ *"Backdoor" listing of PRC enterprises.* Also on the increase since 1992 is the number of backdoor listings, a term used to describe the acquisition by a mainland Chinese enterprise of a significant stake in a small, SEHK-listed company with the aim of injecting part of the parent company's business or assets into the Hong Kong-listed company. About 12 "red chips" (that is, companies listed in Hong Kong that are controlled, directly or indirectly, by mainland Chinese enterprises or their subsidiaries in Hong Kong) went through this process in the first seven months of 1993 (as compared with 5 during 1992), raising a total of HK$8 billion of funds from the market since April 1992. These companies account for a market capitalization in excess of HK$65 billion.

▪ *Direct listings of PRC enterprises.* The most significant development for Hong Kong's stock exchange in 1993 (and possibly in its history) was the direct listing on the SEHK of H shares (H for Hong Kong) of PRC state enterprises. Hong Kong's efforts to list PRC-incorporated enterprises on the SEHK have already resulted in the successful listing of five PRC state enterprises. These listings mark the beginning of a new era for Hong Kong's securities markets as Hong Kong becomes China's conduit to international investment capital. These five listings, with a market capitalization of the public float of approximately HK$15 billion, raised more than HK$9 billion in the second half of 1993, and more such listings are expected.

This public float does not reflect the size of the total enterprises because it does not include the market capitalization of the A shares (shares available only to mainland PRC nationals and traded only on mainland PRC stock exchanges) or shares retained by the PRC government.

In addition, Hong Kong is also the principal base for securities firms dealing in B shares (shares available only to non-PRC nationals and traded on the Shanghai or Shenzhen stock exchanges).

The Role of the SFC

The global stock market crash of October 1987 brought to light a number of structural and systemic weaknesses in the market in Hong Kong, as well as a number of gaps in the regulatory system. Following the four-day closing of the SEHK and the near collapse of the futures exchange, the government appointed an independent Securities Review Committee (SRC) to examine the system of financial markets and their regulation and make recommendations for improvements. The report of the SRC, published in May 1988, served as a blueprint for reforms that have since that time been largely implemented.

The SRC's report was 443 pages long and included more than 240 recommendations for reforming the securities and futures markets. The SRC found that Hong Kong had erred on the side of excessive laissez-faire and that the regulatory structure needed substantial strengthening. Its main recommendations were for the following:

- a reconstitution of the stock exchange;
- a reconstitution of the futures exchange and reconstruction of its risk-management and clearing systems; and
- the establishment of an independent statutory market watchdog with the necessary resources to supervise the marketplace adequately.

The establishment of the SFC in May 1989 marked the enactment of the third key recommendation. The SFC is an autonomous statutory corporation that is outside the civil service but part

[2]Figures in this section are from the Hong Kong office of Standard Chartered Bank P.L.C.

of the wider machinery of government. It is composed of ten directors—five executive directors (the chairman and heads of the four operating divisions of the SFC) and five nonexecutives. Market practitioners assist the SFC with a number of its functions. For example, an Advisory Committee consisting of 12 senior market practitioners, business executives, and professionals advises the SFC on policy matters.

Structurally, the SFC is divided into four major operational divisions—for corporate finance, supervision of markets, supervision of intermediaries, and enforcement—each headed by an executive director. Funding is partly by the government and partly by the market through a statutory levy on stock market transactions and fees charged for services provided to market participants. The current staff of 222 people have a broad range of regulatory and market experience; some were recruited from the world's most developed markets.

The SFC states its mission to be the promotion of efficiency and fairness in the markets by balancing measures to enhance market integrity and investor protection with measures to accommodate market development and innovation. The mission statement recognizes the local environment but stresses the need to conform to international standards.

Much of the SFC's work since 1990 has involved a complete overhaul of the regulatory framework, the implementation of international standards, and improvements in standards of corporate and professional behavior. The ordinance that established the SFC set out 14 functions of the commission, including the following (paraphrased) duties:

- to report insider dealing;
- to supervise and monitor the exchanges and clearing houses and to promote self-regulation;
- to safeguard the interests of investors;
- to suppress illegal, dishonorable, and improper practices in securities dealings;
- to promote and maintain the integrity of registered persons; and
- to encourage the use of the markets by domestic and international investors.

Principal Regulatory Changes since 1989

In the first few years after its establishment, the SFC was occupied with ensuring that the blueprint for reform established by the SRC was carried out. Almost all of the SRC's 244 recommendations have been implemented, and the few remaining areas are being addressed. The result of this reform effort is that the Hong Kong market is generally in line with international standards of market regulation and

practice. This section will note some of the key changes in investor protection and then focus on, first, corporate governance of listed companies and, second, standards for intermediaries.

Some of the major improvements and reforms that have been completed are as follows:

■ *Constitutional arrangements.* Reforms in the constitutional arrangements of the stock exchange have established an independent and professional management of the exchange and made the governing council broadly representative of its membership and the various participants other than brokers who have an interest in the market—including, of course, institutional investors and the investing public.

■ *Constitution and risk-management systems.* Reform of the constitution and risk-management systems of the futures exchange included the establishment of a new clearing house and a reserve fund of more than HK$200 million to protect against broker defaults.

■ *Discosure requirements.* The enactment of a disclosure ordinance requiring major shareholders, company directors, and others to disclose shareholdings and dealings above certain levels has enhanced market transparency.

■ *Insider-dealing ordinance.* A new insider-dealing ordinance significantly increased the penalties for this abuse.

■ *Transaction system.* A centralized system for the settlement of stock exchange transactions has significantly enhanced the risk-management systems in the market and, at the same time, paves the way for important market development measures that are in the pipeline: automated trade matching (which began on a limited basis in November 1993), short selling, and stock options trading.

■ *Licensing criteria.* A new system for licensing brokers, dealers, and investment advisers established new criteria for determining the "fitness and properness" of dealers and advisors to be in the securities business. This system is coupled with a much more proactive approach than in the past to ensuring that the intermediaries in the market are efficient, honest, and financially sound and will deal with clients fairly.

■ *Listing rules.* The new stock exchange listing rules meet international standards based on the London Stock Exchange (LSE) model. The new rules have been complemented by a progressive strengthening of the staffing and experience of the SEHK's Listing Division, including the establishment of a Listing Committee and the devolution of listing authority by the SFC to the exchange.

■ *Marketing rules.* An overhaul of the rules governing the marketing of collective investment schemes included the promulgation of three new codes.

■ *Dealing costs.* The SFC is making continuing efforts to reduce dealing costs in Hong Kong. Since 1989, dealing costs have been reduced by 25 percent, primarily through cuts in the rate of the stamp duty on stock exchange transactions.

Corporate Governance of Listed Companies

Any discussion of corporate governance in Hong Kong will be profoundly different from such a discussion in the United States because of the differences in structure of the two markets. Perhaps the most striking difference is the much higher level of corporate control that exists in the Hong Kong market. In Hong Kong, the overwhelming majority of companies are under the effective or legal control of a single shareholder or group of shareholders acting in concert. The majority of important American companies are widely held, and no single shareholder or group has legal or effective control of them.

In the Hong Kong environment, few companies experience problems related to the accountability of management to shareholders. A controlling shareholder has few difficulties in ensuring that management implements its wishes, in detecting mismanagement, or in replacing managers. In many cases, the managers, board of directors, and controlling shareholders are the same.

The central corporate governance concerns in Hong Kong are the accountability of directors/controlling shareholders to public minority shareholders and equity between controlling and minority shareholders. Concerns about accountability of management/controlling shareholders tend to focus on the following:

- non-arms-length transactions between the company and connected persons, such as property or business transactions with controlling shareholders;
- unreasonable compensation arrangements, such as the hiring of relatives not on commercial terms or the payment of unreasonable bonuses or granting of options to directors and their close associates;
- unanticipated changes in business direction, such as a listed company acquiring (often from the controlling shareholder) an entirely different business shortly after listing when no mention of such change in direction was made in the initial public offering (IPO) prospectus; and
- abusive financings, such as very large or frequent rights issues.

Many commentators also argue that any consideration of corporate governance in Hong Kong should take into account the particular character of Hong Kong-listed companies. These companies tend to be family controlled with highly centralized decision making. These characteristics may reflect the stage of evolution of these companies and the market (relatively new businesses run by first- and second-generation entrepreneurs) or some uniquely Chinese or Hong Kong heritage. Regardless of the cause of the differences, investors need to recognize the characteristics of the local market and its stage of development in formulating investment proposals.

Another "local" factor that needs to be considered in any discussion of corporate governance in Hong Kong is the offshore domicile of the majority of listed companies. Hong Kong is probably unique in having more than half its listed companies incorporated in an offshore jurisdiction (primarily Bermuda).

■ *Independent shareholder protection.* The SFC and the SEHK have introduced a number of measures in recent years to enhance corporate governance—on the whole, in line with international standards of corporate governance. In 1989, the listing rules were comprehensively revised to bring them up to international standards (based on the LSE model). The regulation of non-arms-length or connected transactions included both disclosure and procedural requirements to ensure fairness to minority shareholders.

Chief among the techniques used to protect shareholders is the requirement for independent shareholder approval for certain transactions (such as connected transactions and very large rights issues). This protection is supplemented by a requirement that an independent expert (generally, a merchant bank) provide an opinion on the fairness and reasonableness of the proposed transaction. Although this requirement represented a significant step forward, the structure of the market and its characteristics mean that the requirement for independent shareholder voting does not completely address the problem of policing actions by controlling shareholders. The reasons include shareholder inertia (both retail and institutional), compliant financial advisors, "fan clubs" that tend to support controlling shareholders, and ineffectual media.[3]

■ *"Cadbury" changes.* In August 1993, the stock exchange introduced several new listing rules that were influenced, in part, by the U.K. Report of the Committee on the Financial Aspects of Corporate

---

[3]Hong Kong has addressed one problem that continues to vex the United States and other developed markets: the "one share, one vote" problem. By and large, shares with disproportionate voting rights are prohibited in Hong Kong.

Governance (the "Cadbury Report"). These measures were intended to enhance corporate governance:

- a requirement that all listed companies have a minimum of two independent, nonexecutive directors within a year;
- a requirement that, as a minimum, listed companies aim to comply with the guidelines for boards of directors issued by the SEHK from time to time called "Code of Best Practice." These guidelines include a number of Cadbury proposals related to disclosure of directors fees and similar payments, disclosure of terms of appointments of nonexecutive directors, arrangements in certain circumstances for nonexecutive directors to seek outside professional advice, and requirements for full board meetings when a matter involving a conflict of interest for a substantial shareholder or a director arises.

The listing rules also articulate directors' fiduciary duties under Hong Kong law and the broad duties of directors under common law.

◼ *The Corporate Governance Working Party.* The stock exchange has also recently established a Corporate Governance Working Party, with SFC support and participation, to examine various issues of corporate governance. The purpose is to stimulate debate on these issues in Hong Kong and come up with further proposals.

◼ *PRC enterprises listed in Hong Kong.* Developing a framework for PRC-incorporated issuers in Hong Kong presented novel regulatory issues. The framework had to meet the special circumstances of PRC issuers and protect investors. In June 1993, the SFC and the stock exchange announced a wideranging package of measures to enable PRC issuers to list a class of special shares denominated in PRC currency (renminbi), the H shares, that will be subscribed for and traded in Hong Kong dollars and be available to Hong Kong and overseas investors. Companies with a primary listing of their H shares on the Hong Kong exchange may also list class A shares (available to only PRC individuals and entities) on an exchange in China.

The package of amendments enabling PRC-incorporated enterprises to list in Hong Kong takes account of the lack of a developed body of securities and company law in China. Once listed on the stock exchange, a PRC issuer is subject to all relevant Hong Kong laws and requirements, including listing rules and the Code on Takeovers and Mergers. In addition, because PRC companies were not subject to Hong Kong corporate law, the regulators negotiated amendments to PRC corporate administrative requirements that introduce requirements comparable to those in place in Hong Kong.

Key modifications to the listing rules for PRC issuers included requirements to:

- adopt standard articles to entrench shareholder protections;
- have separate votes for holders of A and H shares when the rights of H shareholders are affected;
- prepare accounts in accordance with Hong Kong or international accounting standards and to be audited by an internationally recognized accounting firm; and
- retain a Hong Kong sponsor (generally, the investment bank handling the IPO) for a minimum of three years after the initial listing.

In addition, the Hong Kong authorities signed a Memorandum of Regulatory Cooperation in June 1993 with the PRC stock exchanges and the new China Securities Regulatory Commission.

Risks do remain for investors in PRC stock. The securities and company regulatory framework has only recently been introduced, much of it is in preliminary form, and it is completely untested.

◼ *Changes in financial disclosure.* Apart from the initiative of the Corporate Governance Working Party, the most significant outstanding proposal for reform of corporate governance relates to financial disclosure. The Working Group on Financial Disclosure, which consisted of representatives of the SFC, the SEHK, and the Hong Kong Society for Accountants (HKSA), made the following recommendations in August 1993:

- establish a new Financial Reporting Standards Committee to develop accounting and auditing standards under the auspices of the HKSA but including, among others, representatives from the SFC, the stock exchange, and the investment community. This structure is designed to ensure a wider constituency than at present in the development of accounting standards;
- for the HKSA, consider new or revised accounting standards for the format of profit-and-loss accounts and balance sheets, earnings per share, segment reporting, research and development, valuation of intangible assets, joint ventures, auditors reports, and off-balance-sheet items;

- establish a separate unit at the stock exchange to monitor and enforce compliance with financial disclosure requirements by reviewing the accounts of listed companies;
- recommend changes to the listing rules to require additional disclosure in financial reports regarding directors' compensation, pensions, intangible assets, management discussion and analysis, etc.;
- for the SFC, issue a public consultation paper on statutory backing in respect to the disclosure obligations of listed companies;[4] and
- recommend that the SFC take a more active role than at present in identifying emerging accounting issues, standard setting, and compliance and enforcement to ensure that Hong Kong's requirements, compliance, and oversight are consistent with the leading international financial markets.

The Working Group also suggested that the current exclusion of banks from certain disclosure requirements of the Companies Ordinance should be removed. This exclusion is incompatible with Hong Kong's position as an international financial center. The report proposed that the issue of disclosure by banks be dealt with through amendments to the listing rules to require that financial statements of listed banks disclose their true results and financial positions.

Regulation of Intermediaries

Hong Kong legislation has for years required intermediaries (dealers, advisors, and their representatives) to register with the SFC in order to conduct business. In 1989 and 1990, the SFC introduced a "fit and proper" test for applicants for such registration and set out guidelines for administering the test to applicants and for the continuing obligation of registrants to meet the requirements of the test. The test covers such aspects as financial status, educational qualifications and/or experience, ability to perform efficiently, fairly, and honestly, and reputation, character, and reliability. In effect, it requires applicants to prove that they have the appropriate qualifications and experience, have no criminal record, are mentally sound, and so forth. In consider-

ing a corporate applicant, the SFC takes into consideration the substantial shareholders, directors, and officers of the applicant and its related companies and businesses.

Although the SFC's "Fit and Proper Criteria" contributed greatly to informing both prospective and existing market professionals of the standards to be applied in determining whether a person possesses the requisite qualifications for registration as a market professional, detailed rules setting forth the manner in which these professionals should conduct their business were also deemed necessary. Both the SFC and the SEHK are thus in the process of implementing detailed minimum rules of conduct.

Stock Exchange Code of Conduct

A new Code of Conduct introduced by the stock exchange in November 1993 sets forth the minimum standards of conduct for a member. Some standards may be at variance with the current practices of certain members, particularly in respect to the handling of client orders and transactions. The code recognizes a member's role as agent for its principal clients.

The nine general principles underlying the new code require that a member:

- observe professional standards of integrity, act honestly, fairly, and in the best interests of clients, and conduct business so as to help maintain a fair and orderly market;
- act with due skill and diligence;
- take all reasonable steps to ensure that the member and employees are fit and proper, that adequate resources are used, and that the necessary procedures for the proper conduct of business are in place;
- take all reasonable steps to obtain sufficient financial and other information from each client, and where investment advice is provided, take reasonable steps to obtain sufficient information regarding the client's financial situation, investment experience, and investment objectives to ensure that investments are suitable for a particular client;
- make adequate disclosure to clients of all information relating to dealing on the client's behalf and strictly avoid making misleading or deceptive representations;
- avoid treating a client's interests as subordinate to the member's;
- take all reasonable steps to avoid conflicts of interest, and where such con-

---

[4]The majority of the regulations affecting listed companies are in nonstatutory form—primarily, the listing rules of the stock exchange and the Takeovers Code. Statutory backing would involve codification of disclosure obligations with a view to reinforcing existing requirements by using criminal or administrative sanctions and civil remedies.

flicts cannot reasonably be avoided, take all reasonable steps to ensure that clients are treated fairly;

- ensure that client assets are promptly and properly accounted for and safeguarded; and
- comply with all regulatory and exchange requirements applicable to business conduct so as to promote the best interests of clients and the integrity of the market.

These nine general principles are supplemented by detailed requirements.

SFC Code of Conduct and International Standards

In November 1993, the SFC issued a draft code of conduct for nonmembers of the stock exchange that is broadly comparable to international principles and the SEHK Code of Conduct. The principles were developed and recognized by the International Organization of Securities Commissions (IOSCO) as being fundamental to the undertaking of a registered person's business.

The proposed SFC code does not apply to the conduct of a registered person if that person is acting as a management company under the SFC's Code on Unit Trusts and Mutual Funds. The SFC will be preparing further guidelines in 1994, however, concerning such management companies.

Enforcement of International Standards

After several years of work on a formidable agenda of regulatory reform, during which time virtually every aspect of the market underwent change, the SFC believes that Hong Kong's standards are generally in line with standards in other developed markets. Investors examining the regulatory environment in a foreign market will wish to look beyond the standards, however, to how seriously they are applied by the regulators. Are enforcement proceedings taken against listed companies, market intermediaries, and others for failure to comply with the standards?

Although Hong Kong has always had an enforcement program, the SFC has significantly stepped up its enforcement activities since 1991. The following are some highlights:

Inspectors. SFC investigations resulted in the appointment of inspectors for two high-profile groups of listed companies (one group had a market capitalization in excess of HK$10 billion). The report of one inspection was recently published and is likely to result in criminal, civil, and regulatory proceedings against several listed companies and individuals.

Takeovers. In 1992, the SFC successfully blocked abusive privatizations in two controversial cases, and in 1992 and 1993, SFC inquiries led to the making of general offers to all shareholders in several cases where they would not otherwise have been made.

Insider dealing. Since the SFC's inception, only one insider-dealing case has been prosecuted, but two more are expected to be announced by early 1994.

Unregistered dealing. Forty-eight people were prosecuted and found guilty of unregistered dealing and related offenses in the 1992–93 period.

Disclosure of interests. Following a publicity campaign and after warnings to the market, the SFC prosecuted and obtained convictions in several cases for failure to disclose or late disclosure of dealings in securities by directors and substantial shareholders.

Unauthorized investment arrangement. In 1992 and 1993, 14 persons were convicted of promoting unauthorized investment schemes to the public.

Market manipulation. In 1993, regulators obtained the first conviction for market manipulation in Hong Kong.

Licensed intermediaries. A number of investigations concerning the fitness and properness of licensed intermediaries have been undertaken. Disciplinary action was taken in more than 30 cases, including revocation of licenses of firms and individuals in some cases. A recent settlement with a leading brokerage and merchant banking firm in Hong Kong involved regulatory sanctions against the firm and its officers for actions connected with an IPO and a "voluntary" payment of HK$3.5 million to an investor compensation fund.

This list focuses on statutory proceedings, but a feature of Hong Kong that may be of special interest to investors is the extent to which reliance is placed on nonstatutory requirements. The vast majority of regulatory requirements for listed companies are found in the nonstatutory listing rules of the stock exchange and the SFC's Code on Takeovers and Mergers, neither of which has the force of law.

Nonstatutory requirements have the advantage of being easily changed (which is important in light of the rapid development of the market) and flexibly administered (which is important in light of the approach that certain practitioners and principals take to regulation). The Takeovers Code explicitly states that the "General Principles and the spirit of the Code will apply in areas or circumstances not explicitly covered by any Rule." Nonstatutory requirements are also considered more acceptable than laws in light of the political situation of Hong Kong and are considered more in keeping with local culture.

The stock exchange and the SFC have taken formal disciplinary action, on statutory and nonstatutory grounds, against several listed companies for misleading disclosures and other forms of noncompliance. In addition, listed companies and intermediaries sometimes choose to take remedial action following informal discussions with regulatory authorities. In 1993, remedial action was taken in a number of cases involving several hundred millions of Hong Kong dollars. The role of the regulatory agencies in these cases is not necessarily made public. Again, this informal approach can be effective and is also in keeping with the local environment.

In short, participants in Hong Kong's markets should be convinced by the "balanced portfolio" of enforcement actions that Hong Kong regulatory authorities are serious about enforcing the standards that have been developed.

Conclusion

Regulation of securities markets in Hong Kong is very much a balancing act. Among the various objectives that must be balanced are the following:

- to balance the needs and wishes of local market participants against those of international firms and international investors;
- to balance the need to combat market abuses in a market where capitalism is still very much unbridled against the need to preserve civil liberties in the unique political situation created by the resumption of sovereignty by China in 1997; and
- to balance the need to take account of local history and social values against the need to bring the conduct of business into line with the standards in international securities markets.

Four and a half years after the establishment of the SFC, the Hong Kong market authorities have implemented international standards in most areas, although the process of reform must continue. The environment has changed markedly from 1989, when many issuers, local intermediaries, and others questioned the need for change and worried about "overregulation." The recent success of the Hong Kong markets—in particular, the listing of PRC state enterprises—markedly increased support for international standards among these market participants and the investing public.

Question and Answer Session

Brian E. Hersey, CFA
David H. Beevers
Ermanno Pascutto

Question: Are any practices required in other countries or markets that are considered to be in violation of AIMR's Standards of Professional Conduct; if so, how are they to be handled?

Beevers: I cannot think of any AIMR Standards of Professional Conduct that are prohibited in individual markets. The more usual situation is that *no* applicable standards are in force.

Question: Australia has established its own performance standards; how much of a hurdle will meeting the AIMR Performance Presentation Standards be for Australian managers?

Hersey: Some Australian-based managers are endeavoring to market their financial services in the United States and in other markets, and consultants and plan fiduciaries can play an important role in encouraging them to adopt AIMR standards. In other words, if the managers are interested in having consultants recommend them and plan sponsors seriously consider them for appointments, then it is incumbent upon the managers to meet the standards.

We clearly encourage the adoption of AIMR standards, but we realize that it is not always possible. Sometimes historical returns cannot be reconstructed. Sometimes we can only evaluate specific accounts presented as representative of a particular capability, make judgments about how applicable they are to the assign-

ment at hand, and go from there. The situation is not at all perfect, and we will always be making judgments under uncertainty.

Question: Is technology the main constraint preventing investment management firms from producing offshore composites, specifically in regard to trade data and daily cash flow returns, that are calculated in compliance with AIMR Performance Presentation Standards?

Hersey: The biggest constraint is lack of data. In most cases, the data are not available in a form that can be used to create those histories in compliance with the AIMR standards.

Beevers: In many cases, the organizations concerned have not stored the information, do not have it now, and cannot easily recreate it. When the records were being established, the organizations did not see the need to maintain those information bases.

Question: Do any particularly good publications review regulatory developments around the world?

Beevers: No, nobody has published anything comprehensive. The markets are so diverse, even inside Europe, that you need to read a lot of different works to get a comprehensive review. The individual European countries' regulations are completely different at the moment. In fact, quite recently introduced Italian legisla-

tion, for example, is contrary to the European ISD and will have to be canceled.

Question: One AIMR goal is to obtain common ethical standards worldwide. What approach for working with the regulators toward that goal would you recommend?

Pascutto: IOSCO is playing a growing role in the development of international standards; it has a subcommittee working on harmonizing standards for international offerings and a subcommittee on accounting and auditing standards. IOSCO has also agreed on a set of general principles for the regulation of intermediaries. So, it is working on common international standards in a number of areas. One approach that might make sense, therefore, would be to develop a relationship with IOSCO.[1] This method is probably a better way to move forward than dealing with the issue strictly bilaterally. Bilateral contacts should also be pursued, however.

Question: Is there anything that AIMR or other parties can do beyond working with the regulators that surmounts cultural barriers to increase or improve ethical standards worldwide?

Beevers: Yes. First of all, a lot of the countries are unaware of the standards AIMR sets. So,

---

[1] *Editor's note*: AIMR has applied to become a member of IOSCO.

AIMR needs to disseminate the concepts and the organization's basic guidelines—for example, spend time with practitioners explaining to them that the funds they would like to access will not be available unless they ensure that adequate professional conduct standards are in place. Many people around the world can see the huge flows of money that are possible out of the United States. Access to that money is very tempting, so the threat that it might be diverted elsewhere or withheld would be a good way to focus people's attention on the issues AIMR wants addressed.

The Ethical Implications for Fiduciaries of Using Soft Dollars

Robert A. Anselmi
Managing Director and General Counsel
J.P. Morgan Investment Management, Inc.

One investment management firm provides clear, well-thought-out policies for using soft dollars that are based on two fundamental principles: (1) commissions are the property of the client and (2) a manager should minimize transaction costs.

Soft-dollar practices raise legal, ethical, and fiduciary issues for investment managers. This presentation summarizes the ethical implications of using soft dollars from the perspective of a fiduciary; namely, J.P. Morgan Investment Management.

J.P. Morgan Investment has a strong philosophical commitment to fundamental research as a primary source of adding value in our equity investment process. We also have a strong financial commitment to investment research, with 53 analysts worldwide, 20 of whom are in the United States.

J.P. Morgan Investment is thus relatively self-sufficient in research, but we certainly do not have a monopoly on good investment ideas or on brainpower, so we use outside research, both proprietary and third-party research, to supplement our own. Although we think the quality of outside research is not uniformly high—and that there is probably too much of it—we also believe that the firm and our clients benefit from the ideas these other sources provide.

Defining Soft-Dollar Practices

The term "soft dollars" generally encompasses the payments a fiduciary causes clients to make to a broker (for products and services) that exceed the lowest available commission for executing a securities trade (that is, paying up). The three most prevalent uses of soft dollars are to pay for proprietary and third-party research services, and for directed brokerage.

Clearly, the primary service obtained using soft dollars is proprietary (in-house) research, which is provided as a quid pro quo for commission business by a broker who produces the research. This proprie-

tary research generally does not have an identifiable price; the commissions charged by the broker include the research cost (this practice is known as bundled pricing). The research services are also not generally available for cash or hard-dollar payments.

Soft dollars are also used to obtain third-party investment research services. Brokers do not produce the research themselves but purchase it for the fiduciary from an independent research provider. The fiduciary agrees with the broker to a conversion ratio whereby a portion of every commission dollar generated by the fiduciary will be credited toward paying the broker for the cost of the service. These services typically have an identifiable price, either in soft dollars on the basis of a conversion ratio or in cash or hard dollars.

In purchasing proprietary or third-party research services for soft dollars, the client is paying for more than the cost of execution.

The third use of soft dollars is directed brokerage. In these arrangements, the client directs the investment manager to allocate a certain percentage of transactions in the client's portfolio to a broker designated by the client. In return, the client, by prearrangement with the broker, will be credited a portion of the commissions, which may be used by the client to pay for third-party research, administrative, or other services.

Although much of the debate regarding the propriety of using soft dollars centers on directed brokerage and the purchase of third-party research, J.P. Morgan Investment believes that the purchase of proprietary research with soft dollars also involves legal, fiduciary, and ethical issues and should not be overlooked.

J.P. Morgan Investment's Soft-Dollar Practices

We have two fundamental beliefs with respect to our own soft-dollar practices. The first is that the commissions paid to a broker are fundamentally the property of the client. As a firm, we have to act with the utmost care in using those client assets. They are for the benefit of the client, and they are clearly not to be used for the benefit of the manager.

The second is that money managers have a responsibility to ensure the quality of the transactions effected on behalf of clients; that is, managers have a responsibility to clients to minimize the costs of transactions. The manager's trading function should be geared to ensuring that outcome.

Transaction costs have two essential elements. One is the commission expense, which is highly identifiable and easily understood. The second and more difficult cost to understand and quantify is the market-impact cost. In most transactions, the market-impact cost is higher than the commission expense. Trading strategies and analyses that focus on commission costs alone and give short shrift to market impact are very shortsighted.

Because of the large amount of equity assets J.P. Morgan Investment has under management, our trading function is very important to us. Anything we do contrary to best execution penalizes the returns the client receives from our activities. Moreover, because our performance as managers is measured after, not before, transaction costs, a failure in best execution translates ultimately into a performance penalty.

In short, our practices are based on these two fundamental principles and beliefs: commissions are the property of the client and should be used for the exclusive benefit of the client, and a manager should minimize transaction costs, both commissions and market-impact costs.

General Approach: Selecting Brokers

We believe that the selection of brokers is an important determinant of our ability to add value to our clients' portfolios through our trading function. Managers vary in the way they select brokers and in the types of services they seek from brokers. The first criterion J.P. Morgan Investment applies in selecting a broker is the broker's ability to provide best execution—to provide the best price, including commissions, for each trade. Commissions are a factor in this analysis, but we generally do not seek simply the lowest possible commission cost. Rather, we believe that paying fair and reasonable commissions to brokers will ultimately provide our clients appropriate priority in the execution process.

Second, the broker must be reliable; that is, the broker must be able to perform when needed. Typically, given the amount of equity assets we manage, this criterion involves capital commitment.

Third, we carefully scrutinize the financial condition of potential brokers. Because we are acting in a fiduciary capacity and placing client capital at risk, we are very careful to ensure that the brokers with which we deal are of the utmost integrity and have excellent credit positions.

Finally, we look at the broker's research services. Although independent, third-party research is of value to us, only a small portion of our clients' commissions are used to pay for this type of research, in comparison with what we understand to be an industry average of about 30 percent. To avoid potential distractions to our normal trading processes and to avoid conflicts of interest that could arise from the need to allocate trades for soft-dollar commitments, we have for the last several years been using full-service firms whenever possible, rather than firms with which we might not otherwise do business, for soft-dollar arrangements. Only a few full-service firms are unwilling to engage in soft-dollar arrangements.

Proprietary Research

Because of the volume of business we generate, we receive many proprietary research reports from a large number of brokers; most of these reports are unsolicited although not altogether unwanted or unappreciated. Proprietary research is a factor in selecting brokers, but we do not make commitments to allocate brokerage for proprietary research. Twice a year, our analysts and portfolio managers rank firms based on the value of their proprietary research. We then establish informal targets for brokerage allocations to the firms, but we do not communicate this information to the firms. In general, these informal targets are exceeded in the normal course of our trading activities.

Third-Party Services

Just as we do not have a monopoly on brain power or good investment ideas, neither do proprietary research firms, and we value independent research as a supplement to our own internal research. The benefits of this kind of research are, first, that we can objectively choose what we want (as opposed to merely accepting the generally unsolicited ideas from proprietary research firms); second, that we will know the cost of the research (which is not known with proprietary research because its price is bundled); and third, that the potential conflicts of interest among the proprietary research, trading, and investment banking functions of brokerage firms generally do not exist in independent third-party research firms.

We use two fundamental criteria in determining whether to use any part of client commissions to pay for third-party research. First, the research or the related service must benefit the client rather than the money manager. Are the services value-added investment ideas that are not generally available, or airline tickets, a *Wall Street Journal* subscription, or other questionable services? Second, the research must be of a kind that either enhances our own research efforts or can be integrated into our investment decision-making process.

Directed Brokerage

J.P. Morgan Investment does little directed brokerage business. Only a small number of our clients request that we direct commissions from their accounts to pay for expenses that would otherwise be paid for with cash. We do not encourage directed brokerage because it can affect the efficiency and effectiveness of our trading operation; we generally combine orders for the same security among multiple client accounts, which makes directing orders for one client difficult. Also, directed brokerage can be a distraction to us from our normal trading process and can represent a potential conflict of interest in our efforts to obtain best execution for all clients.

When possible, however, we do attempt to accommodate reasonable requests to direct brokerage.

In such situations, we generally limit the amount to 10 percent of commission volume, require that the request be subject to our judgment of best execution, and encourage clients to make these arrangements with firms with which we would ordinarily do business, namely, full-service firms.

Conclusion

Fiduciaries should consider a number of principles when using client commissions to purchase investment research:

1. Commissions are the property of the client and should be used for the benefit of the client, not the money manager.

2. Using soft dollars to purchase research that either generates value-added investment ideas or can be integrated into an investment decision-making process is a fair and reasonable use of a client's commission dollars.

3. Legal, fiduciary, and ethical issues apply equally to all types of soft-dollar arrangements, whether they involve purchase of proprietary or third-party research services or directed brokerage.

4. The trading function is, or should be, an important part of the value added by money managers in pursuing best execution, and anything managers do that jeopardizes best execution potentially imposes a performance penalty on themselves and their clients.

The Ethical Implications for Brokers of Using Soft Dollars

Thomas J. Healey, CFA
Partner
Goldman, Sachs & Company

Soft-dollar arrangements have legitimate uses, but they have also generated several problems: conflict of interest between client and investment manager, increased potential of poor execution, a decrease in market liquidity, an increase in market volatility, an introduction of incentives to consultants to make recommendations on the basis of soft-dollar use, and a potential incentive to increase portfolio turnover. To combat these problems, the industry needs carefully structured disclosure regulations.

Contrary to conventional wisdom, Goldman, Sachs & Company does not want to eliminate soft-dollar arrangements in the securities industry. Instead, we advocate enhanced disclosure.

Defining Soft Dollars

The phrase "soft-dollar arrangement" refers to an arrangement in which a broker receives commissions in excess of the charge for execution services and in return provides other products and services to investment managers and plan sponsors. In a typical soft-dollar arrangement, the executing broker pays a portion of the broker's commission to one or more third-party or independent providers who, in turn, deliver their products or services to specific investment managers or pension plan sponsors designated by the broker. Because the broker usually advances its own funds to pay for these products and services, the investment manager must commit, at least on an informal basis, to transact a sufficient amount of business with the broker to cover the purchase. The amount of commissions that an investment manager must provide is determined by a conversion ratio, which currently averages 1.6 to 1; that is, the manager or sponsor receives \$1.00 of products and services for every \$1.60 in commissions.

Advocates of soft-dollar services have focused their arguments on the provision of third-party products and services that are directly related to market research. This focus is misleading, because the range of products and services purchased by investment managers with soft dollars goes far beyond straight market research. A money manager can also obtain the following types of products and services with its clients' commission dollars: newspapers, magazines, periodicals, computer hardware and software, government publications, calculators, quotation equipment, office equipment and supplies, copying and fax services, legal and accounting services, telecommunications equipment, and electrical equipment. According to a recent study by the Investors Research Corporation, soft-dollar products and services were obtained from almost 600 companies in 1992, including AT&T, Advent Software, B&F Electric Company, *Barron's*, Bell of Pennsylvania, C&P Telephone Company, Citibank, Computer Directions, Computer Peripheral Systems, Coopers & Lybrand, Copifax, Drs. Baker & Gilmour, M.D., *Forbes*, Harvard University, Hewlett Packard, Pacific Bell, Peat Marwick, the *New York Times*, and the *Wall Street Journal*.

History of Soft-Dollar Arrangements

The genesis of soft-dollar arrangements is linked to the abolition of fixed commissions. Before 1975, securities exchanges fixed the rates of commission charged by their members. Brokerage firms competed for clients by offering superior execution and research capabilities. On May 1, 1975, fixed commission rates were abolished. Investment managers then began to fear that, in an era of competitive rates, they could be charged with a breach of fiduciary duty if they selected brokerage firms on any other criterion but minimum commission rates, even if the selected firm provided superior service.

In response to this concern, Congress added Section 28(e) to the Securities Exchange Act of 1934 to ensure the continued availability of quality execution and market research. Section 28(e) provides investment managers who pay more than a minimum commission rate for brokerage and research services with a "safe harbor" from liability. Under Section 28(e), a person exercising investment discretion lawfully may pay commissions to a broker at rates higher than those charged by other brokers as long as the manager determines in good faith that the commission payments are reasonable in light of the value of the brokerage and research services received.

In 1976, the SEC released an interpretation stipulating that the safe harbor did not apply to "products and services . . . readily available and offered to the general public on a commercial basis." Ten years later, however, in 1986, the SEC replaced the 1976 standard with a much broader definition stating that "the controlling principle to be used to determine whether something is research is whether it provides lawful and appropriate assistance to the money manager in the performance of his investment decision-making responsibilities." This broad definition of "research" made possible the current soft-dollar industry.

Since 1986, the use of soft dollars has grown dramatically. According to a 1991 Greenwich Associates survey, soft-dollar equity commissions accounted for $585 million in 1991, representing 33 percent of commissions paid to brokers. Because that figure does not include directed brokerage commissions, it probably understates the magnitude of soft-dollar use. In fact, some industry participants believe the actual figure for soft-dollar commissions is more than $1 billion.

Problems Connected with Soft Dollars

Goldman, Sachs supports the central purpose of Section 28(e): to protect the investment manager that chooses in good faith to pay higher commissions to obtain services in addition to simple execution. The increased use of soft-dollar arrangements creates potential problems, however, both for clients and the market—problems that could be remedied by enhanced disclosure.

First, soft-dollar arrangements involve an inherent conflict between the client's interest in obtaining the highest quality service per commission dollar and the manager's interest in using those same dollars to obtain products and services for itself.

Second, soft-dollar arrangements may lower the quality of trade execution. Soft-dollar brokers typically offer minimal execution services and do not have the distribution capability or the capital required to find the best prices for their clients. The more complicated and larger the trade and the more illiquid the securities, the more likely that the client whose investment manager uses soft-dollar brokers will receive poor execution relative to best price. Consider this simple point: An eighth of a point improvement in the execution price is worth roughly double the average brokerage commission.

Third, the growth of soft-dollar practices has decreased market liquidity and increased market volatility. Full-service broker/dealers like Goldman, Sachs add liquidity to the market by "block positioning" large blocks of securities and by the market expertise, distribution capabilities, and resources they bring to the handling of large "working orders." The growth of soft-dollar practices has reduced liquidity by causing large institutional customers to divert their large but relatively easy trades away from the full-service broker/dealers. An investment manager that has made substantial commitments to soft-dollar brokers in order to obtain their products or services may be compelled to send large orders to those brokers whenever possible. The effect may be, as noted, to hurt the manager's client when a large order could be handled more successfully by a full-service firm.

Moreover, the diversion of the large, easy orders leaves the full-service broker/dealer with only the most difficult trades, including trades in which the commitment of the broker/dealer's own capital is essential. The predictable result is that the number of firms willing to block position has gone down and the cost that institutions must pay for block positioning and the handling of difficult orders has gone up.

This decrease in liquidity has the further effect of increasing the market's volatility. An important function of block positioning is to cushion the effect of the sudden availability for sale of a large block of shares. A substantial loss of block-positioning capacity caused by the diversion of orders to soft-dollar firms can only reduce the size of that cushion.

Finally, many pension plan administrators and other institutional accounts use soft dollars to hire consultants to recommend and monitor the performance of investment managers. Consultants who are paid with soft dollars have no incentive to recommend investment managers who do *not* use soft-dollar brokers, because the consultants' fees depend on the soft dollars generated by commissions. Highly respected managers have complained that consultants have excluded them from the entire universe of investment managers they are prepared to recommend because the managers do not use the services of soft-dollar brokers.

A related concern is that a certain portfolio turnover rate may be necessary to generate enough commissions to meet the consultants' fees. In this case, payments through soft dollars may actually harm investment performance by encouraging turnover.

Proposed Solution

Goldman, Sachs believes that providing clients with information regarding their managers' soft-dollar practices would help eliminate many of these problems. In the words of former U.S. Supreme Court Justice Louis D. Brandeis, "Sunlight remains the world's best disinfectant."

Accordingly, Goldman, Sachs and Morgan Stanley & Company have placed a joint proposal in front of Congress and the SEC for the enhanced disclosure of soft-dollar arrangements. This relatively straightforward proposal is as follows. An investment manager would be required to disclose the following pieces of information to a client:

1. aggregate commissions paid from the client's account;

2. the amount of commissions directed by the client to specific brokers;

3. a breakdown by type of broker of commissions paid to brokers selected by the manager; brokers would be divided into three types:
- brokers that provide execution services only,
- brokers that provide execution services and nonexecution products or services produced in-house by the executing bro-

ker, and
- brokers that provide execution services and nonexecution products or services produced by someone other than the executing broker (i.e., third-party products or services);

this commission information would be provided on two levels: commissions paid from the client's account and aggregate commissions paid from all accounts over which the manager has investment discretion; and

4. a list of the third-party products and services that are purchased by the manager using its aggregate commission dollars, with a comparison of the costs of these products or services in commission dollars with their commercial costs or fair market value.

Disclosure of this information should accomplish the following: make clients aware of the nature and scope of their managers' total commission expenditures, including soft dollars; inform clients of the percentage of their commission dollars paid to soft dollar brokers; allow clients to monitor the process and assess whether the soft dollars are being used to pay costs that should be covered by fees rather than by commissions; and reveal whether soft dollars are cost-effective as a means of purchasing products and services.

The disclosures we propose will not be costly, because the information is already maintained by both brokers and managers. Disclosure is simply the conclusion of the information process—putting the client, such as a pension fund, in a position to understand how its assets, the brokerage commissions, are being used.

The Ethical Implications for Clients of Using Soft Dollars

William F. Quinn
President
AMR Investment Services, Inc.

The investment management industry failed to self-police the use of soft dollars and now faces probable regulations requiring disclosure of such arrangements. In some minds, however, disclosure will not be enough. One policy is to avoid soft dollars entirely.

Soft dollars—in name and in practice—present a serious ethical problem. The practice casts a cloud on our business, our industry, and our profession. Where else can you find a practice like soft dollars? Surely you cannot pay for a car this way, or buy an airline ticket, or pay your mortgage. The time has come for the profession to do something about soft dollars.

Defining Soft Dollars

The dictionary contains two definitions of "soft," both of which apply to soft dollars. One is "not sharply delineated," and clearly, soft-dollar arrangements are not sharply delineated. The second definition is "apt to change," and these arrangements are so soft they are changing all the time.

Basically, with soft dollars, someone is receiving a specified item—such as research, computer software, subscriptions, magazines, or so forth—for an unspecified amount of commission dollars, which is typically based on some level of business. In most cases, the basic commission cost is higher than it would be without the soft-dollar services.

The use of soft dollars is troublesome for two reasons. First, the arrangement is virtually hidden; who is getting what money for what services is not clear. As a result, whether the client is getting good value for the dollars spent is hard to determine. When AMR Investment Services asked our investment managers to review the soft-dollar arrangements in which they were involved, the managers found that, for about 50–60 percent of the research they were receiving, they did not know why they were receiving it or who ordered the research. People who had previously been with the firm had made the arrangements, yet they continued.

The second troublesome aspect of soft dollars is the lack of disclosure. Few managers provide disclosure of what soft-dollar benefits they receive or what they actually direct on behalf of clients. Management contracts, for example, do not contain references to soft-dollar arrangements.

AMR has argued for years that the money management community has a responsibility to take the lead in developing some procedures or disclosure requirements in the area of soft dollars. Now it is too late for the industry: Congress and the SEC are looking at soft dollars, and the regulations and disclosure requirements that result will probably be much more burdensome than if the industry had agreed to self-police the situation.

Soft-Dollar Conflicts

Although soft-dollar arrangements have probably not created large abuses in the pension fund community, the potential for abuse is clearly present. The biggest potential arena of conflict comes from the divergent interests of the money manager and the client. Generally in a money management agreement, the managers agree to provide a service—that is, investing the clients money—for an agreed fee. Part of the service includes providing the tools—the people, computers, research, and so forth—needed to perform the job. Typically, the cost of commissions is paid directly by the client. By using soft dollars to obtain research, the manager is, in effect, charging client an additional fee in terms of higher commission costs. This cost may be particularly large in the mutual fund industry, which has attracted numerous small, relatively unsophisticated investors.

In every trade, the manager has a potential conflict: Is the method of trading going to benefit the client or the manager economically? "Do I do this trade at a higher cost to get research that economically benefits me (i.e., lowers my cost), or do I do it purely on an execution basis, which will result in the best treatment of the client?"

The dilemma has several solutions, but few are practiced. One solution is to quantify the value of the soft dollars and deduct that value from the management fee. This approach may become the solution if the SEC requires disclosure; that is, once managers disclose the value of the soft dollars, plan sponsors will be able to negotiate fees that reflect the value of soft-dollar benefits to the manager. A second solution is to negotiate a fee that includes the trading commission. In this case, managers would absorb the entire cost and would then choose whether to buy their research directly or through soft dollars.

A second major conflict relates to getting best execution when clients have varied trading guidelines. Some clients require their managers to direct certain trades to designated brokers. Others, like AMR, prohibit soft-dollar arrangements. When two clients have such different guidelines, how does the manager get best execution for both clients? Does the manager separate the trades? If so, who goes first, who goes second? What is the impact on the cost? Getting best execution in such circumstances is a real challenge.

Another conflict relating to divergent client needs is the case of one client benefiting at the expense of another. Some managers attempt to treat all trades uniformly by lumping client orders together. So when they are buying stocks, they are buying stocks for all clients, and when they are selling, they are selling for all clients. In this case, the manager would be inclined to combine the trades of, say, AMR (which has requested no soft-dollar arrangements) with those of a client who requires the use of a specific broker (presumably because the client will receive certain soft-dollar services). If these trades are combined, AMR's commission dollars will be subsidizing another client rather than AMR or its plan.

A fourth area of conflict is the manager's decision on a broker. The manager's role as the client's fiduciary is to negotiate the best execution, including commissions, for the client. It is hard for a client to be objective when a penny higher commission will result in an economic benefit to the manager. Managers will argue that the extra penny is worth the cost

because the broker will provide liquidity in the future if it is needed. This argument may be true, but AMR would feel better about paying that extra penny to get liquidity if the manager was not receiving soft-dollar services. Additionally, we believe our managers have a responsibility to us to monitor the broker's performance. Soft-dollar arrangements reduce our willingness to believe that the manager is totally objective in evaluating a broker.

A fifth conflict, one that involves managers indirectly, is the use of soft dollars by plan sponsors to obtain services that otherwise could not be purchased because of budget constraints. A plan sponsor might, for example, direct a certain volume of commissions to a specific broker in return for a new computer. In these cases, the true beneficiary of the plan is paying more than stated in an approved cash budget for the services of the pension plan administrator.

In light of the various conflicts, in about 1985, AMR developed a simple policy on soft dollars:

1. We ask our managers not to direct any commissions to pay for any of their research.

2. We ask our managers to submit a quarterly report of their trades listing the broker, amount, and what additional services, such as research, they may have received. AMR managers frequently tell us that research is an extra that is thrown in; they really do not want it, but they are getting it anyway. Nonetheless, we like to evaluate that service. We also recognize that we are going to pay more for principal trades, and we are willing to do that.

3. We tell our managers not to direct any commissions on our behalf. We prefer to pay cash if we think we need something rather than obtain it through soft dollars.

By following these simple principles, we believe we have eliminated most of the conflicts that are inherent in soft-dollar environments.

Conclusion

Soft dollars create so many conflicts that we believe they should be eliminated, which is what we advocated at the hearings held by the U.S. House Subcommittee on Telecommunications and Finance on this subject last summer. The consensus of that hearing, however, was to require full disclosure, thereby allowing sophisticated investors to find out the facts and negotiate knowledgeably with their managers. We believe disclosure will not work; too many parties are involved to allow proper policing of them. Therefore, the best practice is to eliminate soft dollars whenever possible.

Question and Answer Session

Robert A. Anselmi
Thomas J. Healey, CFA
William F. Quinn

Question: Are using airline frequent flier miles or similar benefits really any different from using soft dollars?

Quinn: There is a basic difference. In frequent flier programs, the employer knows exactly what is being spent on airfare and has the option of asking the employee to apply the miles to future business trips or of using them to reward the employee for doing all that traveling. Soft dollars should be handled the same way. Clients want to know what is being spent for what services.

Obtaining that information is very difficult currently; the managers do not compile it. With that type of information, however, the client would have the option of saying, "Yes, continue to do what you are doing" or "No, find a lower cost way of executing the trade."

Question: If third-party products and services are by definition commercially available, why not require managers to pay for them directly?

Anselmi: Many managers would be quite willing to pay out of their own pockets for third-party products and services. The way J.P. Morgan Investment uses soft dollars is an alternative. We generally pick brokers without regard for the soft-dollar services they might provide. We are not going to those firms specifically for soft-dollar services, nor are we compromising our objective of best execution. So in that sense,

everything incremental we can receive from those brokers has added value. We are, in effect, extracting added value from those firms by having them provide incremental products and services.

Question: Would J.P. Morgan Investment be willing to disclose information regarding soft-dollar practices?

Anselmi: We have in the past and will in the future provide our clients any data they wish regarding how we have used their commission dollars—including a listing of the products and services purchased with commissions as well as any other commission-related information. As I emphasized, commissions are the property of the client.

Our experience has been, however, that disclosure sometimes causes a dilemma for the client; that is, the client does not know what to do with the information provided or how to evaluate it. A client can certainly judge the value of an airline ticket relative to a research product, but whether or not a particular product has added value to the portfolio is sometimes difficult for clients to assess.

Question: How can calculators or copying, fax, or accounting services pass for "research" under Section 28(e)? Has anyone dealt with this question in an SEC examination, or have any legal or regulatory precedents been set? Please clarify what may be legally acquired with soft dollars.

Healey: The 1986 interpretive release said that the controlling principle to determine whether something is research is whether it provides lawful and appropriate assistance for the money manager in the performance of his or her investment decision-making responsibilities. I do not know whether a specific SEC description of what that language includes exists, but it is generally interpreted by everyone certainly to include data and physical equipment used as part of those responsibilities.

Question: Does AMR Investment Services receive research from, say, Goldman, Sachs or Morgan Stanley? If so, how do you pay for it?

Quinn: No, we do not receive research. We don't manage any money in-house, so we have no need for the services of those types of firms. For the services we do use, such as Value Line's and Standard & Poor's reports, we pay cash.

Question: Some brokers have begun to treat traditional principal transactions—that is, fixed-income transactions—as agency trades for conversion to soft dollars. What is J.P. Morgan Investment's opinion of those practices?

Anselmi: We do not engage in those practices. I believe the SEC has stated that principal transactions are not eligible for the safe-harbor provisions of Section 28(e). Nevertheless, several brokerage firms do categorize riskless principal transactions as eligible for soft-dollar credit. In fact, some brokers now reflect "commissions" on such transactions, rather than the traditional dealer markup.

Question: What are your attitudes toward complete unbundling of research costs from execution expenses?

Quinn: We favor unbundling the services because it would accomplish some of our objectives. That is, brokers would then be able to do execution-only trades for us and do something different for another client. Unbundling would make clear who is getting what.

Healey: The way we look at the world is that clients can receive a valuable service from an execution-only broker and they can also receive a valuable service from a full-service broker, and in a competitive world, if both exist, the clients get to choose which or what combination of the two kinds to use. I am not against unbundling, but I don't believe the whole world needs to be unbundled or that being totally unbundled is going to be better for the client. Let the marketplace sort it out.

Anselmi: Although identifying the cost of proprietary research would generally be helpful to fiduciaries, the question of complete unbundling is complicated. Generally, when an investment management firm deals with a full-service brokerage, the investment manager develops a relationship with that firm that typically encompasses multiple products and services. So, even though the manager might have the brokerage firm unbundle and identify the cost of research on the equity side of the business, that approach might not ultimately result in true unbundling because brokers have never clearly articulated or explicitly priced the variables associated with trade execution (capital commitment, liquidity, etc.) and because brokers generally will consider the breadth and depth of client relationships in setting the prices for such variables. Simply unbundling research, therefore, probably won't solve the entire problem for most firms.

AIMR Performance Presentation Standards: Consultant Perspective

Martin F. Ryan
Managing Director
Russell Data Services

Implementation of the Performance Presentation Standards is well under way, but some aspects remain confusing to managers and plan sponsors; most troublesome are how many composites a manager should have and whether those composites should be verified. In addition, plan sponsors need to understand that the standards do not replace their responsibilities to understand the data they receive on the performance of composites, individual accounts, and portfolios. Because the use of composites is increasing, displaying dispersion within composites by using ellipses may be a beneficial new approach.

Implementing the AIMR Performance Presentation Standards[1] is not always straightforward. Basically, the PPS are an attempt to assist a plan sponsor in the manager selection process by providing comparability among performance results and to provide fairness to money managers by allowing them to demonstrate their skills. Although one of the goals of the standards is to instill confidence among users of performance information, some confusion still exists about what the standards are and how they are being implemented. In some instances, the additional disclosures and footnotes add to the client's confusion rather than clarify the information.

This presentation provides an update on the implementation of the PPS in the United States from a consultant's viewpoint, focusing on the vital role the plan sponsor plays in further implementation of the PPS. The presentation ends with a discussion of a potentially beneficial new way to display dispersion within composites.

Implementation Update

Overall, the implementation process rates a grade of B or B–. Clearly, many managers have a strong desire to comply with the standards and an even stronger desire to be able to claim compliance. Managers are confused, however, about some aspects of implementing the standards. The two areas causing the most confusion are how many composites a manager should have and whether those composites should be verified. In addition, managers' endeavors to provide full disclosure can lead to numerous footnotes. Anyone who has read an annual report that has 50 or 60 notes knows that a host of footnotes creates general unease in the reader.

In grading PPS implementation to date, an important facet is what the expectation was for implementation. Implementing new performance standards takes time, and the AIMR standards are no exception. A good example of the problems encountered by new standards is the experience of the Bank Administration Institute.

BAI performance measurement standards focused on performance calculation of time-weighted and dollar-weighted rates of return and were implemented in 1969 after nine years of discussion about the need for a standard calculation. Twenty years later, an article in the *Wall Street Journal* showed, as reprinted in **Table 1**, ten calculations of the total return of the S&P 500 Index for 1988 by ten relatively prestigious organizations. A 54-basis-point spread resulted for the return as calculated by the ten organizations. All ten no doubt believed they were complying with the BAI standard calculation for total return, but their results depended on judgments and choices.

So, the goal of a single, precise answer to "how to comply" is not easy to attain. Industry partici-

[1]See Appendix B.

Table 1. Total Return Calculations for the S&P 500 Index

Firm	1986	1987	1988
Indata	18.50%	5.10%	16.30%
Salomon Brothers	18.50	5.60	16.34
Frank Russell	18.23	5.16	16.50
CDA Investment	18.60	5.20	16.50
Lipper Analytical	18.71	5.25	16.55
SEI Corp.	18.67	5.25	16.60
Standard & Poor's Corp.	18.50	5.10	16.61
Mellon Bank	18.28	5.11	16.64
American National Bank	18.47	5.23	16.81
Wilshire Associates	18.55	5.23	16.83
Bankers Trust	18.66	5.13	16.84

Source: *Wall Street Journal* (January 26, 1989).

pants should be realistic about what they are going to achieve with any standard. Moreover, recipients of the data need to know that a statement of standards does not assure that everybody is applying the standards consistently.

The Role of the Plan Sponsor

Plan sponsors are key to increasing adoption of the PPS. If plan sponsors demand that data they receive be compliant, it will be. Russell Data Services is receiving more and more demand for compliance, especially in requests for proposal from public funds. Our clients have been fairly clear, however, that they do not want Russell to incur and pass on to them any incremental costs associated with complying with the standards. Clients do not want to pay, for example, for money managers to have their composites audited. Although evaluating money managers is an important activity, it is only a small part of a plan sponsor's job.

The primary responsibility of plan sponsors is to create the proper manager structure for the entire portfolio. In creating that structure, the plan sponsor's job is to look for different investment approaches, different portfolio characteristics, and opportunities to increase return and reduce risk. Basically, with respect to manager structure, the PPS focus on the manager search or selection process. In addressing risk and return, the PPS focus on the composite rather than the portfolio. Thus, the PPS are applicable to only a small part of the task of monitoring manager performance.

Plan sponsors have a major obligation to understand the data they are seeing. When they look at performance data, they need to ask: Am I looking at an individual-manager account or a composite? How was that composite constructed? What is the universe against which it is being compared? For this type of analysis, the underlying individual port-

folios are more useful than a composite. Analytical techniques that illustrate the dispersion of returns within a universe provide more useful information than a composite alone. Composites and benchmark portfolios can be useful, however, if included in these presentations.

Plan sponsors must also be aware of the fact that composites have different risk and return characteristics from individual portfolios. Typically, a composite, unless it has perfect correlation with an individual portfolio, will have lower volatility than that individual portfolio.

Another factor plan sponsors need to understand is that risk is a function of the time period being measured and the portfolios used in the calculation. Most analytical techniques, such as scatter plots, use only those portfolios that met the time-period criterion; they do not use all of the portfolios that might be in a composite for a longer period of time. For example, a three-year scatter plot will include only the accounts in existence for that three-year period, which may be only a subset of the number of accounts in a ten-year composite.

Finally, plan sponsors must understand exactly what has been included in a composite and how appropriate the index or universe is to that composite.

Dispersion in Composites

Despite the limitations of using composites rather than individual accounts to analyze portfolio characteristics and performance, the use of composites is increasing. Therefore, Russell has been researching a way to present the dispersion in composites. The result is an approach that uses ellipses to capture the dispersion factor.

Figure 1 shows a simple three-year risk–return scatter diagram for the Russell growth universe. It also shows an ellipse that includes 60 percent of the

Figure 1. Growth Universe and Growth Ellipse, Three Years Ending March 31, 1993

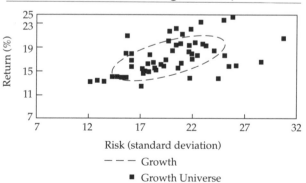

Source: Frank Russell Co.

accounts in that universe of managers. The percentage of accounts included in the ellipse can be varied, and we are still researching what the appropriate percentage should be.

The next step involves adding the composite. **Figure 2** shows the original growth universe ellipse (without the underlying points in order to clarify the

Figure 2. Growth Composite versus Growth Universe, March 31, 1993

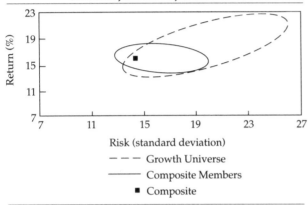

Risk (standard deviation)

− − − Growth Universe
――― Composite Members
■ Composite

Source: Frank Russell Co.

presentation) and a similar ellipse that represents all the portfolios in the composite plus a point for the composite itself. No particular reward results from

taking additional risk with the manager represented by this ellipse.

We believe this graphical presentation provides better information on the risk and return characteristics of composites relative to individual portfolios than a standard scatter plot. This approach shows how tight or loose the dispersion of a composite is. Most people find the more traditional tabular form much harder to comprehend than the ellipses. Another advantage of this approach is that it can be expanded to include the presentation of multiple styles—for example, growth versus value—which allows rapid comparison.

Conclusion

The implementation of the PPS in the United States has encountered some problems, but it is progressing. Plan sponsors are the key to implementation, but standards are not a substitute for understanding; sponsors must know when to use a composite and when to look at an individual account. They must also know how the composite was constructed and when and how to select an appropriate index or benchmark. Finally, ellipse graphs appear to provide a superior mechanism for communicating results from investment managers to plan sponsors and from sponsors to their boards.

AIMR Performance Presentation Standards: Implementation Update

R. Charles Tschampion, CFA
Vice President, Portfolio Strategy and Manager Relations
General Motors Investment Management Corporation

An understanding of current implementation of the Performance Presentation Standards, including recommended verification standards, requires an understanding of their ethical framework: full disclosure, fair representation, comparability, and minimum requirements. Enforcement rests primarily on increasing client pressure, which also increases peer pressure, on AIMR, and on the support of the SEC. A committee and subcommittee structure buttress the ethical underpinnings while adapting the details of the standards to changes in the industry.

When the committee for Performance Presentation Standards was formed in 1986, one of the biggest areas of concern was the lack of standardization in performance reporting within the industry. This deficiency left the door wide open for practitioner misrepresentation and for confusion and mistrust among clients and potential clients. Industry leaders believed that, in the presentations of their historical investment results, some money managers—certainly not all of them, and not all to the same degree, but some—were misrepresenting their firms' abilities to invest.

The techniques for presenting performance in the best light, although subtle, were numerous. One technique involved careful selection of the beginning and ending points of a performance period. Managers would make the period selections in such a way that they could claim above-market performance even if only for a 24-hour period. Another technique was to use "representative portfolios," which may or may not have been truly representative of a manager's actual portfolio returns but, from the examples one can see from that period, were all clearly able to beat the market. An even more subtle method involved allowing the magic of survivorship bias to work its wonders on past history—that is, ignoring the records of clients who had left the manager (probably because of poor performance) and reporting only the history of those clients who remained. In addition, some managers were comparing results against inappropriate benchmarks.

The committee's task was to develop a set of presentation standards that would promote consistent and ethical representation of managers' investment results. The outcome, now known as the Performance Presentation Standards (PPS), was a set of guiding ethical principles that are intended to achieve, first and foremost, full disclosure and fair representation.[1] A secondary objective was to ensure uniformity in reporting so that results would be directly comparable among investment managers.

This presentation begins with the most important prerequisite to understanding today's implementation of the standards: understanding the standards' ethical framework. The discussion then turns to a current major implementation issue—verification—to an update on enforcement of the standards, and to the ongoing activities of the PPS Implementation Committee.

Ethical Framework

The PPS are not a set of rules that must be adhered to rigidly as in following a cookbook recipe. Instead, some aspects of the standards are mandatory and others are recommended. Of course, not every situation can be anticipated, so meeting the goals of full disclosure and fair representation also means making a conscientious, good-faith effort to present investment results in a manner consistent with the

---

[1] See Appendix B for a copy of the Performance Presentation Standards.

underlying ethical principles of the standards. The ethical framework adopted by the committee comprises four elements: full disclosure, fair representation, comparability, and minimum requirements.

■ *Full disclosure.* Managers should tell a client everything the client needs to know to assess the performance of the firm. If in doubt about whether information should be disclosed, disclose it.

■ *Fair representation.* Managers must present the entire record of the firm—that is, all assets for all time periods.

■ *Comparability.* In order to facilitate comparisons among managers, managers should adhere to the recommended calculations, such as the use of a time-weighted rate of return, and use appropriate benchmarks. Such procedures enable a client to examine any manager's numbers and feel comfortable that nothing in the calculation biases the numbers in one way or another.

■ *Minimum requirements.* The PPS provide only minimum standards of performance presentation. To meet the ethical standard of full disclosure and fair representation, managers may have to go beyond the minimum mandatory requirements and disclosures. Each firm has to determine the most appropriate presentation. No body of rules is going to make a person ethical who does not want to be ethical.

Verification

Verification has attracted considerable comment from clients, managers, and verifiers and thus merits some clarification. The standards recommend, but do not require, verification of claims that performance is in compliance. Verification must be performed by an independent party, which does not have to be a Certified Public Accountant.

Two levels of verification are possible. Level I verification applies to the firm; Level II includes Level I verification and applies to specific composites.

Level I is the important one from the standpoint of whether the performance presentation is in compliance with the standards. Level I verification attests to the fact that all of a firm's actual, discretionary, fee-paying portfolios are included in at least one composite. Examination procedures generally include verification of the following: Portfolios are in appropriate composites, additions and deletions to the composites have been made in accordance with the standards, exclusions are accurate, all time periods are included, time-weighted rates of return have been used, composites are asset weighted, and the

required disclosures are included.

Level II is like a standard audit of an account. A Level II verification examines both the investment management process (tests of validity and propriety of underlying shares, income, and pricing data) and the measurement of performance (computation and presentation of performance data).

Enforcement

Four elements are contributing to the PPS enforcement program. The first is peer pressure resulting from investment managers' clients endorsing the PPS. Investment managers should realize that doing a good ethical job and making a full and fair presentation of their performance will be an advantage to them in the eyes of clients. Furthermore, as awareness and understanding of the standards grow, clients will begin to require presentation using the standards, which will attract even more managers to the standards. Eventually, the minority of managers not adhering to the standards could very well draw suspicion to themselves about their reasons for not complying.

The second element of enforcement may prove to be the SEC. From the beginning, the SEC has been informed about the standards, and the commission's responses have been quite supportive of AIMR's work in this area. SEC staff examiners are also aware of the standards and have been known to refer to them during compliance audits.

The third element of enforcement is AIMR itself. The PPS have been incorporated in AIMR's Standards of Professional Conduct as Standard III F. The key requirement is that members present fair, accurate, and complete performance information. Members must also inform their employers of the standards, encourage their employers to adopt and use the standards, and use a reasonable effort to ensure firm compliance with the performance standards.

If members comply with the PPS, then they are in compliance with Standard III F and they can make the following statement on their performance presentation material: "This report has been prepared and presented in compliance with the Performance Presentation Standards of the Association for Investment Management and Research."

Where members get into trouble is in making that statement even though they are *not* in compliance. In that case, they are subject to penalties varying from private censure to revocation of the CFA charter or AIMR membership. Of course, this element applies only to AIMR members, so it does not deter all potential abusers of performance presentation ethics.

The ultimate enforcers are the clients. They must take responsibility for understanding the specific requirements and ethical framework of the standards and thereby become effective monitors of the performance presentation of their managers. In other words, the best enforcement of the PPS is going to be that the end users, such as the pension plan sponsors, know what the standards contain, know what is required, and be able to evaluate the accuracy, fairness, and representativeness of a performance presentation.

Verification provides clients with some comfort that a presentation is in compliance with AIMR standards, but clients should never totally delegate to a verifier their responsibility for both monitoring the performance of managers and assuring that full and fair disclosure is made in performance presentation.

Ongoing Implementation Activities

Because the PPS are considered to be dynamic, AIMR has established a PPS Implementation Committee to maintain and support the standards. The committee's overall goal is to continue to respond to industry change while maintaining focus on the strong ethical framework established with the PPS. To achieve this goal, the committee has appointed several subcommittees to address outstanding implementation issues

■ *International*. Probably the most active subcommittee today, this group is working hard to develop guidelines for implementing the standards outside the United States and Canada.

■ *Bank Trust*. This subcommittee is dealing with the specific problems that bank trust departments have with respect to compliance.

■ *Real Estate*. The unique characteristics of real estate and how they might relate to the standards is the focus of this subcommittee.

■ *Venture Capital and Private Placements*. This subcommittee is focusing on the use of time-weighted rates of return and whether those rates are appropriate for long-term private placements with payoff patterns of the type that venture-capital and many corporate finance debt/equity investments may have.

■ *Wrap Fee*. This subcommittee is looking at the issue of wrap fees. Primarily, it is trying to differentiate what part of the fee institutional managers should be taking out of their "gross of fees" performance calculation, such as commissions and market-impact costs, and what part they should not be taking out, namely, their investment management fees.

■ *Taxable Portfolios*. This subcommittee is dealing with the various issues of taxable portfolios.

Conclusion

The PPS are here to stay, and the Implementation Committee is here to assure that the PPS remain attuned to the dynamics of the investment profession. Although the committee will amend the standards' details as necessary to make the PPS responsive to the needs of AIMR's heterogeneous constituency, the committee's main purpose will be to maintain a basic ethical framework for the presentation of performance.

AIMR Performance Presentation Standards: International Implementation

Iain W. McAra
Senior Performance Analyst
Baring International Investment, Limited

Applying the AIMR Performance Presentation Standards to global investment portfolios and composites is complicated by the need to consider exchange rates, base currencies, country weights, hedging, different benchmarks, regional compositions, and local laws, tax treatments, and restrictions. In addition to these factors, uncertainties as to the future direction of AIMR's and other standards and of client demands places a premium on managerial flexibility and a sophisticated, automated system for gathering and combining data.

Performance presentation is an area of concern not only for those who actually produce the data but also for those who present the data throughout the industry. The AIMR standards have received a lot of attention, but other organizations are struggling with similar problems around the world. In the United Kingdom, for example, the National Association of Pension Funds reported in December 1990 that it had "... found signs of less desirable practices, especially in the use of performance measurement statistics by Consultants, Investment Managers and Pension Funds themselves."

This presentation addresses implementation of the AIMR Performance Presentation Standards (PPS) outside the United States and Canada—that is, the so-called "international standards."[1] Implementation of the standards for U.S. and Canadian portfolios occurred in 1993; implementation for international portfolios is scheduled for 1994. The discussion considers what firms can do to facilitate complying with the PPS for international portfolios today and tomorrow, and it outlines the conditions needed for the PPS to become the world standard for performance presentation in the future.

Implementing the PPS Internationally

The international PPS are based on the fundamental principles that underlie the domestic standards: to promote full and fair representation and to ensure uniformity in reporting, thereby enabling comparisons among portfolios. Users of PPS-compliant results should be able to look at the information and understand what it is, from what it is derived, what it is representing, and what it is not implying. The fundamental requirements underlying the domestic standards are: (1) no selectivity in the presentation of results and (2) no selectivity in the production of results. In other words, the investment manager cannot pick and choose the time frames to use and cannot cherry-pick the ingredients that go into the production of the results. Performance of the entity must be presented in total to claim compliance with PPS.

International managers must deal with performance presentation issues that go beyond those faced by domestic managers. For example, they deal with exchange rates and base currencies, country weights, hedging, and various different local laws. In addition, the construction of benchmarks is more complicated internationally than domestically. Because of the added complexity, the PPS contain additional requirements and call for additional disclosures when presenting PPS-compliant international portfolio results. The standards also provide flexibility in definitions to accommodate variation, making implementation a reasonable and realistic undertaking for most firms. The following discussions illustrate how the standards have been adapted for the realities of cross-border investing.

---

[1]See Appendix B for a copy of AIMR's Performance Presentation Standards.

Compliance

Being in compliance is a concept that applies uniquely to the total of the assets being presenting. For example, a manager cannot state that a single composite is "in compliance," because that composite represents only a part of the total assets under management and, therefore, does not meet the full-representation requirement. Compliance with the standards must be on a firmwide or total-entity basis.

This concept is fairly straightforward when the standards are being implemented for a clearly defined entity such as a domestic market, but it becomes complicated when the standards are to be implemented in a global market with different currencies, regions of investments, tax laws, etc. The PPS include the following statement to aid implementation in an international environment: "If an autonomous investment firm is itself owned by a larger holding company, or if a subsidiary or division is registered or holds itself out to the public as a separate entity, it may claim full compliance for itself without its parent organization being in compliance."[2]

Firms can work quite effectively within these requirements because they can consider all the assets under management and ask whether a certain group is an "entity" as defined. For some firms, putting all their operational entities in compliance with the standards would be pointless at this time. For example, taking a Japanese domestic portfolio and making it comply would be pointless because the Japanese have little interest in AIMR and Japanese clients are not necessarily interested in U.S-style performance measurement statistics.

The next question is: Having arrived at a set of assets under management that are recognized as an entity, what portfolios must be considered and included in the composites in order to be in compliance?

Composite Construction

The PPS state that all actual fee-paying discretionary portfolios must be included in at least one composite and each composite must comprise portfolios or asset classes that represent a similar strategy or investment objective. But what constitutes a discretionary portfolio in international terms?

AIMR states that the definition of "nondiscretionary" depends on the particular strategy the manager is following. Thus, in international applications, AIMR has given managers the flexibility to "manipulate" the standards to meet their own needs.

However, although what was a rigid set of guidelines has apparently been destroyed to accom-

modate international managers, an iron fist lies within the flexible velvet glove, namely, the additional set of clearly defined disclosures that must accompany the definitions. **Figure 1** illustrates this concept for an entity.

Figure 1. Flexibility of the PPS

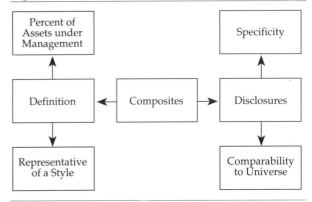

Source: Baring Asset Management.

The schematic in Figure 1 shows the trade-off between definitions and disclosures in defining composites. A tight definition of a composite leads to fewer disclosures, increased specificity, and a smaller percentage of the assets under management complying with the definition. A loose definition, complemented by increased disclosures, leads to less specificity but a higher percentage of assets under management being included under the definition. For a particular composite, the sum of the definitions and disclosures should result in full and fair disclosure of the assets within that composite. The more specific the definition, the more composites; the looser the definition, the more disclosures. In the end, all the elements sum to a full and fair disclosure and representation of the entity.

With the variation existing in international portfolios, (base currency, benchmarks, regional composition, tax treatments, hedging policy, country restrictions, weighting regimes, and so on), a measurer could present several sets of composites for each entity—each set of composites compiled using a different selection of portfolio characteristics, and each set of composites summing to the entity. In addition, for each set of composites, all the disclosures have to be provided. Therefore, the volume of work required is enormous.

The Baring group's approach to this issue has been to create a data base of portfolios that can be aggregated into composites based on similar mandates or restrictions. This approach gives us the ability to construct composites on a variety of levels according to the relevant audience. The data base

---

[2]Section III of the Performance Presentation Standards; see Appendix B.

comprises, for each portfolio, all the mandated restrictions and policy restrictions that are used when managing those assets. The data are stored on a monthly basis, so when we receive a request from a consultant or from a party that is interested in Baring International, for example, we can actually construct composites that are in compliance by using the restrictions that are used when managing the money to define the composite style. Thus, we have integrated the concept of managing money and reporting results, and we have automated it so as to respond quickly to the questions being asked.

Basically, the approach rests on effective data capture and control. We control the numbers and the concepts/ideas involving asset management; then, we can respond effectively to the marketplace concerning our products and results.

Recommendations for Managers

The current state of AIMR and other standards regarding performance presentation around the world places a premium on managerial flexibility and sophisticated data gathering. Specifically:

▪ *The standards are dynamic.* The AIMR standards are under continuous study, and other national organizations are also interested in some form of standardization in performance presentation. Therefore, a thorough data base that can respond to different international presentation and disclosure requirements is critical.

▪ *The standards contain both recommended and mandatory elements.* As people live with the AIMR and other standards methods that are now "strongly recommended" will migrate into the "mandatory" category. Again, flexibility and a comprehensive data base will allow managers to adapt to this inevitable evolution.

▪ *Definitions and disclosures require a balancing act.* Managers have to cope with the trade-off between definitions and disclosures, particularly with regard to the AIMR definition of composites and their representation of the asset base. Clearly, automation helps in this balancing.

▪ *A variety of requests for proposals.* At present, particularly in the international marketplace, managers must cope with a huge variety of requests for performance information. Even if requests for proposals (RFPs) become more standardized in the future, which should occur as the PPS become more widely adopted, flexibility and automation will be needed to respond to varied RFPs.

▪ *Future verification mandates are unknown.* Probably the biggest unknown with respect to performance presentation standards worldwide is how verification will evolve within the industry. So,

again, a premium is placed on flexibility and automation in international investment management.

Looking Ahead

By now, most investment managers have encountered the PPS either because they are members of AIMR or because they have seen the PPS reflected in RFPs. Many, however, do not yet understand the standards or the purpose of the standards. To ensure the integrity of the standards and their adoption internationally, at least three things have to happen.

First, the standards must be used properly within the industry. We cannot allow interpretations that are slightly dubious or too free to become part of the psyche of the industry; if we do, the very reason for the standards' existence will become diluted.

Second, if verification is to be the one thing that keeps the standards on the straight and narrow, then we have to pay a lot of attention to verification and to what verification implies. Performance must be verified on a total-entity basis. Verification of a particular presentation or a particular composite does not provide the necessary full and fair representation of all the assets under management.

Finally, the goal for the industry should be global consistency and global acceptance of the PPS. We must not underestimate the complexity of the industry. The approach should be to move the PPS forward as a multinational concept rather than restricting it to a U.S. client base. AIMR should work with other organizations—such as the National Association of Pension Funds in the United Kingdom, which is interested in performance calculation standards—to integrate standards.

In the end, the task boils down to one of education. It is up to us to help people around the world realize exactly what the standards are and to educate them about the benefits they will derive from the standards. If we can do that, then we will have international standards that are workable.

Conclusion

The French writer and diplomat Joseph de Maistre said in the early 19th century, "Every nation has the government it deserves." We could say the same today for our industry with regard to performance presentation standards. All international investors have the opportunity, and are asked, to provide input into the specific requirements to be included in worldwide PPS; if nobody bothers to provide the input, the industry will end up with exactly the standards it deserves, which will not be the best or the most pertinent. The choice is ours.

Question and Answer Session

Martin F. Ryan
R. Charles Tschampion, CFA
Iain W. McAra

Question: How much did coming into compliance with the PPS cost the Baring group? How much would it have cost if you had not created the new computer system?

McAra: That question is very difficult to answer because the new computer system offers a lot of benefits beyond coming into compliance with the AIMR standards, such as improved ways of analyzing the data and analyzing performance attribution. For a firm the size of the Baring group, implementing the standards could probably cost £250,000 for time and materials, including computers and related developments.

The biggest cost in coming into compliance is actually the time spent by professionals determining how to implement the standards. Firms do not need complex systems to come into compliance if they are presenting their data only in one standard format, but monthly calculations of even ten composites covering 30 funds will take appreciable amounts of time. People have to understand the standards, and working out how they are actually going to implement them takes a lot of time and thought.

Question: In your most recent searches for investment managers, are you requiring or is your client requesting independent verification of performance numbers?

Ryan: Verification of the per-

formance information is not relevant to our consulting clients because we provide analyses for them that use the underlying portfolio data. Our trust company, however, is seeing an increasing desire, particularly from the public funds, for data that are in compliance with the AIMR standards.

Tschampion: General Motors Investment Management does not require verification, primarily because we believe we can perform the verification ourselves. Increasing numbers of clients, however, are requiring verification. Personally, as I said, I believe the verification function is the responsibility of the plan sponsor and should not be dealt with simply by requiring it in RFPs. RFPs should not require compliance, and verification, without also providing a forum for disclosure. Cases may exist in which a manager is not in technical compliance but has a reasonable explanation for the circumstances. That manager should have the right to be considered in a search. This aspect relates to the issues of sponsors assuming the responsibility for enforcement and the reasonable promulgation of the standards that are meant to help them.

Question: Does General Motors Investment Management require that its managers be in compliance with the standards? If so, does their history have to be in compliance?

Tschampion: The standards are

intended primarily for prospective managers and marketing efforts. Obviously, we want our managers to present their performance in accordance with the basic principles of the standards, such as using a time-weighted rate of return, but we do not require them to comply with the standards.

Question: Some people think the guidelines for presenting supplemental information are not clear. From an ethical perspective, please discuss how supplemental information should be presented?

Ryan: This issue is not excessively complex. With minimal expenditure of time and money, a firm should be able to present supplemental information on a separate sheet of paper that makes adequate disclosure of the situation. The client can then make a judgment about the relative performance numbers.

The client must also consider the qualitative factors surrounding the supplemental information, particularly if the supplemental information relates to portability situations. From the consultant's perspective, in the case of portability, the notion that performance stays with the firm does not mean that the consultant's recommendation stays with the firm. Our recommendation is based on two criteria: first, whether we are comfortable that the performance in the past will continue; second, whether the key people in the investment process—research analysts, portfolio managers, and so forth—are still with the firm.

Many questions surround the idea of presenting the data separately, such as whether the risk profile of a manager who becomes the owner of a firm remains the same as when that person was a portfolio manager. We have a lot of evidence that it does not; the risk profile changes greatly when managers go out on their own. In these situations, as in others, the end users have to be alert and aware of what they are seeing.

McAra: Disclosure is the key. Clients can always come back and ask for additional information and clarification of a situation. The disclosures in the standards are probably the minimum that are required. Managers should provide sufficient information to answer the questions in a full and fair way, and the answers required cannot be automated because the questions vary so much. We must not forget, however, that performance numbers are not the sole criterion for hiring or firing a manager; to put all the emphasis on the numbers alone would be wrong.

Question: Can an institutional investment management group of a bank that also has a substantial private banking operation define the two divisions separately? Could one division come into compliance and the other not come into compliance?

Tschampion: Basically, the standards say that the firm is the entire bank and everything has to be included. The rationale is that the bank entity includes every account, no matter how small. Some people believe this interpretation is unfair to bank trust departments, but look at it from the

client's perspective: Clearly, the standards are intended to improve the presentation to the small clients.

AIMR is aware of the administrative burden the standards place on bank trust departments, however, and is reviewing recommendations from the subcommittee on these issues. The focus of the recommendations is to enhance the definition of "nondiscretionary." The spirit of the standards is that managers cannot exclude a whole bunch of clients from the performance presentation just because including them is costly.

Moderator: If a bank has spun off a separately registered investment subsidiary that is recognized as a separate entity, however, the bank can be in compliance for the investment subsidiary without being in compliance for the bank trust department. The interpretation depends on how the bank is structured.

McAra: This issue has two aspects—one relating to discretion and one to definition of the entity. Once you have defined your entity, you can also define your discretionary portfolios. You can consider "discretion" in three ways.

First, all portfolios will have some form of restriction on them, even if it is only "prudent management" of those assets. Those portfolios are in no way considered nondiscretionary, so you simply practice prudent asset management.

Second, a set of portfolios might have well-recognized restrictions, such as mandates against investing in South Africa or against hedging. Those sets can be considered separate composites of which only the assets within a composite must comply with a particular set of restric-

tions. The result may well be, say, eight different determinants resulting in, maybe, 32 different composites into which all the assets go.

Finally, some portfolios may have restrictions that are so strict the manager does not, in fact, have investment discretion. Those composites are not reflective of the manager's style, and they are the nondiscretionary portfolios. This situation is particularly likely to occur in private banking operations.

Question: Many brokers present the performance of their research recommendations; that is, they show the results of their recommended list. Is this practice in compliance with the standards?

Moderator: The performance of a recommended list would not be in compliance because it does not represent the actual performance of assets under management. It would be more like a model portfolio.

Question: Given the complexities of handling wrap fees in composites, should all wrap accounts of the same type be grouped together in composites separate from fee-plus-commission accounts, or should the accounts be combined?

Tschampion: That question is hard to answer because the issue is really how to deal with wrap accounts within the construct of the requirement to present results gross of fees as well as the fee schedule that applies. As I noted, a subcommittee is examining this issue. The challenge is to harmonize the wrap accounts so they can be integrated with fee-plus-commission accounts, not merely integrated within the firm but integrated in terms of comparisons between one firm and another that the client might want to make. Brokers could certainly group all their wrap-fee accounts, if they were otherwise groupable, into a single composite and identify it as such. Perhaps that approach would help the client, but it is not really addressing the main issue the Wrap Fee Subcommittee is addressing.

Question: What is AIMR doing to clarify the issues relating to performance presentation for taxable accounts?

Tschampion: The Taxable Portfolios Subcommittee of the PPS Implementation Committee is reviewing the key issues relating to reporting the performance of taxable accounts. This report will be published in early 1994.

The issue is very complex. The subcommittee continues the recommendation, as in the original guidelines, that performance be reported gross of taxes (following the same idea of reporting gross of management fees), which allows people to apply their own tax rates. On the other hand, the subcommittee is analyzing what information would be helpful to people when they are making comparisons specific to their own situations. The subcommittee has looked at the *Morningstar* reports and the type of information these reports recommend. The subcommittee is looking at additional recommended disclosures, such as breaking out realized gains and unrealized gains so that people can get an idea of the future taxable impact of breakout income. So, additional disclosures may be recommended, but no changes will be made to the current requirements.

Appendix A. AIMR Code and Standards

Code Of Ethics[1]

A financial analyst should conduct himself[2] with integrity and dignity and act in an ethical manner in his dealings with the public, clients, customers, employers, employees, and fellow analysts.

A financial analyst should conduct himself and should encourage others to practice financial analysis in a professional and ethical manner that will reflect credit on himself and his profession.

A financial analyst should act with competence and should strive to maintain and improve his competence and that of others in the profession.

A financial analyst should use proper care and exercise independent professional judgment.

Standards Of Professional Conduct

I. Obligation to Inform Employer of Code and Standards

The financial analyst shall inform his employer, through his direct supervisor, that the analyst is obligated to comply with the Code of Ethics and Standards of Professional Conduct, and is subject to disciplinary sanctions for violations thereof. He shall deliver a copy of the Code and Standards to his employer if the employer does not have a copy.

II. Compliance with Governing Laws and Regulations and the Code and Standards

A. *Required Knowledge and Compliance*

The financial analyst shall maintain knowledge of and shall comply with all applicable laws, rules, and regulations of any government, governmental agency, and regulatory organization governing his professional, financial, or business activities, as well as with these Standards of Professional Conduct and the accompanying Code of Ethics.

B. *Prohibition Against Assisting Legal and Ethical Violations*

The financial analyst shall not know-

ingly participate in, or assist, any acts in violation of any applicable law, rule, or regulation of any government, governmental agency, or regulatory organization governing his professional, financial, or business activities, nor any act which would violate any provision of these Standards of Professional Conduct or the accompanying Code of Ethics.

C. *Prohibition Against Use of Material Nonpublic Information*

The financial analyst shall comply with all laws and regulations relating to the use and communication of material nonpublic information. The financial analyst's duty is generally defined as to not trade while in possession of, nor communicate, material nonpublic information in breach of a duty, or if the information is misappropriated.

Duties under the standard include the following: (1) If the analyst acquires such information as a result of a special or confidential relationship with the issuer or others, he shall not communicate the information (other than within the relationship), or take investment action on the basis of such information, if it violates that relationship. (2) If the analyst is not in a special or confidential relationship with the issuer or others, he shall not communicate or act on material nonpublic information if he knows, or should have known, that such information (a) was disclosed to him, or would result, in a breach of a duty, or (b) was misappropriated.

If such a breach of duty exists, the analyst shall make reasonable efforts to achieve public dissemination of such information.

D. *Responsibilities of Supervisors*

A financial analyst with supervisory responsibility shall exercise reasonable supervision over those subordinate employees subject to his control, to prevent any violation by such persons of applicable statutes, regulations, or provisions of the Code of Ethics or Standards of Professional Conduct. In so doing the analyst is entitled to rely upon reasonable procedures established by his employer.

---

[1]Reprinted, with permission, from *Standards of Practice Handbook*, 6th ed. (Charlottesville, Va.: AIMR, 1992): 2–9.

[2]Masculine pronouns, used throughout the code and standards to simplify sentence structure, apply to all persons regardless of sex.

III. Research Reports, Investment Recommendations and Actions

A. *Reasonable Basis and Representations*

1. The financial analyst shall exercise diligence and thoroughness in making an investment recommendation to others or in taking an investment action for others.

2. The financial analyst shall have a reasonable and adequate basis for such recommendations and actions, supported by appropriate research and investigation.

3. The financial analyst shall make reasonable and diligent efforts to avoid any material misrepresentation in any research report or investment recommendation.

4. The financial analyst shall maintain appropriate records to support the reasonableness of such recommendations and actions.

B. *Research Reports*

1. The financial analyst shall use reasonable judgment as to the inclusion of relevant factors in research reports.

2. The financial analyst shall distinguish between facts and opinions in research reports.

3. The financial analyst shall indicate the basic characteristics of the investment involved when preparing for general public distribution a research report that is not directly related to a specific portfolio or client.

C. *Portfolio Investment Recommendations and Actions*

1. The financial analyst shall, when making an investment recommendation or taking an investment action for a specific portfolio or client, consider its appropriateness and suitability for such portfolio or client. In considering such matters, the financial analyst shall take into account (a) the needs and circumstances of the client, (b) the basic characteristics of the investment involved, and (c) the basic characteristics of the total portfolio. The financial analyst shall use reasonable judgment to determine the applicable relevant factors.

2. The financial analyst shall distinguish between facts and opinions in the presentation of investment recommendations.

3. The financial analyst shall disclose to clients and prospective clients the basic format and general principles of the investment processes by which securities are selected and portfolios are constructed and shall promptly disclose to clients any changes that might significantly affect those processes.

D. *Prohibition Against Plagiarism*

The financial analyst shall not, when presenting material to his employer, associates, customers, clients, or the general public, copy or use in substantially the same form, material prepared by other persons without acknowledging its use and identifying the name of the author or publisher of such material. The analyst may, however, use without acknowledgment factual information published by recognized financial and statistical reporting services or similar sources.

E. *Prohibition Against Misrepresentation of Services*

The financial analyst shall not make any statements, orally or in writing, which misrepresent (1) the services that the analyst or his firm is capable of performing for the client, (2) the qualifications of such analyst or his firm, and/or (3) the expected performance of any investment.

The financial analyst shall not make, orally or in writing, explicitly or implicitly, any assurances about or guarantees of any investment or its return except communication of accurate information as to the terms of the investment instrument and the issuer's obligations under the instrument.

F. *Performance Presentation Standards*

1. The financial analyst shall not make any statements, orally or in writing, which misrepresent the investment performance that the analyst or his firm has accomplished or can reasonably be expected to achieve.

2. If an analyst communicates directly or indirectly individual or firm performance information to a client or prospective client, or in a manner intended to be received by a client or prospective client ("Performance Information"), the analyst shall make every reasonable effort to ensure that such Performance Information is a fair, accurate, and complete presentation of such performance.

3. The financial analyst shall inform his employer about the existence and content of the Association for Investment Management and Research's Performance Presentation Standards . . . [3] and this Standard III F, and shall encourage his employer to adopt and use the Performance Presentation Standards.

4. If Performance Information complies with the Performance Presentation Standards, the analyst shall be presumed to be in compliance with III F 2 above.

5. An analyst presenting Performance Information may use the following legend on the Performance Information presentation, but only if the analyst has made every reasonable effort to ensure that such presentation is in compliance with the Performance Presentation Standards in all material respects:

"This report has been prepared and presented in compliance with the Performance Presentation Standards of the Association for Investment Management and Research."

G. *Fair Dealing with Customers and Clients*

The financial analyst shall act in a manner consistent with his obligation to deal fairly with all customers and clients when (1) disseminating investment recommendations, (2) disseminating material changes in prior investment advice, and (3) taking investment action.

IV. Priority of Transactions

The financial analyst shall conduct himself in such a manner that transactions for his customers, clients, and employer have priority over transactions in securities or other investments of which he is the beneficial owner, and so that transactions in securities or other investments in which he has such beneficial ownership do not operate adversely to their interests. If an analyst decides to make a recommendation about the purchase or sale of a security or other investment, he shall give his customers, clients, and employer adequate opportunity to act on this recommendation before acting on his own behalf.

For purposes of these Standards of Professional Conduct, a financial analyst is a "beneficial owner" if he directly or indirectly, through any contract, arrangement, understanding, relationship or otherwise, has or shares a direct or indirect pecuniary interest in the securities or the investment.

V. Disclosure of Conflicts

The financial analyst, when making investment recommendations, or taking investment actions, shall disclose to his customers and clients any material conflict of interest relating to him and any material beneficial ownership of the securities or other investments involved that could reasonably be expected to impair his ability to render unbiased and objective advice.

The financial analyst shall disclose to his employer all matters that could reasonably be expected to interfere with his duty to the employer, or with his ability to render unbiased and objective advice.

The financial analyst shall also comply with all requirements as to disclosure of conflicts of interest imposed by law and by rules and regulations of organizations governing his activities and shall comply with any prohibitions on his activities if a conflict of interest exists.

VI. Compensation

A. *Disclosure of Additional Compensation Arrangements*

The financial analyst shall inform his customers, clients, and employer of compensation or other benefit arrangements in connection with his services to them which are in addition to compensation from them for such services.

B. *Disclosure of Referral Fees*

The financial analyst shall make appropriate disclosure to a prospective client or customer of any consideration paid or other benefit delivered to others for recommending his services to that prospective client or customer.

C. *Duty to Employer*

The financial analyst shall not undertake independent practice which could result in compensation or other benefit in competition with his employer unless he has received written consent from both his employer and the person for whom he undertakes independent employment.

VII. Relationships with Others

A. *Preservation of Confidentiality*

A financial analyst shall preserve the confidentiality of information communicated by the client concerning matters

---

[3]Ellipses indicate references to other sections of the handbook.

within the scope of the confidential relationship, unless the financial analyst receives information concerning illegal activities on the part of the client.

B. *Maintenance of Independence and Objectivity*

The financial analyst, in relationships and contacts with an issuer of securities, whether individually or as a member of a group, shall use particular care and good judgment to achieve and maintain independence and objectivity.

C. *Fiduciary Duties*

The financial analyst, in relationships with clients, shall use particular care in determining applicable fiduciary duty and shall comply with such duty as to those persons and interests to whom it is owed.

VIII. Use of Professional Designation

The qualified financial analyst may use, as applicable, the professional designation "Member of the Association for Investment Management and Research," "Member of the Financial Analysts Federation," and "Member of the Institute of Chartered Financial Analysts," and is encouraged to do so, but only in a dignified and judicious manner. The use of the designations may be accompanied by an accurate explanation (1) of the requirements that have been met to obtain the designation, and (2) of the Association for Investment Management and Research, the Financial Analysts Federation, and the Institute of Chartered Financial Analysts, as applicable.

The Chartered Financial Analyst may use the professional designation "Chartered Financial Analyst," or the abbreviation "CFA," and is encouraged to do so, but only in a dignified and judicious manner. The use of the designation may be accompanied by an accurate explanation (1) of the requirements that have been met to obtain the designation, and (2) of the Association for Investment Management and Research and the Institute of Chartered Financial Analysts.

IX. Professional Misconduct

The financial analyst shall not (1) commit a criminal act that upon conviction materially reflects adversely on his honesty, trustworthiness, or fitness as a financial analyst in other respects, or (2) engage in conduct involving dishonesty, fraud, deceit, or misrepresentation.

Appendix B. Performance Presentation Standards[1]

I. Preamble

The Association for Investment Management and Research (AIMR) and its subsidiary organizations, the Financial Analysts Federation (FAF) and the Institute of Chartered Financial Analysts (ICFA), formulated these performance presentation standards for investment management results and subsequently endorsed and adopted them. These standards represent the work of the Committee for Performance Presentation Standards, commissioned in 1986 by the FAF; the Performance Presentation Standards Implementation Committee, commissioned by AIMR in 1990; and various subcommittees of the Implementation Committee.

The work toward establishing these standards has been consistently guided by the investment community's need for a common, accepted set of ethical principles ensuring fair representation and full disclosure in investment managers' presentations of their results to clients and prospective clients. A secondary objective is to achieve greater uniformity and comparability among such presentations. Some aspects of the standards are mandatory (i.e., they *must* be observed), and other aspects are recommended (i.e., they *should* be observed). Although the standards specify minimum calculation requirements, they are intended primarily to be performance *presentation* standards, not performance *measurement* standards. It is neither envisioned nor intended that the standards enhance or detract from the potential value or usefulness of the information contained in historical results.

No finite set of guidelines can cover all potential situations or anticipate future developments in industry structure, technology, or practices. Meeting the primary objectives of fair representation and full disclosure requires a conscientious, good-faith commitment to the spirit of the standards under any specific circumstances. Disclosure must be relied upon to convey the elements of any material interpretations that are not covered in the standards. Meeting the full intent of the standards may, and probably will, require more than meeting the minimum requirements and mandatory disclosures. No portion of the standards should be interpreted as inhibiting managers from providing additional information that prospective clients or consultants might request or believe would more clearly represent the manager's investment results.

II. Parties Affected

The standards affect those who present performance information and those who use performance information. All AIMR members, CFAs, and candidates for the CFA designation are required to inform their employers about the existence and content of the standards and to encourage their employers to adopt and use the standards. Such employers include investment advisory firms, banks, insurance companies, consultants and broker–dealer firms acting as investment advisors, as well as other organizations offering investment management services.

For the user audience, the primary application of the standards is in presenting performance to prospective clients. Current clients also must be provided returns that are calculated according to methods that conform to the standards and that are consistent with the calculation methods applied to the manager's composites. Performance presentations in compliance with the standards do not obviate the need for due diligence on the part of prospective clients or consultants in evaluating performance data.

III. Compliance

All portfolios solely invested in U.S. and/or Canadian securities managed for U.S.- or Canada-based clients must be presented in composites that adhere to the AIMR standards to claim compliance as of January 1, 1993, or before. The standards will be implemented for portfolios invested in non-U.S. and/or non-Canadian investments ("international portfolios") as of January 1, 1994. An exemption to the implementation of the standards for taxable portfolios has been granted until January 1, 1994. Firms electing to take advantage of this exemption must disclose in all presentations that they are not in compliance for taxable portfolios. Managers marketing taxable and international portfolios are encouraged to come into compliance during 1993 in preparation for the mandatory January 1, 1994, implementation date.

For periods prior to January 1, 1993, a firm has the option of restating historical performance num-

[1]Reprinted, with permission, from *Performance Presentation Standards* (Charlottesville, Va.: AIMR, 1993): 1–18.

bers in accordance with the standards. As long as appropriate disclosures are made, a firm can claim compliance with the standards as of January 1, 1993, and going forward without restating its historical record. The requirements and disclosures for retroactive compliance are presented in Section VII.

The Performance Presentation Standards were incorporated into the AIMR Code of Ethics and Standards of Professional Conduct as of January 1, 1993. Section III E of the Standards of Professional Conduct prohibits misrepresentation of performance. Section III F specifically endorses the practices set forth in the standards . . .[2]

Compliance must be met on a firmwide basis, i.e., selected composites may not be presented as being in compliance unless *all* of the firm's qualifying portfolios have been accounted for in at least one composite. If an autonomous investment firm is itself owned by a larger holding company, or if a subsidiary or division is registered or holds itself out to the public as a separate entity, it may claim full compliance for itself without its parent organization being in compliance. To claim compliance, firms must meet all the requirements and mandatory disclosures and any other additional requirements or disclosures necessary to that firm's specific situation. If results are not in full compliance, performance cannot be presented as being "in compliance except for . . .".

IV. Performance Calculations

Achieving comparability among performance results requires at least some uniformity in methods used to calculate returns. The standards allow flexibility as long as the calculations chosen represent performance fairly and without intent to misrepresent. For additional calculations that apply to international and real estate portfolios, see Sections X and XI . . .

A. *Required Calculations*
The minimum requirements for calculating returns are as follows:
1. Total return, including realized and unrealized gains and losses plus income, is required.
2. Accrual accounting is required for fixed-income securities and all securities for which income is anticipated, with the exception of dividends. Accrual accounting for dividends as of their ex-dividend date is recommended, but cash-basis accounting is acceptable as long as it does not distort

performance. Estimated accrual is acceptable, although exact accrual is preferred. Accrued income must be included in both the beginning and ending portfolio market values or be otherwise accounted for when performance is being calculated. Accrual accounting is recommended but not required when calculating performance prior to January 1993.
3. Time-weighted rate of return is required using a minimum of quarterly valuation and geometric linking of these interim returns. Approximation methods are acceptable. Because distortions in performance from cash flows will decrease as portfolios are valued more frequently, daily valuations are recommended.
4. The pricing of all assets must be based on a reasonable estimate of current value of assets sold on that date to a willing buyer. In cases of frequently traded securities, standardized pricing quotations must be used and, if necessary, verified. The valuation of real estate assets is described separately in Section XI.
5. Performance results for any portfolio must be presented with cash, cash equivalents, or substitute assets. This applies to single-asset portfolios, multiple-asset portfolios, and the segments of multiple-asset portfolios when used as single-asset composites or when included in single-asset composites. To account for cash or cash equivalents appropriately, cash must be assigned at the beginning of each reporting period after January 1993.
6. The calculation of portfolio return for inclusion in a composite is required to commence either at the beginning of the first full reporting period for which the portfolio is under management or according to reasonable and consistently applied manager guidelines.

B. *Recommended Calculations*
The recommendations for calculating returns are as follows:
1. Revaluation of a portfolio is recommended whenever cash flows and market action combine to cause a material distortion of performance,

---

[2]Ellipses indicate references to other sections in *Performance Presentation Standards*.

deemed to be likely when cash flows exceed 10 percent of the portfolio's market value.

2. Trade-date accounting is recommended for calculating performance, although settlement-date accounting is acceptable if disclosed.

3. The calculation of performance prior to the deduction of investment management fees is recommended unless net-of-fee calculations are required to meet Securities and Exchange Commission (SEC) advertising requirements . . . When different kinds of fees are embedded in a single fee, as in the case of wrap fees, the manager must deduct from gross performance all fees that cannot be unbundled. Estimated transaction costs are not permitted.

4. The calculation of performance results before taxes is recommended. If results are presented after taxes, the tax rate assumption must be disclosed.

V. Composites

The standards require the use of composites in investment performance presentations. The standards governing composites help ensure that prospective clients have a fair and complete representation of a manager's past performance record. Each composite must comprise portfolios or asset classes representing a similar strategy or investment objective. The construction of multiple composites is required if the use of a single composite would be misleading or otherwise inappropriate in the context of the presentation for which the composite results are being used. For a multiproduct firm, a composite of all of the firm's portfolios is unlikely to be meaningful and is not recommended. A composite could include only one portfolio if the portfolio is unique in its approach but fully discretionary. Mutual funds, commingled funds, or unit trusts may be treated as separate composites or be combined with other portfolios or assets of similar strategies. The performance of portfolios invested in one commingled fund, mutual fund, or unit trust should be represented by the performance of the fund or unit trust. For portfolios invested in more than one fund or unit trust, a total return must also be calculated and performance included in a multiple-asset composite. Balanced portfolios with differing allocations may be defined by allowable bands of asset mix.

A. *Construction and Maintenance of Composites*
    1. All actual, fee-paying, discretionary portfolios must be included in at least one composite. Performance records must be presented fairly and completely without intent to bias or misrepresent by excluding selected portfolios.

2. Firm composites must include only actual assets under management. Model results may be presented as supplementary information, but the model results must be identified as such and must not be linked to actual results.

3. Non-fee-paying portfolios may be included in composites if such inclusion is disclosed.

4. If investment restrictions hinder or prohibit the application of an intended investment strategy, the affected portfolio may be considered nondiscretionary. Examples of such restrictions include:
    a. Tax considerations that prevent the manager from realizing profits on existing holdings.
    b. Client requirements that the portfolio include or exclude certain securities or types of securities.
    c. Minimum portfolio-size limits that exclude portfolios a manager deems too small to be representative of the manager's intended strategy. The size limit must be disclosed and adhered to rigidly, and no portfolios under the size cutoff can be considered discretionary. Composites of larger sized portfolios must not be used as representative of performance results when marketing to prospective clients whose assets are below the size cutoff.
    d. The definition of a nondiscretionary portfolio depends on a manager's particular strategy. For example, a manager may exclude a South-Africa-free portfolio if that restriction makes its construction different from the manager's other portfolios. Another manager may choose to create a separate composite of several such portfolios. A third manager may include all such portfolios in a more broadly defined composite

if the restriction does not result in holdings that are different from the other portfolios' holdings.

5. Asset-weighting of the portfolio returns within a composite is required using beginning-of-period weightings (or beginning-of-period market values plus weighted cash flows, or by aggregating assets and cash flows to calculate performance as for a single portfolio). The additional presentation of equal-weighted composite returns is recommended but not required.

6. New portfolios must not be added to a composite until the start of the next performance measurement period (month or quarter) after the portfolio comes under management or according to reasonable and consistently applied manager guidelines.

7. Portfolios no longer under management must be included in historical composites for the periods they were under management; that is, "survivor" performance results are prohibited. They must be excluded for all periods after the last full period they were in place.

8. Portfolios must not be switched from one composite to another unless documented changes in client guidelines make this appropriate.

9. Changes in a firm's organization must not lead to an altering of composite results. A change in personnel should be disclosed, but personnel changes must not be used to alter composite performance results. Performance results of a past affiliation must not be used to represent the historical record of a new affiliation or a newly formed entity. Using the performance data from a prior firm as supplemental information is permitted as long as the past record is not linked to the results of the new affiliation. The guiding principle is that performance is the record of the firm, not of the individual . . .

10. Convertibles or other hybrid instruments should be treated consistently across and within composites, except when meeting client directives. Convertibles should be treated as equity instruments, unless the manager and the client have decided otherwise.

B. *Presentation of Composites*
The presentation of composites is subject to certain mandatory requirements as well as recommended guidelines for providing information that will allow prospective clients to evaluate fairly the representativeness of the composites being presented . . .

1. Prospective clients must be advised that a list and description of all of a firm's composites is available.

2. At least a 10-year record (or the record since inception of the firm, if shorter) must be presented; presentation of a 20-year record is recommended if the company has been in existence for 20 years.

3. Retroactive compliance is recommended but not required. Section VII details the requirements for presenting performance for periods prior to 1993.

4. For any period for which compliance is claimed, the presentation of annual returns for all years is required to avoid selectivity in time periods presented. Annualized cumulative performance is recommended. Performance for periods of less than one year must not be annualized.

5. When composites include both taxable and tax-exempt securities, the manager should state the percentages of each class and, where possible, present results for each of the portions separately.

6. Managers should show both internal and external dispersion of portfolio returns in the composite. Section VIII details the recommendations for the presentation of measures of risk and dispersion.

7. Presentation of supplemental information is recommended when the manager deems this additional information to be valuable to clients. Such disclosures might include the average market capitalization of stocks held, the average quality and duration of bond holdings, and additional information on international portfolios (Section X), real estate portfolios (Section XI), and portfolios using leverage

or derivative securities (Section XII). This information must not supplant the required information, and it must be accompanied by the appropriate composite returns.

C. *Disclosures*

The following disclosures are required for each period for which composite results are presented. Additional disclosures will probably be needed to meet the fair-representation and full-disclosure objectives. The disclosures are expected to be specific to each circumstance and are therefore not required in all situations. For additional disclosures that apply to international and real estate portfolios, see Sections X and XI.

1. For each time period for which composite results are presented, a manager must disclose the number of portfolios in the composite, total composite assets, and composite assets as a percentage of firm assets. For composites of five or fewer portfolios, the disclosure "five or fewer portfolios" may be made rather than disclosing the exact number of portfolios. Additional disclosures, such as portfolio size range and the percentage of total assets managed in the same asset class as represented by the composite, are recommended.

2. Disclosure is required of whether segments of multiple-asset, or balanced, portfolios are included in single-asset composites. If they are, a description must be provided of how cash has been allocated to the included asset segments.

3. Disclosure is required of whether performance results are calculated gross or net of investment management fees. In either case, an appropriate schedule of fees must be presented. When net-of-fee results are presented, the weighted average fee must also be presented so that performance can be computed on a gross-of-fee basis.

4. The existence of a minimum asset size below which portfolios are excluded from a composite must be disclosed.

5. The use of settlement-date rather than trade-date accounting must be disclosed.

6. The use and extent of leverage must be disclosed . . .

7. The inclusion of any non-fee-paying portfolios in composites must be disclosed.

8. If a manager claims current compliance with the standards, but the pre-1993 historical record is not in compliance for all periods, the manager must follow the rules and guidelines in Section VII, Retroactive Compliance.

VI. Multiple-Asset Portfolios

Multiple-asset portfolios are any portfolios that include more than one asset class. Total return on the entire portfolio is required for purposes of composites whenever the manager has discretion over changes from one asset class to another. If the segments of multiple-asset portfolios are broken out separately as supplemental information to the total return or as stand-alone composites of single-asset strategies or if the segments are added to single-asset composites, the manager must meet certain specific requirements to claim compliance with the standards. The standards do not require these subcomponents to be broken out or included in single-asset composites, although managers may choose to do so.

A. *Total Return of the Multiple-Asset Composite*
When a manager uses the total return of a multiple-asset composite to market a multiple-asset portfolio strategy, cash allocation to each of the segments of the multiple-asset composite is not required.

B. *Segment Returns as Supplemental Information*
When a manager uses the total return of a multiple-asset composite to market a multiple-asset portfolio strategy, but the manager wishes to present the segment returns of the multiple-asset composite as supplemental information, the segment returns may be shown without making a cash allocation as long as the returns for each of the composite's segments (including the cash segment) are shown along with the composite's total return . . .

C. *Segment Returns as Single-Asset Composites or Added to Single-Asset Composites*
When the segment returns of a multiple-asset composite are added to, or are being used to market, single-asset strategies, a cash allocation to each of the segments must be made at the beginning of each reporting period, and the methodology must be disclosed. The segment may then be included on the firm's list of composites. Asset-only returns must not be mixed with asset-plus-cash returns. Section VII details

the requirements for retroactive compliance.

VII. Retroactive Compliance

The requirements and disclosures for retroactive compliance apply to any composites constructed for periods prior to January 1993. After this date, all composites must be constructed and maintained in accordance with the standards. For periods prior to January 1993, a firm has the option of restating historical performance numbers in accordance with the standards. As long as appropriate disclosures are made, a firm can claim compliance with the standards as of January 1993 and going forward without restating its historical record. Presentation of a minimum of a 10-year performance record (or since firm inception, if shorter) is required even if the record is not restated.

   A.   *Presentation of Historical Data*

       If a manager claims current compliance with the standards, but the pre-1993 historical record is not in compliance for all periods and the noncompliance periods are linked to periods that are in compliance, the manager must:

       1. Disclose that the full record is not in compliance.

       2. Identify the noncompliance periods.

       3. Explain how the noncompliance periods are out of compliance.

   B.   *Guidelines for Retroactive Compliance*

       The standards for retroactive compliance for periods prior to January 1993 are somewhat more relaxed than the standards that apply after that date.

       1. Valuation periods may be as long as one year, although if cash flows were significant during the year, valuations should be done more frequently to reduce performance distortion. To qualify for inclusion in a composite that is valued annually, a portfolio must have been under management according to a strategy appropriate to the composite for at least one year.

       2. Composites may be asset weighted using annual beginning-of-period market values.

       3. Accrual accounting need not be applied if cash-basis accounting was used historically.

       4. Within multiple-asset portfolios, if cash allocations are made to each of the composite segments, the manager must use a reasonable and consistent approach, and the manager must disclose the methodology used for assigning cash. If information is not available for making a reasonable allocation, then retroactive allocations of each must not be attempted.

VIII. Measures of Risk and Dispersion

The standards recommend presentation of risk measures appropriate to the strategy represented by a composite. Both external and internal risk measures should be considered in presenting performance results . . .

   A.   *External Risk Measures*

       External risk measures represent the riskiness of investment strategies and include standard deviation across time, beta, duration, and others that are based on current and historical data. Benchmarks, including market indexes, manager universes, and normal portfolios, provide a relative measure for the riskiness of a strategy.

       1. Managers should designate a benchmark and explain this choice.

       2. Benchmarks must be consistently applied and must parallel the risk or investment style the client portfolio is expected to track. A portfolio with, for example, 50 percent of its total assets in small- to medium-capitalization stocks and 50 percent in large-capitalization stocks should be compared to a similarly weighted composite of appropriate indexes rather than to just one index. Disclosure of differences in portfolio structure relative to the benchmark is recommended.

       3. If an index is used as a benchmark, it should be investable, although this may be impossible with certain indexes such as some fixed-income and international indexes.

       4. For multiple-asset portfolios, managers and clients should agree in advance on the frequency and the assumptions to be used in rebalancing to the benchmark or target allocation.

   B.   *Internal Risk Measures*

       Internal risk measures represent the consistency of a manager's results with respect to the individual portfolio returns within a composite. For an equal-weighted composite, standard deviation across portfolios is the appropriate measure of internal risk. For an asset-weighted composite, a reformulation of the standard deviation to an asset-weighted dispersion measure or an alternative approach to exhibit consistency is recommended. Also recommended is inclusion of the range of portfolio returns within the composite, high–low portfolio return statistics, and other measures a manager deems valuable.

IX. Verification

The standards recommend verification of claims that performance is in compliance. Verification must be performed by an independent party. Two levels of verification are possible. Level I verification applies to the firm; Level II verification includes Level I verification and applies to specific composites.

As in an audit, a relatively small sample of data may satisfy the verifier that appropriate procedures and computer software are in place to calculate performance correctly if no discrepancies are found. The lack of explicit audit trails or apparent errors, however, may warrant a larger sample or additional verification procedures. The verifier may conclude that, based on insufficient backup, some performance records simply do not lend themselves to an attest. A qualified opinion must be issued in such cases, clarifying why a completely satisfactory opinion was not possible . . .

A. *Level I Verification*

A Level I verification attests to the fact that all of a firm's actual, discretionary, fee-paying portfolios are included in at least one composite. Examination procedures generally include verification of the following:

1. Each portfolio, including those no longer under management, is in fact either included in a composite or has been documented as being excluded for valid reasons.

2. All portfolios sharing the same guidelines are included in the same composite and shifts from one composite to another are based on documented client guidelines.

3. Portfolio returns within the composites are weighted by size.

4. Performance is being calculated using a time-weighted rate of return, with a minimum of quarterly valuations and accrual of income.

5. Disclosures offered to ensure that performance has been presented accurately and in keeping with a full and fair presentation of investment results.

B. *Level II Verification*

A Level II verification examines both the investment management process (tests of validity and propriety of underlying shares, income, and pricing data) and the measurement of performance (computation and presentation of performance data). Examination procedures generally include verification of the following:

1. All of a firm's actual, discretionary, fee-paying portfolios are included in at least one composite (i.e., a Level I verification).

2. Performance calculations use the time-weighted return formula.

3. Asset prices.

4. Capital gains/losses.

5. Trades, on a sample basis, checking the accounting trail, cost records, and actual shares or bonds still held.

6. Income streams, on a sample basis, including the timing and actual receipt of dividends, accrued interest, and the treatment of fees.

7. Cash flows are accounted for properly.

X. Treatment of International Investments

For managers marketing international products, the following additional requirements, disclosures, and recommendations apply . . .

A. *Performance Calculations*

In addition to the requirements in Section IV, Performance Calculations, the following requirements and recommendations apply specifically to international portfolios:

1. Managers must disclose whether composite and benchmark returns are net or gross of foreign withholding taxes on dividends, interest, and capital gains. If net performance is shown, managers must also disclose the assumed tax rate for the benchmark.

2. Managers should calculate portfolio returns net of withholding taxes on dividends, interest, and capital gains, and disclose the percentage of the portfolio for which potential capital gains taxes on unrealized gains have not been subtracted. This particularly applies to emerging market investments.

3. Because of the volatility and lengthy settlement periods of some markets,

trade-date rather than settlement-date reporting is strongly recommended.

4. A consistent source of period-end exchange rates should be used. Managers should disclose any inconsistencies among portfolios in the treatment of exchange rates.

B. *Composites*

In addition to the requirements in Section V, Composites, the following requirements and disclosures apply specifically to international composites:

1. Subsectors, or carve-outs, of larger international portfolios may be used to create stand-alone composites only if the subsectors are actually managed as separate entities with their own cash allocations and currency management. Disclosure that the composite is a subsector is required. If a stand-alone composite is formed using subsectors from multiple composites, its return must be presented with a list of the underlying composites from which the subsector was drawn, along with the percentage of each composite the subsector represents.

If the subsector is not treated as a separate entity, the subsector-only performance must be provided as supplemental information to the composite or composites from which the subsector was drawn. In this case, the percentage of the composite's assets represented by the subsector must be disclosed; returns of the larger composite must be made available. Subsector results should include all qualifying portfolios; the presentation of subsector results as supplemental information, however, may be based on representative portfolios as long as this is disclosed. Carve-outs presented as supplemental information must not be combined with stand-alone portfolios.

2. For portfolios managed to a specific international benchmark, the manager must disclose the percentage of composite assets invested in countries or regions outside the benchmark. The manager should also disclose the range or average of country weights in the composite.

3. If a composite is to be compared to an unhedged benchmark, portfolios that are allowed to use currency hedging should not be included with portfolios that cannot use hedging instruments, unless the use of currency hedging is judged to be immaterial. Similarly, if portfolios managed against hedged benchmarks are materially different from portfolios managed against unhedged benchmarks, they should be placed in separate composites.

C. *Currency and Currency Overlay Portfolios*

The requirements below, except for C.1, apply to portfolios managed as stand-alone currency overlay portfolios . . .

1. When expressing the return of a portfolio excluding the effect of currency, the return should be shown fully hedged back to the base currency of that portfolio. If this hedged return is not calculated, disclosure must be made that the return is in the local currency and does not account for interest rate differentials in forward currency exchange rates.

2. The benchmark for any currency overlay portfolio must be calculated in accordance with the mandates of the portfolio (unless the benchmark is actually the currency return on a published benchmark).

3. Currency overlay portfolios should be valued whenever there are notified changes in the underlying currency exposures (as the result of a shift in the underlying assets). In accordance with the overall standards, currency overlay portfolios must be valued at least quarterly; however, the volatile nature of these portfolios may make the use of shorter time periods necessary to obtain full and fair disclosure.

4. In terms of currency exposure, composites must be determined according to similar benchmarks and restrictions. In currency management, the underlying currency exposure might not matter if portfolios are managed according to similar index benchmarks. If, however, the manager is being measured according to the value added over existing positions, then the underlying currency exposure becomes critical. In this case, grouping currency overlay portfolios into composites of more

than one portfolio would not be meaningful. A series of one-portfolio composites may be used if composites of multiple currency overlay portfolios would not provide useful information.

XI. Treatment of Real Estate

Because of its unique characteristics, particularly the lack of a readily verifiable secondary market to determine asset values, real estate performance presentation guidelines warrant separate treatment. Consistent with the requirements presented in Section V, Composites, all properties must be included in at least one composite and a list of the composites must be made available. Because of the unique nature of individual real estate investments, however, composites containing single properties will be appropriate in many cases. Presentations should disclose inclusions and exclusions . . .

A. *Performance Calculations*

In addition to the requirements in Section IV, Performance Calculations, the following requirements and recommendations apply specifically to real estate portfolios:

1. The attribution and separate presentation of returns from income and capital appreciation is required. When presenting the components of total return, the recognition of income at the investor level is preferred over income at the operating level. Appreciation includes realized and unrealized gains and losses.

2. The value of a real estate portfolio must be reviewed at least quarterly. Valuations must be performed by independent, objective appraisers with sufficient frequency, not longer than every three years, and the frequency of the valuation must be disclosed. The appraisers must be asked to originate and communicate value rather than merely confirm prior knowledge. The source of the valuation and the valuation policy must be fully disclosed. If client agreements do not require independent appraisals, independent valuations are not required, but the absence of independent valuations must be disclosed.

3. Investment income must be calculated on an accrual basis rather than on a cash basis.

4. Returns associated with cash, cash equivalents, and substitute assets held in the portfolio must be included in the presentation.

B. *Disclosures*

In addition to the required disclosures outlined in previous sections, the following disclosures must be made in the presentation of real estate performance:

1. Return formulas and accounting policies for items such as capital expenditures, tenant improvements, and leasing commissions. A statement as to whether the returns have been audited must be included.

2. The amount of leverage used, if any.

3. The management fee structure, including its relationship to asset valuation.

XII. Treatment of Portfolios Using Leverage and/or Derivative Securities

The standards require that the use and extent of leverage be disclosed when reporting performance. Examples of leverage include, but are not limited to, buying securities on margin, writing covered call options, buying protective put options, using futures for either hedging or speculation, and short-selling. The important issue relating to leverage is the altered risk and return profile of the portfolio. Disclosure of portfolio strategies included in the composite is required when such strategies have significant potential to influence the risk and/or return characteristics of the composite . . .

A. *Restatement to an All-Cash Basis*

Return results should be restated to an all-cash basis when the portfolio used leverage and the same securities could have been purchased at the same prices if the portfolio had the cash to do so. Results should be restated to an all-cash basis only when the necessary restatement can be based entirely on actual transactions and can be verified in accordance with applicable accounting standards, including third-party documentation (such as client agreements about asset allocation or client guidelines on portfolio strategies and objectives).

B. *Disclosure of Strategies*

The standards recommend complete disclosure regarding the nature of the strategies for portfolios using derivative securities. The disclosures must include:

1. A description of the use of derivatives.

2. The amounts of derivatives used.

3. The frequency of their use.

4. A discussion of their characteristics. These disclosures must be detailed enough for clients or prospective clients to judge the impact of all the pertinent factors regarding the returns and risks of the strategy or portfolio.

C. *Incremental Return Calculation*

The incremental return from derivative securities is equal to the difference between the total fund return and the return on the fund without the contribution of the derivative securities. The incremental return should be calculated whenever (1) such a calculation is representative of the true incremental return attributable to derivatives, and (2) the necessary calculation is based entirely on actual transactions or on third-party documentation that can verify the calculation. Causes of nonrepresentative calculations include, but are not limited to, the use of derivatives affecting the execution of the portfolio strategy in the remainder of the fund or affecting prices of transactions in the remainder of the fund.

Self-Evaluation Examination

1. Identify three threats to ethical behavior in the investment industry according to Avera.

2. The concern over ethical behavior in the investment industry first surfaced during the 1980s.
   a. True.
   b. False

3. Identify the five key elements of the enforcement process in the AIMR Professional Conduct Program.

4. According to the Standards of Professional Conduct, investment professionals must allocate some of an initial public offering to every account in order to treat all customers fairly.
   a. True.
   b. False.

5. According to the Standards of Professional Conduct, investment professionals must wait 48 hours after receiving new information about a security before making a transaction for a personal account.
   a. True.
   b. False.

6. According to the Standards of Professional Conduct, investment professionals are not permitted to accept any gifts, no matter what the amount.
   a. True.
   b. False.

7. According to *Ethics in the Investment Profession: A Survey* (see the Foreword), the most important deterrent to unethical actions is:
   a. Moral and religious beliefs.
   b. Having a published code of ethics.
   c. Concern about sanctions from the SEC or state.
   d. Concern that family or friends will find out.

8. According to *Ethics in the Investment Profession: A Survey*, the most frequent serious ethical violation is:
   a. Plagiarizing another's work.
   b. Failure to use diligence and thoroughness in making recommendations.
   c. Trading based on inside information.
   d. Writing reports that support predetermined conclusions.

9. According to Vass, the most important element of a compliance program is the support of senior management and its insistence that ethical conduct be part of the company's culture.
   a. True.
   b. False.

10. What criteria must a compliance program meet to be an affirmative defense in lessening penalties for violations involving proper supervision of employees at the firm level?

11. Which of the following statements is *not* an advantage of having a formal compliance program?
    a. A compliance program is an effective way of meeting a firm's legal requirements to supervise its employees.
    b. A compliance program can foster an ethical culture within the firm.
    c. Adherence to a compliance program once in place is voluntary.
    d. A compliance program can deter crime, negative publicity, and misconduct.

12. What is the difference between the two types of compliance officers—direct supervisors and indirect supervisors?

13. The primary purpose of a Chinese Wall is to avoid insider-trading violations.
    a. True.
    b. False.

14. Identify the elements of a Chinese Wall policy.

15. For a violation of the insider-trading law to exist, material nonpublic information must be involved and a breach of duty must occur.
    a. True.
    b. False.

16. Identify four key aspects in running an insider-trading compliance program according to Haaga.

17. According to U.S. Sentencing Guidelines for ethics violations, all the following are mitigating factors that may reduce any penalties and fines levied against corporations *except*:
    a. Voluntarily reporting the offense.
    b. Cooperating with the federal or regulatory investigations.
    c. Having an effective program to deter and detect violations.
    d. Designating a mid-level employee to ensure compliance.

18. What are the seven fundamental elements of an effective ethics or compliance program according to Tansey?

19. Tansey identifies all the following as key reasons for ethical misconduct *except*:
    a. Ignorance.
    b. Greed.
    c. Failure to have a compliance officer.
    d. Individuals' desires for the organization to succeed.

20. According to Tansey, the most critical task in developing an effective corporate ethics program is to:
    a. Establish what needs to be evaluated or measured.
    b. Determine the program's objectives.
    c. Determine the tools and methods needed for measuring compliance.
    d. Set a benchmark for the level of employee knowledge of company standards.

21. What does Beese mean by the statement: "Good ethics is good business if one intends to be around for the long term in our markets"?

22. What is the meaning of the following statement by Beevers about the regulation of financial markets and services in the United Kingdom: "The system creates a lot of confusion without necessarily enhancing the quality of regulation"?

23. According to Hersey, the major catalyst for the growth in non-U.S. private pension assets is:
    a. The overall maturing of plans abroad.
    b. Extension in non-U.S. plans of the service definitions for the determination of benefits.
    c. Privatizing of retirement obligations abroad.
    d. All of the above.

24. Hersey identifies the *major* area of departures from AIMR's Standards of Professional Conduct in non-U.S. markets as:
    a. Use of material nonpublic information.
    b. Standards for performance presentation.
    c. Priority of transactions.
    d. Disclosure of conflicts.

25. According to Pascutto, the Hong Kong market is generally in line with international standards of market regulation and practice.
    a. True.
    b. False.

26. What are the three most common uses of soft dollars for fiduciaries according to Anselmi?

27. Which of the following are potential problems of using soft-dollar arrangements?
    I. Conflict of interest between client and investment manager.
    II. Increased potential of poor execution.
    III. An increase in market liquidity.
    IV. An increase in market volatility.
    V. An incentive to increase portfolio turnover.
    a. I and II only.
    b. I, III, and IV only.
    c. II, III, and IV only.
    d. I, II, III, IV, and V.

28. Why does Quinn believe that the biggest potential arena of conflict involving soft dollars comes from the divergent interests of the money manager and the client?

29. According to Richardson, having a conflict of interest is ethically wrong.
    a. True.
    b. False.

30. According to McAra, AIMR's Performance Presentation Standards (PPS) have the same requirements and disclosure provisions internationally as they do domestically.
    a. True.
    b. False.

31. According to Ryan, the key to implementing the PPS in the United States is in the hands of plan sponsors.
    a. True.
    b. False.

32. Identify the four elements of the ethical framework for the PPS.

33. The PPS require that a Certified Public Accountant verify the claims that performance is in compliance with the standards.
    a. True.
    b. False.

34. Identify two actions that companies can take to counteract unfavorable perceptions about ethical behavior in the investment industry.

35. How did Congress respond to violations of the securities laws during the 1980s?

36. What two major areas does Sporkin single out as needing reform in the investment industry?

higher cost in order to obtain research that economically benefits the manager, or to trade so as to achieve the best treatment of the client.

29. b. False. Richardson asserts that nothing is wrong ethically with simply having a conflict of interest. What is unethical is *acting* in one's own best interest instead of the client's.

30. b. False. McAra says that the PPS contain additional requirements and call for additional disclosures for international portfolios because of the added complexity in international portfolios.

31. a. True. Ryan contends that adoption of the PPS depends primarily on demand on the part of plan sponsors.

32. The four elements of the ethical framework of the PPS are (see Tschampion): (1) full disclosure, (2) fair representation, (3) comparability, and (4) minimum requirements.

33. b. False. As Tschampion discusses, the PPS recommend, but do not require, verification of claims that performance is in compliance. Moreover, although an independent party must perform the verification, this party does not have to be a CPA.

34. According to Lummer, companies can counteract unfavorable perceptions about ethical behavior in the investment industry by: (1) providing continuing education and training to employees about ethical behavior and (2) providing leadership through management examples.

35. According to Lynch, the securities law violations of the 1980s radically changed the penalty structure in U.S. regulation of the securities markets. Congress responded to the violations by empowering the SEC to penalize any violation of the securities laws, not merely insider-trading violations. In short, Congress increased the SEC's power to levy penalties to apply to any matter brought before the SEC.

36. Sporkin says that two areas in great need of reform in the investment industry are the commission compensation system for broker/dealers and the way in which investment managers conduct their personal investing activities.

Selected AIMR Publications*

A Practitioner's Guide to Factor Models, 1994 . . . . $20

Quality Management and Institutional Investing, 1994 . . . . $20
  Keith P. Ambachtsheer, *Editor*

Managing Emerging Market Portfolios, 1994 . . . . $20
  John W. Peavy III, CFA, *Editor*

Global Asset Management and Performance Attribution, 1994 . . . . $20
  Denis S. Karnosky, Ph.D., and Brian D. Singer, CFA

Franchise Value and the Price/Earnings Ratio, 1994 . . . . $20
  Martin L. Leibowitz and Stanley Kogelman

Investing Worldwide, 1993, 1992, 1991, 1990 . . . . $20 each

The Modern Role of Bond Covenants, 1994 . . . . $20
  Ileen B. Malitz

Derivative Strategies for Managing Portfolio Risk, 1993 . . . . $20
  Keith C. Brown, CFA, *Editor*

Equity Securities Analysis and Evaluation, 1993 . . . . $20

The CAPM Controversy: Policy and Strategy Implications for $20
Investment Management, 1993
  Diana R. Harrington and Robert A. Korajczyk, *Editors*

The Health Care Industry, 1993 . . . . $20
  James Balog, *Editor*

Predictable Time-Varying Components of International Asset Returns, 1993 . . . . $20
  Bruno Solnik

The Oil and Gas Industries, 1993 . . . . $20
  Thomas A. Petrie, CFA, *Editor*

Execution Techniques, True Trading Costs, and the Microstructure
of Markets, 1993 . . . . $20
  Katrina F. Sherrerd, CFA, *Editor*

Investment Counsel for Private Clients, 1993 . . . . $20
  John W. Peavy III, CFA, *Editor*

Active Currency Management, 1993 . . . . $20
  Murali Ramaswami

The Retail Industry, 1993 . . . . $20
  Charles A. Ingene, *Editor*

Equity Trading Costs, 1993 . . . . $20
  Hans R. Stoll

Options and Futures: A Tutorial, 1992 . . . . $20
  Roger G. Clarke

*A full catalog of publications is available from AIMR, P.O. Box 7947, Charlottesville, Va. 22906; 804/980-3647; fax 804/977-0350.

Order Form₀₃₀

Additional copies of *Good Ethics: The Essential Element of a Firm's Success* (and other AIMR publications listed on page 127) are available for purchase. The price is **$20 each in U.S. dollars**. Simply complete this form and return it via mail or fax to:

AIMR
Publications Sales Department
P.O. Box 7947
Charlottesville, Va. 22906
U.S.A.
Telephone: 804/980-3647
Fax: 804/977-0350

Name _____

Company_____

Address _____

_____ Suite/Floor _____

City_____

State _____ZIP _____ Country _____

Daytime Telephone _____

Title of Publication	**Price**	**Qty.**	**Total**
_____	_____	_____	_____
_____	_____	_____	_____

Shipping/Handling
- ❏ All U.S. orders: Included in price of book
- ❏ Airmail, Canada and Mexico: $5 per book
- ❏ Surface mail, Canada and Mexico: $3 per book
- ❏ Airmail, all other countries: $8 per book
- ❏ Surface mail, all other countries: $6 per book

Discounts
- ❏ Students, professors, university libraries: 25%
- ❏ CFA candidates (ID #_____):   25%
- ❏ Retired members (ID #_____):   25%
- ❏ Volume orders (50+ books of same title): 40%

Discount	$–
4.5% sales tax (Virginia residents)	$_____
8.25% sales tax (New York residents)	$_____
7% GST (Canada residents, #124134602)	$_____
Shipping/handling	$_____
Total cost of order	$_____

❏ Check or money order enclosed payable to **AIMR**   ❏ Bill me
Charge to: ❏ VISA   ❏ MASTERCARD   ❏ AMERICAN EXPRESS

Card Number:_____ ❏ Corporate ❏ Personal

Signature:_____ Expiration date: _____